CentOS Quick Start Guide

Get up and running with CentOS server administration

Shiwang Kalkhanda

BIRMINGHAM - MUMBAI

CentOS Quick Start Guide

Commissioning Editor: Pavan Ramchandani
Acquisition Editor: Siddharth Mandal
Content Development Editor: Kirk Dsouza
Technical Editor: Adya Anand
Copy Editor: Safis Editing
Project Coordinator: Hardik Bhinde
Proofreader: Safis Editing
Indexer: Rekha Nair
Graphics: Alishon Mendonsa
Production Coordinator: Tom Scaria

First published: December 2018

Production reference: 1241218

Published by Packt Publishing Ltd.
Livery Place
35 Livery Street
Birmingham
B3 2PB, UK.

ISBN 978-1-78934-487-5

www.packtpub.com

To the two most beautiful ladies and pillars of my life, my mother, Mrs. Vijay Lata, and my better half, Reetu.

`mapt.io`

Mapt is an online digital library that gives you full access to over 5,000 books and videos, as well as industry leading tools, to help you plan your personal development and advance your career. For more information, please visit our website.

Why subscribe?

- Spend less time learning and more time coding with practical eBooks and videos from over 4,000 industry professionals

- Improve your learning with Skill Plans built especially for you

- Get a free eBook or video every month

- Mapt is fully searchable

- Copy and paste, print, and bookmark content

Packt.com

Did you know that Packt offers eBook versions of every book published, with PDF and ePub files available? You can upgrade to the eBook version at `www.packt.com` and, as a print book customer, you are entitled to a discount on the eBook copy. Get in touch with us at `customercare@packtpub.com` for more details.

At `www.packt.com`, you can also read a collection of free technical articles, sign up for a range of free newsletters, and receive exclusive discounts and offers on Packt books and eBooks.

Contributors

About the author

Shiwang Kalkhanda (RHCA, RHCSS, MCSE) is a Linux geek and consultant with expertise in the automation of infrastructure deployment and management. He has more than 10 years' experience in security, system, and network administration, and training on open source tech. For most of his automation work, he uses Shell Scripting, Python, and Go. He holds a master's and a bachelor's degree in computer applications. He enjoys traveling and spending time with his children. He is also the author of a book on text processing utilities in Unix-like environments, *Learning Awk Programming*.

First and foremost, I would like to thank my Guru, Shri Snehamoy Banerjee, for introducing me to the world of Linux and open source.

I would like to thank my parents and grandparents for their unconditional love and encouragement throughout my life. To my brother, Pranjal, and my friends, Sanjay Rana, Shreyas Zare, Jugaldeep Sinha, Kapil Bhatnagar, and Lehar Gupta, and all the Packt Publishing staff for their help and guidance throughout the writing process.

About the reviewer

Denis Fateyev holds a master's degree in computer science and has been working with Linux for more than 10 years (mostly with Red Hat and CentOS). He currently works as a Perl and Go system programmer and DevOps for a small international company. For Packt Publishing, he has reviewed several books, mostly related to CentOS, DevOps, and high-availability technologies, including *GitLab Cookbook, CentOS High Availability*, and *CentOS High Performance*. A keen participant in the open source community, he is a package maintainer in the Fedora project. Foreign languages (German, Spanish) and linguistics are other passions of his. He can be reached at `denis@fateyev.com`.

Packt is searching for authors like you

If you're interested in becoming an author for Packt, please visit `authors.packtpub.com` and apply today. We have worked with thousands of developers and tech professionals, just like you, to help them share their insight with the global tech community. You can make a general application, apply for a specific hot topic that we are recruiting an author for, or submit your own idea.

Table of Contents

Preface

This book will provide an introduction to essential Linux skills using CentOS 7. It describes how a Linux system is organized and provides an introduction to key command-line concepts that an individual can practice on their own. It guides an individual in performing basic system administration tasks and day-to-day operations in a Linux environment.

Today, Linux is everywhere. It is an essential ingredient of most technical innovations, powering anything from the tiniest smart devices to the world's most gigantic supercomputer. Linux kernel development has been the world's largest collaborative project hitherto. Readers will learn the basics of Linux and open source technology in modern computing environment. This book will introduce users to CentOS 7 in a concise and practical way. Most of the command lines used in the book are explained with graphics for better understanding.

By the end of this book, you will have a solid understanding of working with Linux using command lines. You will learn core system administration skills for managing a system running CentOS 7, or a similar operating system, such as RHEL 7, Scientific Linux, and Oracle Linux. After reading this book, you will be able to perform installation, establish network connectivity and user and process management, modify file permissions, manage text files using command lines, and implement basic security administration.

Who this book is for

This book is intended for any individual who wants to learn how to use Linux as a server or desktop machine in their environment. Whether you are a developer, fledgling system administrator, or tech lover with no previous Linux administration background, you will be able to start your journey in Linux using CentOS 7 with the help of this book.

Even though this book is written for novice Linux users, a seasoned Linux user will also have something to take away from each chapter. You don't need any prior experience of working with the Linux command line for this book. Most new users of Linux find it difficult to work with the command line and, occasionally, the choice as to which Linux distribution to start with may be confusing. You will learn Linux using CentOS 7, which is one of the most popular and stable Linux distributions based on RHEL 7.

Some of the key features of this book are as follows:

- No previous Linux environment experience is required prior to reading this book
- Readers will become comfortable with a popular and stable Red Hat Enterprise Linux distribution
- Concise content, with a thorough coverage of important utilities

The book is written in such a manner that any computer user with basic familiarity with operating systems can start using it. The only prerequisite is to have some decent hardware on which you can install CentOS 7 and practice the commands covered.

What this book covers

Chapter 1, *Getting Started with CentOS 7*, establishes the environment for practicing the Linux commands to be covered in forthcoming chapters. You will begin with the installation of CentOS 7, followed by an introduction to the Bash shell environment.

Chapter 2, *Command Line and File system Navigation*, introduces users to the file system hierarchy, and basic command-line skills, such as navigational commands and backup utilities.

Chapter 3, *Managing Text Files*, focuses on working with common text manipulating utilities. Readers will learn how to work with the vi editor and input/output redirection in files or in programs.

Chapter 4, *User and Group Management*, focuses on user management. Readers will learn how to create, modify, or delete users and groups. They will also learn how to manage passwords and their aging policies.

Chapter 5, *Managing File Permissions*, focuses on managing ownership, permissions, and ACL. Readers will learn how to apply discretionary access controls via permissions and ownership, while also learning how to apply special permissions and ACL to files and directories.

Chapter 6, *Process Management*, focuses on process management and command-line monitoring. Readers will learn how to interact with processes and modify their priorities to keep systems running smoothly.

Chapter 7, *Managing Networking in CentOS*, focuses on network management in CentOS 7. Readers will learn how to validate and manage network configurations, including host name, DNS servers, and IP addressing. Readers will also learn remote logins using SSH, and file transfer using SCP and Rsync.

Chapter 8, *Software Package Management*, focuses on managing software using RPM and Yum. Readers will learn how to keep their systems up to date and install or remove applications by enabling official or third-party repositories.

Chapter 9, *Overview of Essential Advance Utilities*, focuses on a number of advance utilities related to system logging, system services management, and the securing of systems using firewalld and SELinux.

To get the most out of this book

As always, we have put our best efforts into making this book's content relevant to user requirements. All command lines covered in this book are based on CentOS 7. You can use any minor release of CentOS 7, from CentOS 7.1 through to CentOS 7.6. A CentOS 7 operating system is the only requirement for this book. For beginners, however, it is recommended installing and practicing CentOS 7 in any desktop virtualization application, such as VirtualBox, and VMWare Workstation.

For Windows and macOS users who would like to use a virtual environment, they can use VMWare or VirtualBox to set up CentOS 7 and execute the given command-line examples. For those who are new to Linux, the installation of CentOS 7 is covered in Chapter 1, *Getting Started with CentOS 7*.

Conventions used

There are a number of text conventions used throughout this book.

CodeInText: Indicates code words in text, database table names, folder names, filenames, file extensions, pathnames, dummy URLs, user input, and Twitter handles. Here is an example: "For example, DIRECTORY.. in mkdir usage means we have to insert the directory name we want to use with the mkdir command."

Any command-line input or output is written as follows:

```
$ mkdir -p -v demo/linux/centos
```

Bold: Indicates a new term, an important word, or words that you see on screen. For example, words in menus or dialog boxes appear in the text like this. Here is an example: "Thereafter, the **Begin Installation** button will be enabled."

 Warnings or important notes appear like this.

 Tips and tricks appear like this.

Get in touch

Feedback from our readers is always welcome.

General feedback: If you have questions about any aspect of this book, mention the book title in the subject of your message and email us at customercare@packtpub.com.

Errata: Although we have taken every care to ensure the accuracy of our content, mistakes do happen. If you have found a mistake in this book, we would be grateful if you would report this to us. Please visit www.packt.com/submit-errata, selecting your book, clicking on the Errata Submission Form link, and entering the details.

Piracy: If you come across any illegal copies of our works in any form on the internet, we would be grateful if you would provide us with the location address or website name. Please contact us at copyright@packt.com with a link to the material.

If you are interested in becoming an author: If there is a topic that you have expertise in, and you are interested in either writing or contributing to a book, please visit authors.packtpub.com.

Reviews

Please leave a review. Once you have read and used this book, why not leave a review on the site that you purchased it from? Potential readers can then see and use your unbiased opinion to make purchase decisions, we at Packt can understand what you think about our products, and our authors can see your feedback on their book. Thank you!

For more information about Packt, please visit packt.com.

Getting Started with CentOS 7

Community Enterprise Operating System, commonly referred to as **CentOS**, is a fast, stable, and open source enterprise-grade Linux distribution used on laptops, desktops, and servers. It is derived from the source code of **Red Hat Enterprise Linux** (**RHEL**), which is developed and maintained by the CentOS community. All proprietary content related to Red Hat Inc. is removed from the CentOS packages, which are then recompiled with CentOS community assets, such as logos and so on. CentOS 7 is an exact replica of RHEL 7, but is available for free with community support and updates. The CentOS project is now officially sponsored by Red Hat Inc. and is most suitable for environments where commercial support for operating systems is not mandatory.

In this chapter, we will give you a walk-through on how to install CentOS 7 on your computers. After installation, we will introduce you to the command-line console of Linux in order to use **Bash** (short for **Bourne Again Shell**). This chapter teaches you how to set up your environment to perform all the exercises in the following chapters of this book.

In this chapter, we will cover the following:

- Preparing to install CentOS 7
- Performing manual installation
- Accessing the command line using the console
- Introducing the Bash shell
- Bash shell and command execution

Preparing to install CentOS 7

The CentOS community released its latest operating system version with the name CentOS 7.6-1810, where 7.6 comes from RHEL 7.6 and 1810 shows its release date (October 2018). CentOS 7.6 can be installed on physical or virtual hardware. You can use any of the main desktop virtualization software utilities, such as Oracle VirtualBox (`https://www. virtualbox.org/wiki/Downloads`) or VMWare Workstation (`https://www.vmware.com/ products/workstation-pro/workstation-pro-evaluation.html`), as per your environment. My choice for desktop virtualization software is VirtualBox as it is free, open-source, and easy to use. You will also need a working internet connection to download the CentOS image from the community download page.

 Those are using Linux as their base operating system can also use KVM for virtualization.

Getting the right hardware

For a minimal installation of CentOS 7.6, the following hardware requirements must be met:

- 512 MB RAM
- 4 GB HDD space
- A network card

However, to practice all the exercises described in this book, we recommend that the following hardware requirements are met:

- 64-bit architecture support
- 1 GB RAM
- 10 GB HDD space
- DVD drive or USB memory stick
- A network card

Getting the software

There are different ways to get the software required to perform all the exercises in this book. However, the easiest and most flexible way is to download the `iso` file from the CentOS website and burn it to a DVD, or create a bootable USB drive with CentOS. Then, boot your PC using the ISO DVD image if you are using a virtual machine. If you are installing onto a physical system, then use a bootable USB drive or burned CentOS DVD for installation.

Use the following link to download the CentOS 7.6 (64 bits) ISO image file:

```
http://centos.mirror.net.in/centos/7.6.1810/isos/x86_64/CentOS-7-x86_64-DVD-
1810.iso
```

> You can download MD5 and SHA1 hashes of the image file downloaded from CentOS site. The downloaded image should have the same hash as the one posted on the CentOS website.

Finalizing server setup details

Once you have the right hardware and software for the CentOS installation, you should decide on the basic setup parameters to be specified while performing the installation. The following table lists the details we will use during the installation of our CentOS 7.6 server described in this chapter:

Setup parameter	Sample values
IP address	192.168.0.100
Netmask	255.255.255.0
Hostname	Server.example.com
Root password	Linux@12345
User name	Student
User password	Student@12345

Performing manual installation

Nowadays, the fastest and easiest way to install CentOS is to use a bootable USB drive; however, in our case, I have chosen to use the DVD ISO image with a virtual machine. First, we need to boot the computer system/virtual machine using the DVD. On booting from the DVD, you will get a cool CentOS screen displaying the basic installation options, and testing the media and troubleshooting options. Once your system/virtual machine is up and running with a bootable DVD of CentOS 7, follow these steps to install CentOS on your system:

1. We have to choose the **Install CentOS 7** option and press *Enter*, as shown in the following screenshot. This will start the graphical installer and ask about the language to be used during the installation process:

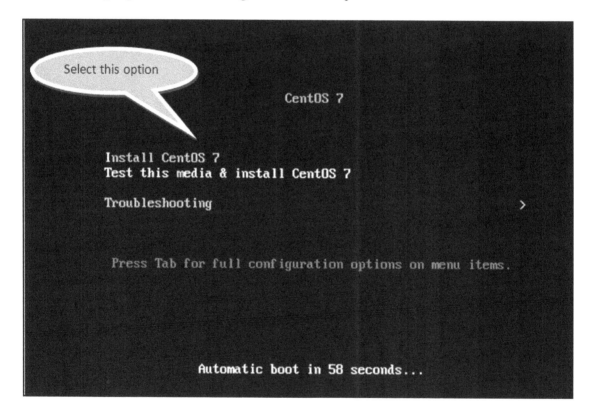

2. Now, you will see a **WELCOME TO CENTOS 7** screen, prompting you to choose your language and keyboard settings. Choose your respective language and keyboard settings and click on the **Continue** button, as shown in the following screenshot. In my case, I have chosen **English**:

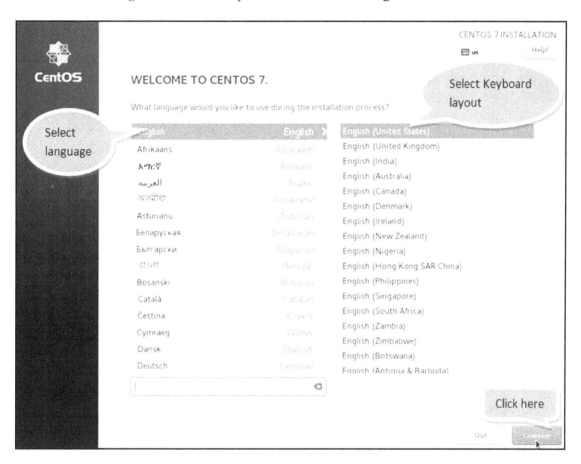

3. After this, you will see an **INSTALLATION SUMMARY** screen. From this screen, you can specify the settings you want to use for the three different sections and their sub-sections, as shown in the following screenshot:

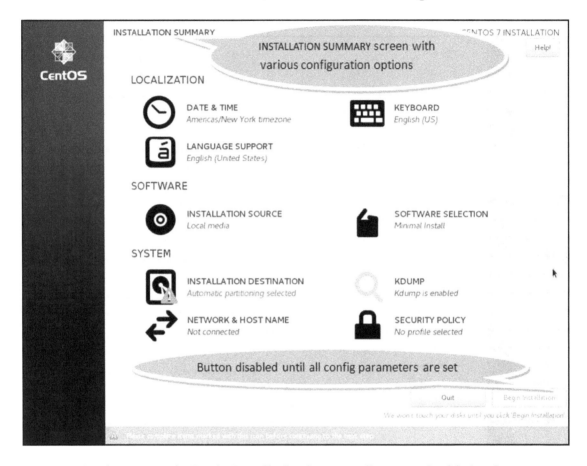

On this screen, the **Begin Installation** button will remain disabled as long as any setting from a section or subsection displayed on the **INSTALLATION SUMMARY** screen is still incomplete. If all the sections and subsections displayed on this screen are complete with minimum installation instructions, only then will the **Begin Installation** button be enabled.

By default, the installer does automatic partitioning for our hard disk. If we want to use the default layout, then we must click on **INSTALLATION DESTINATION**, and then approve the disk device we want to use for automatic partitioning by clicking on the **Done** button on the next screen. Thereafter, the **Begin Installation** button will be enabled and we can install CentOS with a minimal configuration, as shown in the following screenshot:

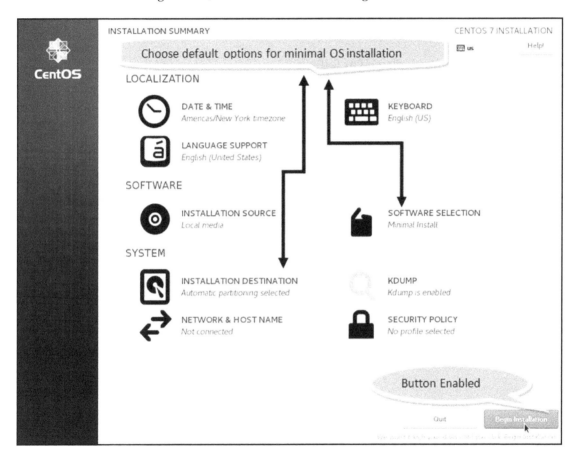

The minimal installation of CentOS 7 doesn't have a graphical interface—it has a bare minimum set of packages installed, with limited features available in the command-line interface.

4. If you are a beginner and want to use CentOS 7 with a **graphical user interface** (**GUI**), then follow these installation instructions. In this step, we'll learn about the usage of CentOS and then modify certain options that need to be configured during installation. The **INSTALLATION SUMMARY** screen has three sections, as follows:
    - **LOCALIZATION**
    - **SOFTWARE**
    - **SYSTEM**

These three sections are explained as follows:

- **LOCALIZATION**: This section further contains the following three sub-sections for configuration:
    - **DATE & TIME**
    - **KEYBOARD**
    - **LANGUAGE SUPPORT**

Or these three, the **DATE & TIME** sub-section is often required to be configured. The other two we have already configured in the previous steps.

In the **DATE & TIME** option, select the time zone that you are in by clicking on your location on the world map. You can also configure your current specific **DATE & TIME** from this window, as shown in the following screenshot:

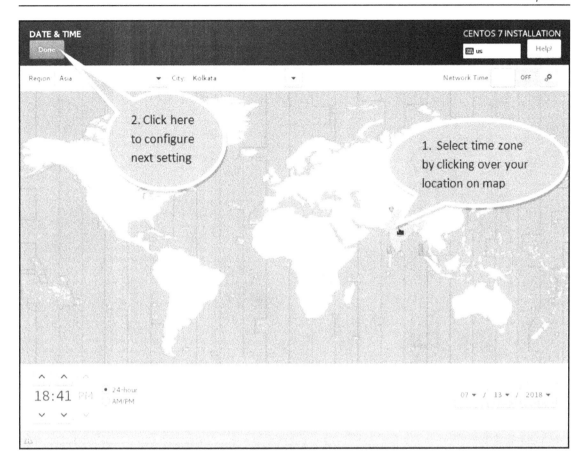

We leave the **KEYBOARD** and **LANGUAGE SUPPORT** settings at their defaults, and move to the next section to be configured—in this case, **SOFTWARE**.

- **SOFTWARE**: This section further contains two sub-sections for configuration:
  - **INSTALLATION SOURCE**
  - **SOFTWARE SELECTION**

Under the **SOFTWARE** section, we keep **INSTALLATION SOURCE** set to its default local media (DVD-ROM), as shown in the following screenshot:

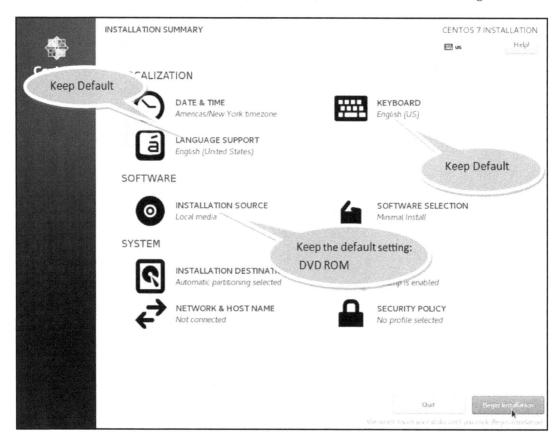

The next sub-section for configuration is **SOFTWARE SELECTION**. This forms an important part of the installation procedure. Click on this option and you will get the screen shown in the following screenshot. From here, you can choose the default base environment and add-ons that are available for the selected environment. For our practice demonstration, we will install the **GNOME Desktop** base environment with four add-ons: **GNOME Applications**, **Office Suite and Productivity**, **Development Tools** and **System Administration Tools** as shown in the following screenshot:

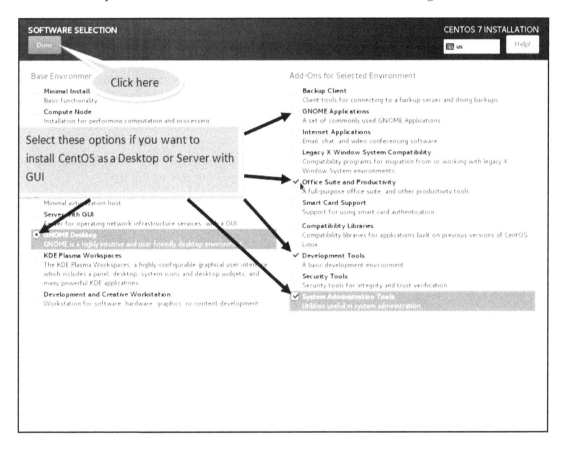

- **SYSTEM**: This section further contains four sub-sections for configuration:
  - **INSTALLATION DESTINATION**
  - **KDUMP**
  - **NETWORK & HOST NAME**
  - **SECURITY POLICY**

In this section, we keep the **KDUMP** and **SECURITY POLICY** sub-sections set to their default parameters, and configure the two remaining sub-sections as follows:

In the **INSTALLATION DESTINATION** sub-section, we specify where we want to install CentOS. Automatic partitioning is selected by default, but we can create a manual partitioning scheme of our own as per our requirements. As a bare minimum standard, we will create the following three partitions:

- **Boot partition**: This partition stores bootable files such as the kernel image, and so on.
- **Swap partition**: This is for swapping files and programs in and out of the RAM. It is generally twice the size of the RAM.
- **Root (/) partition**: This contains the Linux filesystem.

The following screenshot shows where to click to create manual partitions:

5. Choose the device onto which to install the OS, and select **I will configure partitioning**. Finally, click on the **Done** button to proceed with the creation of multiple partitions as shown in the following screenshot:

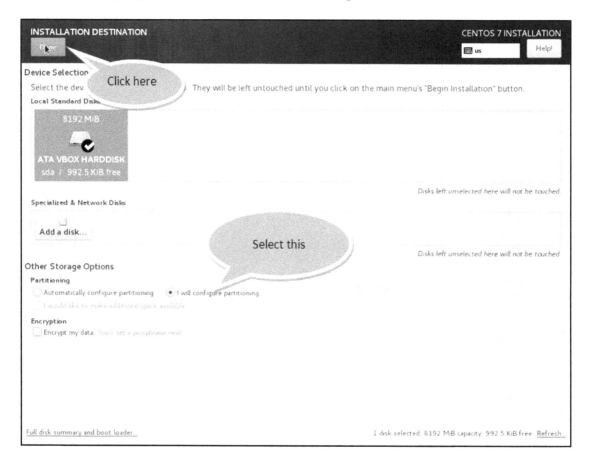

6. Now, we create a minimum of three partitions in the partition table (`boot`, `swap`, and `/`). In my case, I have kept **File System** as **xfs**, with the **Standard Partition** type for the `boot` and / partitions. For the `swap` partition, the **File System** type is kept as `swap`, as shown in the following screenshot:

7. Next, on pressing **Done**, you will get the **SUMMARY OF CHANGES** dialog box. Click on the **Accept Changes** button to begin creating on the disk the partitions that we specified in the partition table, as shown in the following screenshot:

8. **NETWORK & HOST NAME**: In this final part of the installation summary, which we'll configure networking. You can leave the default settings as they are to get the IP address from the DHCP server, or click on **NETWORK & HOST NAME** to set up networking manually. From the dialog box, click on the **IPv4 Settings Tab**, then choose the method as **Manual** from drop-down menu and specify the private IP address, as shown in the following screenshot:

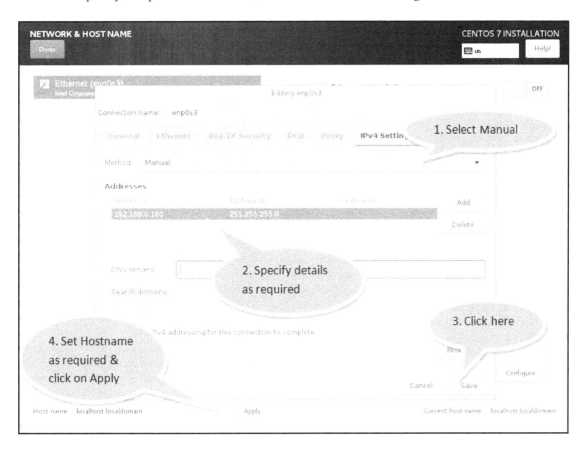

Further in the **NETWORK & HOST NAME** settings, change the network connection state from Off to On, as shown in the following screenshot:

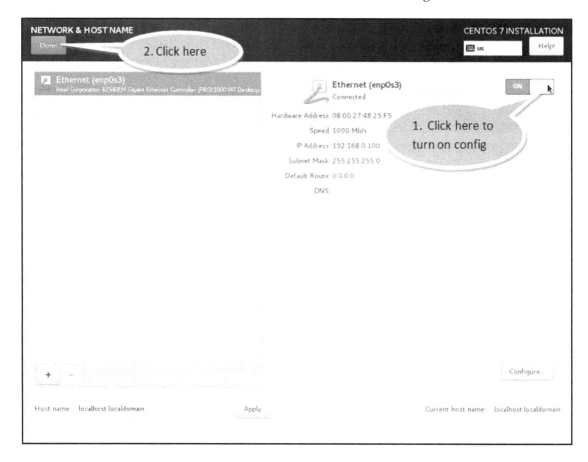

9. Now that all the **INSTALLATION SUMMARY** sections are configured as required, the **Begin Installation** button is enabled. Click on the **Begin Installation** button to start the process of installation, as shown in the following screenshot:

10. Next, the screen prompts for user settings. Here, we click **Root Password** first and set the password to Linux@12345.

11. Next, we click on **CREATE USER** to create a user. For both the **Full name** and **User name** fields, enter student, and set **Password** as Student@12345. Here also we have to click on the **Done** button twice to confirm the password, as shown in the following screenshot:

12. Have a cup of coffee while the installation process is in progress. Once the installation is complete, remove any installation media (the instructions only apply to the DVD method) and click on the **Reboot** button, as shown in the following screenshot:

13. Once the system has rebooted, we will get the INITIAL SETUP screen, where we have to accept an EULA agreement before logging in to the system. Here, we click on **LICENSE INFORMATION** to accept the license agreement, as shown in the following screenshot:

14. Once the license agreement has been accepted, the **FINISH CONFIGURATION** button will become enabled. Click on it to reach the login screen.

15. On the login screen, click on the **student** username and enter the password as Student@12345, as shown in the following screenshot:

16. After a successful login, you will see the welcome screen that is displayed only when the user LOGS IN for the first time. Click on the **Next** button to reach the desktop.

17. Congratulations! You have successfully installed the latest version of CentOS 7 on your computer system or virtual machine. You can explore your new CentOS 7 environment and perform other tasks, such as updating the system or installing other useful software for daily operational requirements. To power down the system, click on the right corner of desktop. You will get a drop-down menu; from there you can click on **Shut down**, as shown in the following screenshot:

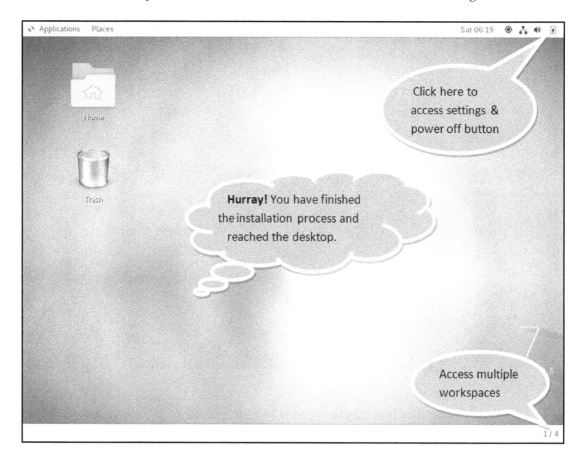

With this, your installation process is complete. In the upcoming section, we will learn how to access the command-line console.

Accessing the command line using the console

When using CentOS, system administration or applications development tasks are performed using either the **command-line interface** (**CLI**), such as the Bash shell, or with the help of a GUI, such as GNOME, KDE, and so on. In this section, we will learn how to enter commands in the Bash shell at the Linux console.

Starting a Terminal

When you log in to a Linux system in CLI mode or open a Terminal, it displays a string where it waits for user input (a command). This is known as a **shell prompt**.

To access a shell prompt in the GUI environment, you have to start a Terminal application, such as GNOME Terminal. There are multiple ways to launch a Terminal. The most frequently used ways to access a Terminal are as follows:

- Select **Applications** | **System Tools** | **Terminal**
- Right-click anywhere on your Terminal and select **Open in Terminal** from the context menu that pops up
- From the activities overview, select **Terminal**

If you have started the Terminal application as a normal user, then the default prompt ends with a $ character, as shown in the following screenshot:

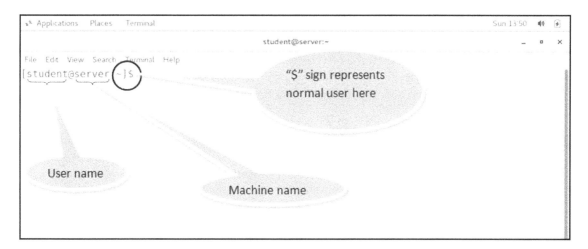

A normal shell prompt lists the following three details:

- The login name of the current user
- A short hostname of the machine, also known as the machine name
- The name of the current working directory

 The tilde (~) sign in the shell prompt represents the user's home directory. We will learn more about this in the following chapter.

If you have started or switched to the shell as a root user, also known as a **superuser** or **administrator**, then the prompt ends with a # character, as shown in the following screenshot:

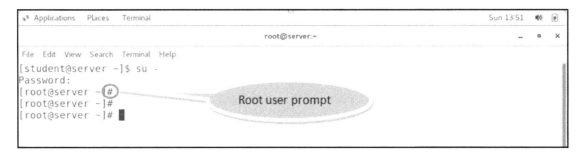

The default shell of CentOS 7 is Bash, which provides a scripting facility for the automation of repeated tasks. The main functionality of any shell is to interpret the commands entered by the user at the prompt, and to provide a platform to launch any other program.

 The default shell of Unix distributions is generally set as the Bourne shell. It is similar to the Microsoft Windows's Command Prompt application, cmd.exe. Windows 7 and Windows Server 2008 R2 onwards include Microsoft PowerShell, which is very similar in functionality to Bash.

There are two ways to access the shell. The first method is via the Terminal. When you install Linux without a GUI (as in a text-based installation), this can be the Linux machine's physical console, consisting of a keyboard for user input and a display to show output.

The second method is by using the shell from a virtual console. The Linux machine's physical console supports multiple virtual consoles, which act as separate Terminals with independent login sessions. If the GUI is installed, then the first virtual console is the GUI in CentOS/RHEL. In addition to the first graphical environment, five pure text-based environments are also available on a virtual console with which you can access a login shell. *Ctrl + Alt + (F2 through F6)* are text-based and *Ctrl + Alt + F1* is the graphical desktop.

Command-line syntax and structure

Any command entered at the shell prompt can be broken down into three parts:

Part	Description
Command	The name of the application to be executed
Options	This modifies the behavior of the command; options are generally prefixed with one or two hyphens
Arguments	These generally indicate the target on which the command is be applied

A command can consist of one or more options and can take one or more arguments, depending upon its syntax. Understanding the syntax of commands will tell you all about the options and arguments it can take, and in what order. To view the syntax of a command, we can use the `--help` option or view the manual page. The usage of the `mkdir` command with its options is shown in the following screenshot:

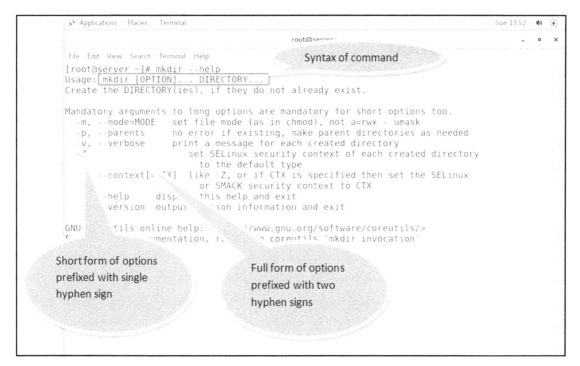

Initially, you may find the output of the `--help` option a bit confusing. However, it becomes much simpler once you understand the basic conventions used in the syntax, discussed as follows:

- Square brackets, `[ ]`, enclose optional items. For example, it is not mandatory to execute the `mkdir` command with any option, as shown in the following command line:

      $ mkdir mydirectory

- Ellipses, …, represent a list of more than one item of a given type. For example, we can use multiple options, such as `-m` and `-p` or `-v`, together with the `mkdir` command as shown in the following command line:

      $ mkdir -p -v demo/linux/centos

- Text given in angled brackets, `<>`, represents variable data. Sometimes, variable data is also written in capital letters. For example, `DIRECTORY..` in `mkdir` means we have to insert the directory name we want to use with the `mkdir` command.
- Multiple items separated by pipes (`|`), mean that only one of those items can be specified.

Exiting the shell

There are multiple ways to quit the shell, when you have finished using it and you want to end your session. Some of the most popular options to exit the shell are as follows:

- Typing the `exit` command anytime on the console terminates the current session.
- Pressing the `Ctrl + D` keys together is also a shortcut quite often used to terminate the current session.

Introducing the Bash shell

The GNU Bash is primarily a program that interprets commands entered by the user at the prompt. As we learned in the previous *Command line syntax and structure* section, each command entered by the user can have three parts:

- The command
- The options (beginning with – or ––)
- The arguments

Each word entered in the shell is separated from the others with a space. Commands are the names of various applications installed on our system, where each command has its own options and arguments.

When you want to execute a command entered at the prompt, the *Enter* key is pressed. After the *Enter* key is pressed, output from that command is displayed on the shell, which is followed again by the prompt as shown in the following screenshot:

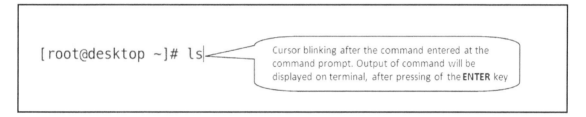

Each command is entered on a single line; however, if you wish you can enter multiple commands on a single line using the semicolon (;), which acts as a command separator.

The various functions performed by the shell include the following:

- It provides an interface between the user and operating system
- It is a way for the user to execute commands and other programs
- It acts as an command-line interpreter for commands entered at the command prompt
- Shell also enables the automation of tasks by reading commands from a special text file, known as a shell script
- Shell provides an environment for users and programs running on the operating system

There are multiple types of shell installed on each Linux distribution, with slight differences in features among them. The **Bourne shell** (**sh**) is the most primitive, and the Bash shell is the most advanced. The differences between these shells are listed in the following table:

Feature	Bourne	Korn	C	Tcsh	Bash
Background processing	Yes	Yes	Yes	Yes	Yes
Command history	No	Yes	Yes	Yes	Yes
I/O redirection	Yes	Yes	Yes	Yes	Yes
Shell scripts	Yes	Yes	Yes	Yes	Yes
Command alias	No	Yes	Yes	Yes	Yes
File name completion	No	Yes	No	Yes	Yes
Command completion	No	No	No	Yes	Yes
Command line editing	No	Yes	No	Yes	Yes
Job control	No	Yes	Yes	Yes	Yes

Bash shell and command execution

In this section, we will learn about the different features of the Bash shell with which you can reduce errors and increase the speed at which you work on the Terminal.

Tab completion

Linux shell syntax is case-sensitive as well as space-sensitive, so typing errors are the first major hurdle in learning for any beginner. However, if the tab completion feature is adopted by a beginner, then it makes life very easy and smooth by reducing typing errors to a minimum.

Tab completion enables you to complete command names or file names once you have typed enough characters at the prompt to make it unique. If the characters entered at prompt are not unique, pressing the *Tab* key twice displays all commands that can begin with the character already entered into the command line. An example of command completion using the *Tab* key is shown in the following screenshot:

```
                                    root@server:/home/student/Desktop

 File   Edit   View   Search   Terminal   Help

[root@server Desktop]# pas <Press tab><Press tab> (list combination which exists)
passwd          paste           pasuspender
[root@server Desktop]# pass <Press tab> (completes unique command given characters)
[root@server Desktop]# passwd
Changing password for user root.
New password:
[root@server Desktop]#
```

The Tab completion feature can be used to complete file names or path names when typing them as argument to commands. Pressing the *Tab* key once completes the filename or path if it is unique; otherwise, pressing the *Tab* key a second time lists all the possible combinations of filenames or path names based on the current pattern. Thereafter, you can type additional characters to make the name or path unique, and press the *Tab* key again for completion of the command line. An example of path and filename completion using the *Tab* key is shown in the following screenshot:

```
                               root@server:/home/student/Desktop                    _  □  ✕

 File   Edit   View   Search   Terminal   Help
[root@server Desktop]# ls /etc/pas <Press tab><Press tab> (completes the unique name)
[root@server Desktop]# ls /etc/passwd <Press tab> (it list various combination which exists)
passwd      passwd-
[root@server Desktop]# ls /etc/passwd
/etc/passwd
```

Command-line editing shortcuts

Bash has a very useful command-line editing feature that can increase your productivity while working on the Terminal. It enables the user to use some shortcut commands to move around or delete characters on the command prompt.

The following table lists the most useful command line shortcuts available in Bash:

Shortcut	Description
	To move the cursor
Ctrl + A	Moves the cursor to the beginning of the command line
Ctrl + E	Moves the cursor to the end of the command line
Ctrl + Left arrow	Moves the cursor to the beginning of the previous word on the command line
Ctrl + Right arrow	Moves the cursor to the beginning of the next word on the command line
	To delete characters
Ctrl + U	Deletes the characters from the current cursor position to the beginning of the command line
Ctrl + K	Deletes the characters from the current cursor position to the end of the command line
Ctrl + W	Deletes the last word from the current cursor positing on the command line
Ctrl + L	Clears the screen (you can also type the `clear` command)
	To modify the size of the Terminal window
Ctrl + +	Increases the size of the Terminal window
Ctrl - -	Decreases the size of the Terminal window

The history command

The `history` command is used to display a list of previously executed commands prefixed with a command number showing the order of their execution, as shown in the following screenshot:

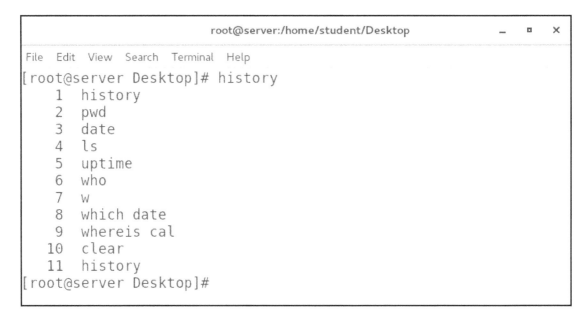

The exclamation point character (!) is a metacharacter in Bash, used for previously executed command expansion from history list on prompt.

The following table lists various `history` commands that are quite useful for beginners:

Command	Description
!<number>	Expands to the command matching the specified number from history
!<string>	Expands to the most recently used command that begin with the string specified at the prompt
history -d <number>	Used to delete the numbered command from history
history -c	Empties the history list
Ctrl + R	Searches the history list of commands for a pattern, and executes the most recent match when found

The following screenshot displays the usage of the `history` command:

```
 File   Edit   View   Search   Terminal   Help
[root@server Desktop]# history
     1   history
     2   pwd
     3   date
     4   ls
     5   uptime
     6   who
     7   w
     8   which date
     9   whereis cal
    10   clear
    11   history
[root@server Desktop]# !3
date
Sun Jul 22 16:36:42 IST 2018
[root@server Desktop]# !upt
uptime
 16:36:52 up  2:53,  2 users,  load average: 0.10, 0.04, 0.05
[root@server Desktop]# history -c
[root@server Desktop]# history
     1   history
[root@server Desktop]#
```

Besides the already listed options, we can use the arrow keys for navigation between the previous and next command line in the shell's history. The Up arrow key brings up the previous command executed from the history list. The Down arrow key brings up the next command from the history list.

Command aliases

The `alias` command is used to create an alias name or nickname for frequently used commands. It simplifies the administration process by providing alias names for long commands or even combinations of commands.

Listing current aliases

To list the currently configured aliases for your shell, just type `alias` without any argument at the prompt, as shown in the following command line:

```
$ alias
```

Setting an alias

The following syntax is used to set an alias x for the `exit` command. Thus, after setting this alias, whenever you want to exit from Terminal, you just have to enter x at the prompt:

```
$ alias x="exit"
$ alias c="clear"
```

Removing an alias

To remove an `alias`, the `unalias` command is used. For example, to remove the previously set `alias`, we use the `unalias` command as follows:

```
$ unalias x
```

The `alias` command will set its alias for the current session only. If you want to set an alias for any command persistently, you have to make an entry for it in `/etc/bashrc` for system-wide changes, and if you want to make user-specific changes, than put its entry in the `.bashrc` file stored in the user's home directory.

Summary

In this chapter, we started our journey learning CentOS 7. First, we began with the installation process, which was followed by an introduction to the Bash shell and command line syntax and structure. We then mastered the basic features of running commands from the shell with fewer strokes with the help of the *Tab* key, command-line shortcuts, `history`, and `aliases`.

In our next chapter, we will continue our journey through CentOS 7, looking at the Linux file system hierarchy and other essentials.

Command-Line and Filesystem Navigation

2

In this chapter, our objective is to identify the purpose of important directories in the CentOS 7 filesystem, and to learn various basic command-line skills. When we are working on the command line, it is essential that we have a clear picture of the filesystem hierarchy, layout, and organization in mind. We will go through the variety of documentation that exists on CentOS 7, including man pages, info pages, `help` command options, and so on. Thereafter, we will learn various filesystem navigation and management commands for changing directories, copying, moving, and renaming files, and so on. Finally, we'll learn about archiving and compressing files, which are very often required when creating backups.

In this chapter, we will cover the following:

- Understanding the CentOS 7 filesystem hierarchy
- Using man pages and the `help` command
- Managing filenames with path expansion
- Managing files using command-line tools
- Managing archives and compressed files

Understanding the CentOS 7 filesystem hierarchy

We can compare a filesystem to a refrigerator, or any other storage with multiple shelves that is used for storing different items. These shelves or compartments help us to organize grocery items in our refrigerator by certain characteristics, such as shape, size, type, and so on. The same analogy is applicable to a filesystem, which is the epitome of storing and organizing collections of data and files in human-usable form.

A filesystem is organized in an inverted root tree design with / (a forward slash; pronounced root) as the root of the filesystem, and underneath /, we see the rest of the directories and subdirectories, as shown in the following diagram:

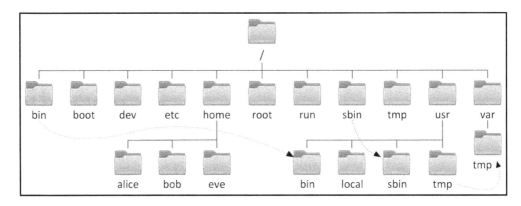

Important filesystem directories in CentOS 7

This layout of the filesystem hierarchy is described in the Linux Filesystem Hierarchy Standard.

Here, / represents two things:

- The root directory at the top of the filesystem hierarchy.
- It is also used as a directory separator to separate one directory from another. For example, the home directory is inside the / directory; hence, it is referred to as /home/. Similarly, if we have another directory, alice, above the /home directory, it is represented as /home/alice/.

Each directory is used for the standard purpose of organizing files of a particular type and purpose. Any directory can contain four types of content, as shown in the following table:

Content type	Description
Static	This type of content remains unmodified until explicitly edited

Dynamic or variable	This type of content generally gets modified continuously
Persistent	This type of content retains changes made even after reboot, for example, configuration files
Runtime	This type of content mostly resides in memory and its contents are cleared on reboot, for example, files used by processes of the system

The following table lists the location and purpose of important directories in CentOS 7:

Location	Purpose
/boot	Contains files required to start the boot process of CentOS 7, including the GRUB configuration file, the kernel image (vmlinuz), the RAM disk file (initramfs), and so on.
/dev	Contains special device files used by the system to access hardware and software devices such as /dev/sda (for the hard disk drive), or /dev/pts1 (for representing a psuedo Terminal).
/etc	Contains configuration files for applications (resolv.conf, passwd, and so on) installed on this particular system for system-wide changes.
/root	The home directory of the root user, also known as superuser.
/home	Contains home directories of normal users for storing their personal files.
/run	Contains runtime data, variables, process IDs, lock files, and so on for processes started since the last boot. The contents of this directory are regenerated upon restarting the system (in CentOS 6, its contents were stored in /var/run and /var/lock). One of the important subdirectories in this directory is as follows: • /run/media: Used as a mount point for removable devices such as USB, CDs, DVDs, and so on
/var	Contains the variable data, specific to the system that persists across reboots. The content and size of these files change dynamically (for example log files, printer-spooled documents, website content, and FTP content) as the system is running. The /var directory can be put in its own filesystem so that the growth of files does not fatally affect the system.

`/tmp`	Contains temporary files; has write permissions enabled for all users on the system. The files that have not been accessed, modified, or changed in last 10 days are deleted automatically from this directory. Another temporary storage directory in our system is `/var/tmp`.
`/usr`	Contains application files, shared libraries, and documentation. The files in this directory are static, read-only, and shareable. It also has three important sub-directories, as follows: • `/usr/bin`: Contains essential user commands (`ps`, `ls`, `cp`, and so on) • `/usr/sbin`: Contains system administration commands (`fsck`, `shutdown`, and so on) • `/usr/local`: Contains data and program specific to the local machine • `/usr/include`: Contains header files used to compile applications
`/bin`	A symbolic link to `/usr/bin`.
`/sbin`	A symbolic link to `/usr/sbin`.
`/lib`	A symbolic link to `/usr/lib`; contains shared libraries used by applications stored in `bin` and `/sbin`.
`/lib64`	A symbolic link to `/usr/lib64` and contains the 64-bit shared libraries used by applications stored in `/bin` and `/sbin`.
`/mnt`	This directory is used as temporary mount point for partitions and devices in the filesystem tree, such as for the mounting of NFS filesystems.
`/proc`	Contains the virtual filesystem (as in, it exists only in memory); also known as a psuedo-filesystem of the kernel. It contains dynamic runtime system information (for example, system memory, devices mounted, hardware configuration, and so on) and is considered the control and information center of the kernel. Some utilities directly call the files stored in this directory and display the information such as free memory using the `/proc/meminfo` file and arp table info using the `/proc/net/arp` file, and so on.

 For detailed info on the Linux Filesystem Hierarchy Standard, you can refer to the *Using the man command* section, and `https://www.tldp.org/LDP/Linux-Filesystem-Hierarchy/html/` for an online reference.

Using man pages and the help command

We could spend a good amount of time learning CentOS 7; it is equivalent to serving you cooked food, but in place of this, we could actually learn how to cook, so that you'll be able to make your own different recipes. Linux has one of the best and largest bodies of documentation in the operating system for most of the commands and their options. Whether you are an experienced user or a beginner, you will never remember the exact use of all the Linux commands and utilities, each with its own multiple options. It is in this case that Linux documentation comes to our rescue.

Different types of documentation available in Linux

There are multiple sources of documentation available in Linux for learning how to use different commands and their options, as shown in the following diagram:

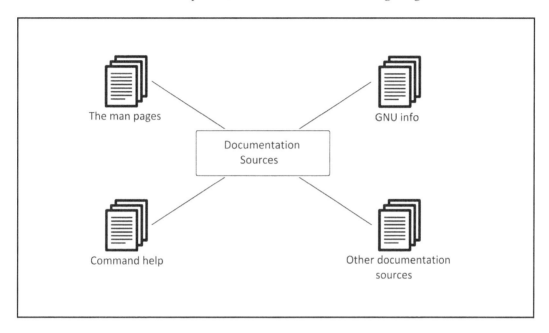

Different types of documentation in Linux

Using the man command

Man (short for **manual**) pages are the most used source of Linux documentation for various programs, utilities, system calls, library files, configuration files, and kernels that exist within the system. The whole man documentation is organized in nine sections, where each section caters for a particular type of documentation. By default, if there are multiple sections for one command, it displays the documentation from the first section it encounters. The syntax for man command usage is as follows:

```
$ man <topic name>
```

Upon execution of the preceding command, the specified topic's contents will be displayed on one screen at a time. Use the arrow keys for scrolling line by line, or press the Space bar for the next screen. By default, man pages are opened in the less viewer.

The following table lists the man page navigation command keys and their description:

Key	Description
Space bar/*Page Down*	Scroll down one screen
Page Up	Scroll up one screen
Down arrow (↓)	Scroll down a single line
Up arrow (↑)	Scroll up a single line
/string	Search forward (down) for the given string in the man page
?string	Search backward (up) for the given string in the man page
n	Repeat the previous search forward in the man page
N	Repeat the previous search backward in the man page
q	Exit the man and return to the prompt
g/Home	Go to the start of the man page
G/End	Go to the end of the man page

Some useful options that are used with the man command include the following:

- `$ man -f <topic name>`: Gives a brief description of that topic (the equivalent of the `whatis` command). See the following screenshot for usage:

```
[root@server Desktop]# man -f date
date (1)                - print or set the system date and time
date (1p)               - write the date and time
[root@server Desktop]# |
```

- `$ man -k <topic name>`: Lists all the matching pages that discuss a specified topic in their man pages (the equivalent of `apropos`). See the following screenshot for usage:

```
[root@server Desktop]# man -k passwd
chpasswd (8)              - update passwords in batch mode
fgetpwent_r (3)          - get passwd file entry reentrantly
getpwent_r (3)           - get passwd file entry reentrantly
gpasswd (1)              - administer /etc/group and /etc/gshadow
grub2-mkpasswd-pbkdf2 (1) - Generate a PBKDF2 password hash.
kpasswd (1)              - change a user's Kerberos password
lpasswd (1)              - Change group or user password
lppasswd (1)             - add, change, or delete digest passwords.
pam_localuser (8)        - require users to be listed in /etc/passwd
passwd (1)               - update user's authentication tokens
sslpasswd (1ssl)         - compute password hashes
passwd (5)               - password file
passwd2des (3)           - RFS password encryption
pwhistory_helper (8)     - Helper binary that transfers password hashes
saslpasswd2 (8)          - set a user's sasl password
smbpasswd (5)            - The Samba encrypted password file
vncpasswd (1)            - change the VNC password
[root@server Desktop]#
```

- `$ man -a <topic name>`: Displays, in sequence, all the man pages with the given topic name from all sections. For example, `man -a passwd` will list all the man pages containing `passwd` in any section.

- `$ man <section number> <topic name>`: Forces the `man` command to display topic documentation from a given section. Otherwise, by default, it displays the most popular section when used without a section number, as shown in the following command:

  ```
  $ man passwd
  ```

Output on execution of the preceding command is shown in the following screenshot:

```
PASSWD(1)                    User utilities                    PASSWD(1)

NAME
       passwd - update user's authentication tokens

SYNOPSIS
       passwd [-k] [-l] [-u [-f]] [-d] [-e] [-n mindays] [-x maxdays]
       [-w warndays] [-i inactivedays] [-S] [--stdin] [username]

DESCRIPTION
       The passwd utility is used  to  update  user's  authentication
       token(s).

       This  task  is  achieved  through  calls  to the Linux-PAM and
       Libuser API.  Essentially, it initializes itself as a "passwd"
       service  with  Linux-PAM and utilizes configured password mod-
       ules to authenticate and then update a user's password.
```

The man command with a specified section lists the documentation from that particular section as shown in following command:

```
$ man 5 passwd
```

Output on execution of the preceding command is shown in the following screenshot:

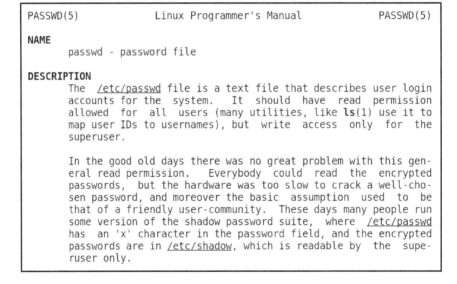

```
PASSWD(5)              Linux Programmer's Manual              PASSWD(5)

NAME
       passwd - password file

DESCRIPTION
       The  /etc/passwd file is a text file that describes user login
       accounts for  the  system.   It  should  have  read  permission
       allowed  for  all  users (many utilities, like ls(1) use it to
       map user IDs to usernames), but  write  access  only  for  the
       superuser.

       In the good old days there was no great problem with this gen-
       eral read permission.   Everybody  could  read  the  encrypted
       passwords,  but the hardware was too slow to crack a well-cho-
       sen password, and moreover the basic  assumption  used  to  be
       that of a friendly user-community.  These days many people run
       some version of the shadow password suite,  where  /etc/passwd
       has  an 'x' character in the password field, and the encrypted
       passwords are in /etc/shadow, which is readable by  the  supe-
       ruser only.
```

Using the GNU info command

The next source of documentation in Linux is GNU info pages, where the topics are connected using hyperlinks. The documentation contained in info pages can be read through the command line using `info` or `pinfo` commands, or with the help of a graphical utility. Some commands and utilities have both info and man documentation, but info documentation will usually be more in-depth.

The topic viewed in the info page is known as a **node**. Each node can include menus and subtopics known as **items**. Item names are prefixed with an asterisk (*) symbol. You can browse through the topic list using the regular keys (the arrow keys, *Page Up* and *Page Down*). The following table lists the most commonly used keys for navigation inside info pages:

Key	Description
Page Down or Space bar	Scroll forward one screen
Page Up or b	Scroll up one screen
n	Go to the next node
p	Go to the previous node
u	Move one node up in the index
Tab	Move to next hyperlink (node)
Enter	Select the node and display the content of the current cursor location
q	Quit viewing the info page
/string	Search for a string in the open document
/<Enter Key>	Repeat the previous search forward

Typing the `info` command without any argument in Terminal displays an index of available topics as shown in following command:

```
$ info <topic name>
```

Output on execution of the preceding command is shown in the following screenshot:

```
File: *manpages*,  Node: passwd,  Up: (dir)

PASSWD(1)                        User utilities                        PASSWD(1)


NAME
       passwd - update user's authentication tokens

SYNOPSIS
       passwd  [-k]  [-l]  [-u  [-f]]  [-d] [-e] [-n mindays] [-x maxdays] [-w
       warndays] [-i inactivedays] [-S] [--stdin] [username]


DESCRIPTION
       The passwd utility is used to update user's authentication token(s).

       This task is achieved through calls to the Linux-PAM and  Libuser  API.
       Essentially, it initializes itself as a "passwd" service with Linux-PAM
       and utilizes configured  password  modules  to  authenticate  and  then
       update a user's password.

       A simple entry in the global Linux-PAM configuration file for this ser-
       vice would be:
```

Using the help command and the --help option

The help command is another important source of documentation that exists in Linux. Most Linux commands have a short description that can be viewed using the --help or the -h option, along with the command or application name.

For example, you can learn more about the mkdir command by running it with the --help option, as shown in the following command:

```
$ mkdir --help
```

Output on execution of the preceding command is shown in the following screenshot:

```
[root@server ~]# mkdir --help
Usage: mkdir [OPTION]... DIRECTORY...
Create the DIRECTORY(ies), if they do not already exist.

Mandatory arguments to long options are mandatory for short options too.
  -m, --mode=MODE   set file mode (as in chmod), not a=rwx - umask
  -p, --parents     no error if existing, make parent directories as needed
  -v, --verbose     print a message for each created directory
  -Z                set SELinux security context of each created directory
                       to the default type
      --context[=CTX]  like -Z, or if CTX is specified then set the SELinux
                       or SMACK security context to CTX
      --help        display this help and exit
      --version     output version information and exit

GNU coreutils online help: <http://www.gnu.org/software/coreutils/>
For complete documentation, run: info coreutils 'mkdir invocation'
[root@server ~]#
```

The `--help` option is quite handy as a quick reference, as it displays limited information for using various options associated with the given command. Executing the `help` command on its own displays the list of built-in internal commands in Bash. You can also display the help info for these built-in commands by typing `help`, followed by the internal command name, as shown in following command:

```
$ help exit
```

Output on execution of the preceding command is shown in the following screenshot:

```
[root@server ~]# help exit
exit: exit [n]
    Exit the shell.

    Exits the shell with a status of N.  If N is omitted, the exit status
    is that of the last command executed.
[root@server ~]#
```

Other sources of documentation

In addition to `man` and `pinfo`, page developers may also include documentation in the application's RPM package. This documentation is installed on package installation and is conventionally stored in the `/usr/share/doc/<packagename>` directory. It contains any other relevant information that the developers want to share but that is not available in the man page of that package. You may find PDF, HTML, or TXT file-based documentation, license agreements, sample configuration files, and so on inside these directories.

Besides the preceding sources of documentation, if you have a GUI installed, then `gnome-help` or `Khelpcenter` are other sources of documentation available on the system. The online community of CentOS 7 also contains vast resources of documentation and help. Each Linux distribution has its own user-driven forums and Wiki sections.

The CentOS documentation is available at `https://www.centos.org/docs/`, but is being merged with the RHEL documentation at `http://access.redhat.com`, as CentOS has limited resources by comparison.

Some useful commands that give descriptions of other commands are as follows:

- `Whatis`: This command displays a short description of binaries available in the Linux system. Its database is updated daily in CentOS 7 with the help of another command, `makewhatis`.
- `Whereis`: This command locates the binary, source, and manual pages of the given command.
- `Which`: This command takes one or more command names as argument, and returns the absolute path of the given command name.

Managing filenames with path expansion

In this section, we will see the meta-characters and expansion technique that can improve file management efficiency.

File globbing

The bash shell can match a pathname based on some meta-characters. This feature is known as **file globbing**. The pathname matching capability was historically called globbing (also known as pattern-matching or wildcard matching) for managing a large number of files. It expands the meta-characters used in filenames and pathnames.

When using file globbing for matching filenames or pathnames, the meta-characters are replaced by the list of matching pathnames prior to command execution. The following table lists the pattern and its corresponding result:

Pattern	Result
?	Matches any single character
*	Matches any string of characters (0 or more)

`[set]`	Matches any character in the set; for example, `[akl]` will match any single occurrence of a, k, l
`[!set]` or `[^set]`	Matches any character not specified in the set of characters
`~`	Matches the current user's home directory (known as tilde expansion)
`~username`	Matches username's home directory

Wildcard expansion

To search for a file using the ? wildcard, replace each unknown character with ?, as shown in this example:

- `$ ls /etc/???.conf` will list the `conf` files with names that consist only of three characters

To search for files using the * wildcard, replace the unknown string with *, as shown in this example:

- `$ ls /etc/*.conf` will list all `conf` files inside the `/etc/` directory

The result of the preceding command will look as follows:

```
[student@server ~]$ ls /etc/???.conf
/etc/nfs.conf  /etc/ntp.conf  /etc/sos.conf  /etc/yum.conf
[student@server ~]$ ls /etc/*.conf
/etc/asound.conf                /etc/mke2fs.conf
/etc/autofs.conf                /etc/mtools.conf
/etc/autofs_ldap_auth.conf      /etc/nfs.conf
/etc/brltty.conf                /etc/nfsmount.conf
/etc/cgconfig.conf              /etc/nsswitch.conf
/etc/cgrules.conf               /etc/ntp.conf
/etc/cgsnapshot_blacklist.conf  /etc/numad.conf
/etc/chrony.conf                /etc/oddjobd.conf
/etc/dleyna-server-service.conf /etc/pbm2ppa.conf
/etc/dnsmasq.conf               /etc/pnm2ppa.conf
/etc/dracut.conf                /etc/radvd.conf
```

Tilde expansion

The tilde character, ~, if immediately followed by a forward slash, /, matches the current user's home directory, as shown in the screenshot:

```
[student@server ~]$ pwd
/home/student
[student@server ~]$ cd ~/Desktop
[student@server Desktop]$ pwd
/home/student/Desktop
[student@server Desktop]$ |
```

The tilde character, ~, if immediately followed by a string and then a forward slash, /, matches the username as specified in the string, as shown in the following screenshot:

```
[root@server ~]# pwd
/root
[root@server ~]# cd ~student/Desktop/
[root@server Desktop]# pwd
/home/student/Desktop
[root@server Desktop]# |
```

Brace expansion

Brace expansion generates a set of strings of characters. Inside braces, we specify a comma-separated list of strings or a sequence expression, which is either preceded or followed by text to append in the string supplied between braces, as shown in the following screenshot:

```
[root@server Desktop]# echo {Good,Average,Poor}_marks
Good_marks Average_marks Poor_marks
[root@server Desktop]#
[root@server Desktop]# echo file{1..4}.txt
file1.txt file2.txt file3.txt file4.txt
[root@server Desktop]# |
```

Command substitution

Command substitution allows the output of a command to be stored in a variable; the command can be replaced by itself. There are two methods for performing command substitution:

- Enclosing the command within backticks, as in `` `command` ``. Use of backticks is an older method, and has two disadvantages:
  - Backticks are sometimes confused with single quotation marks
  - Backticks cannot be nested inside other backticks, so nested command substitution is not possible
- Enclosing the command with an initial dollar sign and parentheses, as in `$(command)`. This overcomes the disadvantages of backticks when used in command substitution as shown in the following screenshot:

```
[root@server Desktop]# echo "Todays's date is : `date +%d-%m-%Y`"
Todays's date is : 05-08-2018
[root@server Desktop]#
[root@server Desktop]# echo "Todays's date is : $(date +%d-%m-%Y)"
Todays's date is : 05-08-2018
[root@server Desktop]#
```

Quoting and escaping

There are certain characters in bash shell that have special meaning, they are also known as meta-characters. Bash meta-characters enhance the flexibility, power and usage of bash. Examples of meta-characters are asterisk (*), question mark (?), hyphen (–), exclamation (!), and so on. The usage of expansion meta-character exclamation (!) is explained in Chapter 1, *Getting Started with CentOS 7*, in the *The history command* section. Quoting and escaping are used inside the bash shell to protect meta-character expansion:

- **Escaping**: The backslash (\) is an escape character that protects the special interpretation of the character immediately followed
- **Quoting**: To protect longer character strings, enclose them inside single (') or double (") quotes

- **Double quotes** ("): Using double quotes suppresses globbing and shell expansion; however, it allows command and variable substitution, as shown in the following screenshot:

```
[root@server Desktop]# computername=$(hostname)
[root@server Desktop]#
[root@server Desktop]# echo $computername
server.example.com
[root@server Desktop]# echo "My hostname is ${computername}"
My hostname is server.example.com
[root@server Desktop]#
```

- **Single quotes** ('): Using single quotes suppresses all kinds of expansion, and everything within single quotes is treated as literal characters without any special meaning, as shown in the following screenshot:

```
[root@server Desktop]# echo "My hostname is ${computername}"
My hostname is server.example.com
[root@server Desktop]#
[root@server Desktop]# echo 'My hostname is ${computername}'
My hostname is ${computername}
[root@server Desktop]#
```

File naming conventions

A file or folder name is a string used to identify a file. It can consist of 255 characters, including alphabetical letters, numbers, and special characters, excluding (/), which is used as the directory separator. You can include special characters (meta-characters); however, use of certain characters in filenames is not advisable, including ', ", $, #, !, and so on, because of their special interpretation by the shell.

Linux is case-sensitive as well as space-sensitive, so filenames are also case-sensitive. This means if we create files with the name data.txt and Data.txt in the same directory, then it results in two unique files.

The space is an acceptable character in Linux filenames; however, a space is also used as a delimiter by the command shell for command-line syntax interpretation, so it is generally not advised to use spaces in filenames in case this leads to ambiguity when executing commands.

Managing files using command-line tools

Commands are names of programs installed on the system. Before proceeding with the basic command operation, let's have a look at the two types of path traversal in Linux:

- **Absolute path**: This method specifies the full path of a file, regardless of your current location. This path always begins with a leading / (root directory) and specifies each subdirectory traversed in order to uniquely represent a single file in the filesystem. This removes any ambiguity whatsoever in the pathname. One directory is separated from another by a forward slash (/) in the pathname. While creating shell scripts, this type of naming convention should be used to refer to a file. Absolute pathnames are long to type in comparison to relative pathnames, which are used frequently when working on the command line to refer to a file or directory.
- **Relative path**: This method specifies the file path relative to your current location. It may or may not begin with one or more dot (.) symbol. This path never begins with a /. In this method of traversal, two or more files can have the same relative pathname in the same Linux filesystem, with respect to two different working locations. While working with shell scripts, this type of naming convention should always be avoided, in order to make your script executable from different locations in your Linux filesystem.

For example, if you are working in your home directory, /home/student, and you want to move to the /home/student/backup directory, you can traverse in the following two ways:

- Absolute pathname traversal: $ cd /home/student/backup
- Relative pathname traversal: $ cd backup:

```
[student@server ~]$ mkdir backup
[student@server ~]$ cd /home/student/backup (relative path traversal)
[student@server backup]$ pwd
/home/student/backup
[student@server backup]$ cd ..
[student@server ~]$ cd backup (absolute path traversal)
[student@server backup]$ |
```

The relative path of the backup directory, when a user's current working directory is /home/student, is simply backup. Here, we specify the directory name only with the cd command, since we are already working inside the /home/student directory.

In a standard Linux filesystem, the pathname of a file, including all characters (even the / directory separator), cannot exceed 4,095 bytes. Most of the time, it is easy to use relative paths for navigation, as it requires less typing. It also takes advantage of the shortcuts provided by meta-characters:

- .: Dot represents the current directory
- ..: Double dots represent the parent directory
- ~: Tilde represents the user's home directory

For example, imagine you are working in your home directory, /home/student, and you want to move to the /usr/bin directory; the following two methods can be used:

- Absolute pathname traversal: # cd /usr/bin
- Relative pathname traversal: # cd ../../usr/bin

Navigation commands

These commands fall into the category of navigation, as they are mostly used for navigating paths:

- pwd: The pwd command displays the full pathname of your current working directory. It helps in determining the current syntax to be used with other commands such as cp, mv, rm, mkdir, and so on, using relative pathnames, as shown in the following screenshot:

```
[student@server ~]$ pwd
/home/student
[student@server ~]$ cd Desktop/
[student@server Desktop]$ pwd
/home/student/Desktop
```

- `ls`: The `ls` command is used to list the directory contents of the given directory. If no directory name is given, then it lists the contents of the current directory as shown in the following screenshot:

```
[student@server ~]$ ls
demo      Documents  Music      Public      Videos
Desktop   Downloads  Pictures   Templates
[student@server ~]$ ls demo/
backup   myfile
[student@server ~]$ ls demo/ /opt/
demo/:
backup   myfile

/opt/:
rh
```

The `ls` command has got many options that are often used together to produce more structured and human-readable output. The most commonly used options with `ls` are listed in the following table:

Option	Description
-a	Displays the filenames beginning with a (.), as any filename beginning with (.) is hidden by default
-l	Displays detailed information on contents, also known as the long-listing format
-t	Sorts the listing contents by modification time, with last modified file first
-r	Lists the contents in reverse order while sorting by filename
-h	Prints the sizes of files in human-readable format (for example, 1 K, 50 M, 3 G, and so on)
-S	Sorts the contents by file size
-i	Prints the inode number of each file in listing
-Z	Displays the security context (SELinux parameter) for each file

The examples of `ls` command usage are shown in the following screenshot:

```
[student@server ~]$ ls -l demo/
total 516
drwxrwxr-x. 2 student student     63 Aug  6 08:31 backup
-rw-r--r--. 1 student student 525925 Aug  6 07:40 myfile
[student@server ~]$ ls -al demo/
total 520
drwxrwxr-x.  3 student student     34 Aug  6 08:03 .
drwx------. 16 student student   4096 Aug  6 07:42 ..
drwxrwxr-x.  2 student student     63 Aug  6 08:31 backup
-rw-r--r--.  1 student student 525925 Aug  6 07:40 myfile
[student@server ~]$ ls -ltrh demo/
total 516K
-rw-r--r--. 1 student student 514K Aug  6 07:40 myfile
drwxrwxr-x. 2 student student   63 Aug  6 08:31 backup
[student@server ~]$ ls -il demo/
total 516
6608076 drwxrwxr-x. 2 student student     63 Aug  6 08:31 backup
5178319 -rw-r--r--. 1 student student 525925 Aug  6 07:40 myfile
```

- `cd`: The `cd` command is used to change your working directory. We generally use relative pathnames for brevity while changing directories on the command line. However, while creating scripts, it's good practice to use absolute pathnames. The `cd` command has many options, some of which are described in the following table:

Option	Description
cd -	Changes directory to previous working directory
cd or cd ~	Changes directory to user's home directory
cd ~\<username\>	Changes directory to the specified \<username\> user's home directory
cd . .	Changes directory to up one level to the parent directory

The examples of `cd` command usage are shown in the following screenshot:

```
[root@server ~]# pwd
/root
[root@server ~]# cd /etc/sysconfig/network-scripts/
[root@server network-scripts]# pwd
/etc/sysconfig/network-scripts
[root@server network-scripts]# cd -
/root
[root@server ~]# pwd
/root
[root@server ~]# cd ~student/
[root@server student]# pwd
/home/student
[root@server student]# cd
[root@server ~]# pwd
/root
[root@server ~]# cd ../tmp
[root@server tmp]# pwd
/tmp
```

 The (. .) represents the parent directory of your current working directory, and (.) represents your current directory in relative pathname format.

File management commands

File management is the process of creating, deleting, copying, and moving files or directories for organizing files logically. When doing file management tasks on the command line, awareness of your current working directory is very important. This will help you to give correct absolute or relative pathnames for the immediate task in hand.

`cp` is used to copy a file or directory from one location to another. The various useful options used with this command are listed in the following table:

Command	Description
cp file1 file2	Copies `file1` with the name `file2` in the current directory
cp file1 file2 /tmp/	Copies `file1` and `file2` with the same name to the `/tmp/` directory
cp file1 /tmp/myfile	Copies `file1` with a new name, `myfile`, to the `/tmp/` directory
cp -r backup /tmp/	Copies the backup directory recursively to the `/tmp/` directory

The examples of `cp` command usage are shown in the following screenshot:

```
[student@server demo]$ pwd
/home/student/demo
[student@server demo]$ ls
backup  file1  file2  file3  myfile
[student@server demo]$ cp file1 file4
[student@server demo]$ ls
backup  file1  file2  file3  file4  myfile
[student@server demo]$
[student@server demo]$ cp file1 file2 backup/
[student@server demo]$ ls backup/
file1  file2
[student@server demo]$ cp file3 backup/mybackup
[student@server demo]$ ls backup/
file1  file2  mybackup
```

`mv` is used for two purposes. Firstly, it renames a file or directory if the source and destination path of the file are in the same directory. Secondly, it is used to perform cut and paste (move) operations when the source and destination directory are different.

Some of the most frequently used options with the `mv` command are as follows:

Command	Description
mv file1 file2	Renames file1 with the name file2 in the current directory
mv file1 file2 /tmp/	Moves file1 and file2 with the same name in the /tmp/ directory
mv file1 /tmp/myfile	Moves file1 with a new name, myfile, to the /tmp/ directory
mv backup /tmp/	Moves the directory with the name backup to the /tmp/ directory

The examples of `mv` command usage are shown in the following screenshot:

```
[student@server demo]$ ls
backup  file1  file2  file3  file4  myfile
[student@server demo]$ mv myfile oldfile
[student@server demo]$ ls
backup  file1  file2  file3  file4  oldfile
[student@server demo]$ ls backup/
file1  file2  mybackup
[student@server demo]$ mv oldfile backup/
[student@server demo]$ ls backup/
file1  file2  mybackup  oldfile
[student@server demo]$ mv file1 backup/file99
[student@server demo]$ ls backup/
file1  file2  file99  mybackup  oldfile
[student@server demo]$ ls
backup  file2  file3  file4
```

`mkdir` is used to create a directory. This command is also used with different options on the command line, including the following:

Command	Description
mkdir backup	Creates a sample directory backup in the current directory
mkdir /tmp/backup	Creates a sample directory backup under the /tmp directory
mkdir -p backup/linux/centos	Creates directories with full path backup/linux/centos (if parent directories are missing at destination, it will create full path)
mkdir linux windows mac	Creates directories with the name linux, windows, and mac in the current directory

The examples of `mkdir` command usage are shown in the following screenshot:

```
[student@server demo]$ ls -l backup/
total 536
-rw-rw-r--. 1 student student   3259 Aug  6 13:45 file1
-rw-rw-r--. 1 student student   6826 Aug  6 13:45 file2
-rw-rw-r--. 1 student student   3259 Aug  6 08:02 file99
-rw-rw-r--. 1 student student   2090 Aug  6 13:45 mybackup
-rw-r--r--. 1 student student 525925 Aug  6 07:40 oldfile
[student@server demo]$ mkdir -p backup/linux/centos
[student@server demo]$ ls backup/
file1  file2  file99  linux  mybackup  oldfile
[student@server demo]$ ls backup/linux/
centos
[student@server demo]$ mkdir devshare
[student@server demo]$ ls
backup  devshare  file2  file3  file4
```

`rmdir` is used to delete empty directories only. If a directory contains subdirectories or files, then we have to use the `rm -rf` command as shown in the following command:

```
$ rmdir <empty directoryname>
```

The examples of `rmdir` command usage are shown in the following screenshot:

```
[student@server demo]$ mkdir devshare
[student@server demo]$ ls
backup  devshare  file2  file3  file4
[student@server demo]$ rmdir devshare/
[student@server demo]$ rmdir backup/
rmdir: failed to remove 'backup/': Directory not empty
```

`rm` is used to delete/remove a file from the filesystem. This command also has multiple options, which are to be used with care as a file once deleted cannot be restored from the trash (the recycle bin of Linux) in command-line mode.

This is a table listing options frequently used with the `rm` command and their descriptions:

Command	Description
rm	Removes a file
rm -f	Forcefully removes a file
rm -i	Interactively removes a file by prompting before each removal (use this if you are uncertain of the filename)
rm -rf	Forcefully remove a directory recursively (use this option very cautiously)

The examples of `rm` command usage are shown in the following screenshot:

```
[student@server demo]$ ls
backup  file2  file3  file4
[student@server demo]$ rm file2
[student@server demo]$ ls
backup  file3  file4
[student@server demo]$ rm -i file3
rm: remove regular file 'file3'? y
[student@server demo]$ ls
backup  file4
[student@server demo]$ ls backup/
file1  file2  file99  linux  mybackup  oldfile
[student@server demo]$ rm -rf backup/
[student@server demo]$ ls
file4
```

The `ln` command is used to create links. There are two types of links in Linux, hard links and soft links, which is also known as symbolic link/symlink. The soft links of files and directories can be considered equivalent to the Windows shortcut for files and folders respectively:

- Hard link creation: $ `ln file1 file2`
- Soft link creation: $ `ln -s file1 file2`

The examples of `ln` command usage are shown in the following screenshot:

```
[student@server demo]$ ls -l
total 4
-rw-rw-r--. 1 student student 3259 Aug  6 13:44 file4
[student@server demo]$ ln file4 backupfile
[student@server demo]$ ls -l
total 8
-rw-rw-r--. 2 student student 3259 Aug  6 13:44 backupfile
-rw-rw-r--. 2 student student 3259 Aug  6 13:44 file4
[student@server demo]$ ln -s file4 softbackup
[student@server demo]$
[student@server demo]$ ls -l
total 8
-rw-rw-r--. 2 student student 3259 Aug  6 13:44 backupfile
-rw-rw-r--. 2 student student 3259 Aug  6 13:44 file4
lrwxrwxrwx. 1 student student    5 Aug  6 14:04            -> file4
```

Managing archives and compressed files

Archiving is the process of fetching multiple files from the same or different locations and putting them into a single file bundle. It is generally done together with compression, or immediately followed by compression. This helps in streamlining the backup process, as discussed in the following section.

Compression

File data is generally compressed to save the disk space and reduce traffic, as well as the time to transmit files over a network. Linux has multiple utilities for compression; some of them are listed in the table that follows:

Command	Description
gzip	Most popular Linux compression utility
gunzip	Utility to decompress gzip compressed files
bzip2	Another compression utility, with better compression than gzip
bunzip2	Utility to decompress .bzip2 compressed files
xz	The most space-efficient compression utility that exists in Linux
zip	Popular utility to decompress archives from other operating systems

These utilities have different algorithms for compression and thus different efficiency and resource consumption levels (generally, more efficient techniques take more time). Decompression time does not vary much across different methods.

gzip and gunzip compression

The gzip utility compresses files faster than any other utility.

The following table lists the gzip compression command and its description with some examples:

Command	Description
gzip *	Compresses all files in the current directory and each compressed file is renamed with the .gz extension
gzip -r backup/	Compresses all files in the backup/ directory and subdirectories
gunzip myfile.gz or gzip -d myfile.gz	Decompresses myfile.gz to myfile

The examples of the `gzip` and `gunzip` commands are shown in the following screenshot:

```
[student@server demo]$ ls -l backup/
total 516
-rw-r--r--. 1 student student 525925 Aug  6 07:40 myfile
[student@server demo]$ gzip -r backup/
[student@server demo]$ ls -l backup/
total 76
-rw-r--r--. 1 student student 76039 Aug  6 07:40 myfile.gz
[student@server demo]$
[student@server demo]$ gunzip backup/myfile.gz
[student@server demo]$ ls -l backup/
total 516
-rw-r--r--. 1 student student 525925 Aug  6 07:40 myfile
[student@server demo]$
```

bzip2 and bunzip2 compression

The syntax of the `bzip2` command is similar to `gzip`, but it uses a different compression algorithm and creates a smaller-sized compressed file, at the price of more time taken for compression.

The following table lists the `bzip2` compression command and its description with some examples:

Command	Description
bzip2 *	Compresses all files in the current directory and each compressed file is renamed with the .bz2 extension
bunzip2 *.bz2 or bzip2 –d *.bz2	Decompresses all the files with the .bz2 extension in the current directory

The examples of the `bzip2` and `bunzip2` commands are shown in the following screenshot:

```
[student@server backup]$ bzip2 *
[student@server backup]$ ls -l
total 44
-rw-r--r--. 1 student student 43521 Aug  6 07:40 myfile.bz2
[student@server backup]$ bunzip2 *.bz2
[student@server backup]$ ls -l
total 516
-rw-r--r--. 1 student student 525925 Aug  6 07:40 myfile
[student@server backup]$
```

xz compression

This is the most space-efficient compression utility used in Linux. The trade-off for compression is a slower speed of compression for a higher compression ratio.

The following table lists the `xz` compression command and its description with some examples:

Command	Description
`xz *`	Compresses all files in the current directory and each compressed file is renamed with the `.xz` extension
`xz myfile`	Compresses the `myfile` file to `myfile.xz` with the default compression level (6); deletes the original `myfile` after compression
`xz -dk`	Decompresses `myfile.xz` to `myfile` and preserves `myfile.xz` after decompression
`xz -d *.xz` or `unxz`	Decompresses all files with the extension `.xz` in the current working directory

The examples of `xz` command usage are shown in the following screenshot:

```
[student@server backup]$ ls -l
total 516
-rw-r--r--. 1 student student 525925 Aug  6 07:40 myfile
[student@server backup]$ xz *
[student@server backup]$ ls -l
total 36
-rw-r--r--. 1 student student 36764 Aug  6 07:40 myfile.xz
[student@server backup]$ xz -d *.xz
[student@server backup]$ ls -l
total 516
-rw-r--r--. 1 student student 525925 Aug  6 07:40 myfile
```

zip

This program is not generally used to compress files in Linux, but it is quite often required to decompress archives from a Windows OS.

The following table lists the `zip` command and its description with some examples:

Command	Description
`zip backup *`	Compresses all files in the present working directory and puts them inside `backup.zip`
`zip -r backup.zip /home/student/abc`	Archives the files and directories stored in `/home/student/abc` in the `backup.zip` file
`unzip backup.zip`	Extracts all the files from the `backup.zip` in the current directory

The examples of the `zip` and `unzip` commands are shown in the following screenshot:

```
[student@server backup]$ ls -l
total 516
-rw-r--r--. 1 student student 525925 Aug  6 07:40 myfile
[student@server backup]$ zip backup *
  adding: myfile (deflated 86%)
[student@server backup]$ ls -l
total 592
-rw-rw-r--. 1 student student  76176 Aug  6 07:54 backup.zip
-rw-r--r--. 1 student student 525925 Aug  6 07:40 myfile
[student@server backup]$ unzip backup.zip
Archive:  backup.zip
replace myfile? [y]es, [n]o, [A]ll, [N]one, [r]ename: y
  inflating: myfile
[student@server backup]$ ls -l
total 592
-rw-rw-r--. 1 student student  76176 Aug  6 07:54 backup.zip
-rw-r--r--. 1 student student 525925 Aug  6 07:40 myfile
```

Archiving

In addition to compression, the `tar` (tape archive) utility is very often used to group files into an archive known as a **tarball** and then compress the whole archive together. Creating a single file bundle by putting multiple files together is known as archiving.

The various options used with the `tar` command are given, with their descriptions, in the following table:

tar command option	Description
c	Creates an new archive
v	Verbosity, used to see which files are being added and extracted
f	Filename of the archive to operate on
x	Extracts an archive
t	Lists the contents of an archive
z	Uses `.gzip` compression (`.tar.gz`)
j	Uses `.bzip2` compression (`.tar.bz2`), better than `.gzip`
J	Uses `.xz` compression (`.tar.xz`), better than `.bzip2`

The tarball archives can be compressed using `.gzip`, `.bzip2`, or `.xz` compression with `tar` command itself.

The following table lists the usage of the `tar` command with compression utility:

Command	Description
`Tar cvf abc.tar file1 file2 file3`	Archives the `file1`, `file2`, and `file2` files and puts them into one single file, `abc.tar`
`Tar xvf abc.tar`	Extracts all the files in the `abc.tar` archive in the current directory
`Tar tvf abc.tar`	Lists all the files available inside the `abc.tar` archive
`Tar cvzf abc.tar.gz *`	Creates an `abc.tar.gz` archive of all the files in the current directory and compresses it with `.gzip`
`Tar cvjf abc.tar.bz2 *`	Creates an `abc.tar.bz2` archive of all the files in the current directory and compresses it with `.bzip2`
`Tar cvJf abc.tar.xz *`	Creates an `abc.tar.xz` archive of all the files in the current directory and compresses it with `.xz`
`Tar xvf abc.tar.gz abc.tar.bz2 abc.tar.xz`	Extracts all the files in `abc.tar.gz`, `abc.tar.bz2`, and `abc.tar.xz` in the current directory

Archiving with tar

In the following example, we cover creating and extracting archives:

```
[student@server backup]$ ls
file1  file2  file3
[student@server backup]$ tar cf abc.tar file1 file2 file3
[student@server backup]$ ls
abc.tar  file1  file2  file3
[student@server backup]$ rm file1 file2 file3
[student@server backup]$ ls
abc.tar
[student@server backup]$ tar xf abc.tar
[student@server backup]$ ls
abc.tar  file1  file2  file3
```

Archiving and compression (.gzip) using tar

In the following example, we cover creating and extracting `gunzip` compressed archives:

```
[student@server backup]$ ls
file1  file2  file3
[student@server backup]$ tar czf abc.tar.gz *
[student@server backup]$ ls
abc.tar.gz  file1  file2  file3
[student@server backup]$ tar tvf abc.tar.gz
-rw-rw-r-- student/student 3259 2018-08-06 08:02 file1
-rw-rw-r-- student/student 6826 2018-08-06 08:02 file2
-rw-rw-r-- student/student 2090 2018-08-06 08:25 file3
[student@server backup]$ tar xvf abc.tar.gz
file1
file2
file3
[student@server backup]$ ls
abc.tar.gz  file1  file2  file3
```

Archiving, compression (.bzip2), and listing contents using tar

In the following example, we cover creating and extracting `.bzip2` compressed archives:

```
[student@server backup]$ ls
file1  file2  file3
[student@server backup]$ tar cjf abc.tar.bz2 *
[student@server backup]$ ls
abc.tar.bz2  file1  file2  file3
[student@server backup]$ tar tvf abc.tar.bz2
-rw-rw-r-- student/student 3259 2018-08-06 08:02 file1
-rw-rw-r-- student/student 6826 2018-08-06 08:02 file2
-rw-rw-r-- student/student 2090 2018-08-06 08:25 file3
[student@server backup]$ rm file*
[student@server backup]$ ls
abc.tar.bz2
[student@server backup]$ tar xf abc.tar.bz2
[student@server backup]$ ls
abc.tar.bz2  file1  file2  file3
```

Archiving and compression (.xz) using tar

In the following example, we cover creating and extracting `.xz` compressed archives:

```
[student@server backup]$ tar cJf abc.tar.xz *
[student@server backup]$ ls
abc.tar.xz  file1  file2  file3
[student@server backup]$ rm file*
[student@server backup]$ ls
abc.tar.xz
[student@server backup]$ tar xf abc.tar.xz
[student@server backup]$ ls
abc.tar.xz  file1  file2  file3
```

Summary

In this chapter, we understood the Linux Filesystem Hierarchy Standard and different types of built-in documentation. Thereafter, we covered basic command-line operations, which included filesystem navigation and filesystem management from the command line. Finally, we got our hands dirty with different types of compression techniques and archiving in Linux.

In the next chapter, we will learn about different methods of managing text files.

Managing Text Files

3

Computer systems are mostly used for editing, manipulating, or managing data. On Linux systems, this data is very often in the form of text files. In general, everything in Linux is a file, and having a solid understanding of working with text files is important. All important information in Linux is stored in text format files.

In this chapter, our objective is to learn how to work with text files on the command line, using the most popular default text-based editor, vi, and other text file manipulation utilities. Then, we will learn how input/output redirection is executed in files and programs for further processing.

In this chapter, we will cover the following topics:

- Different methods to create a text file
- Editing files with the vi editor
- Using text file manipulation tools
- Redirecting output to files and programs
- Using grep for text matching
- Finding a file using the locate and find command

Different methods to create a text file

Text files can be viewed and edited using any text editor that exists in Linux. However, before learning the editing part, we must have a basic understanding of different ways that can be used to create plain text files. Depending on the requirement, different methods can be used for text file creation. The most popular ones are described next.

Create a text file using the cat command

The `cat` command can be used to create a text file if we immediately want to add some text to a new blank file. The syntax of the `cat` command to create a file is as follows:

```
$ cat > demo.txt
```

After pressing *Enter*, we will return to the prompt and we can directly start inserting text into our file. Once you are done entering text in the file, press *Ctrl + D* to mark the end of the file and return to the prompt, as shown in the following screenshot:

```
[root@server Desktop]# cat >demo.txt
Welcom to the CentOS 7 Quick Start Guide
This is second line
[root@server Desktop]# ls
demo.txt
[root@server Desktop]# cat demo.txt
Welcom to the CentOS 7 Quick Start Guide
This is second line
```

If you want to use the `cat` command to create a file from a bash script, we have to use an operator known as a here document. It can be any arbitrary string that can be used to mark the beginning of a file and end when repeated in a new line, as shown in the following screenshot:

```
[root@server Desktop]# cat <<EOF>sample.txt
> first line
> second line
> Third..
> EOF
[root@server Desktop]# ls
demo.txt  sample.txt
[root@server Desktop]# cat sample.txt
first line
second line
Third..
```

Create an empty text file using the touch command

The original purpose of the touch command is to update a file's timestamp to the current date and time without modifying it. The touch command can also be used to create an empty file of size 0 bytes. We cannot enter any text in the file with the touch command, but we can create multiple new files with a single command. It is quite often used to create files that are intended to be used in future. The syntax of the touch command is as follows:

```
$ touch <path_for_empty_file>
```

Examples of the touch command are shown in the following screenshot:

```
[root@server Desktop]# ls
[root@server Desktop]# touch file.txt
[root@server Desktop]# ls
file.txt
[root@server Desktop]# touch file1.txt file2.txt file3.txt
[root@server Desktop]# ls
file1.txt   file2.txt   file3.txt   file.txt
```

Create a text file using the redirection symbol (>)

We can also create a text file using the redirection symbol (>), which is used to redirect the output of a command to a file. If we use the redirection symbol alone without prefixing it with any command, then it will create an empty file of 0 bytes and remove the file's content if a file already exists with the given name, as shown in the following command line:

```
$ > demo.txt
```

If we prefix the redirection symbol (>) with any command, then it creates a new file, which contains the output of the command preceding the redirection symbol, as shown in the following screenshot:

```
[root@server Desktop]# ls
[root@server Desktop]# >demo.txt
[root@server Desktop]# ls
demo.txt
[root@server Desktop]# date > d1.txt
[root@server Desktop]# ls
d1.txt  demo.txt
[root@server Desktop]# cat d1.txt
Mon Aug  6 23:22:24 IST 2018
```

We can create one file at a time with the redirection symbol.

Create a text file using the echo or printf command

Sometimes, it is necessary to create a short file that doesn't require us to invoke the full text editor. In those scenarios, the echo or printf command is used with the redirection operator to create an empty file, or a file with a single line. This method of creating a file can be used in scripts also. Use the echo and printf command is shown in the following screenshot:

```
[root@server tmp]# echo "line 1"> file1
[root@server tmp]# ls
file1
[root@server tmp]# cat file1
line 1
[root@server tmp]# printf "line 2\n">file2
[root@server tmp]# ls
file1   file2
[root@server tmp]# cat file2
line 2
```

Create a text file using the vi editor

The vi editor is the most popular command-line editor and is the default editor in most Linux distributions. It has three modes of operation, which will be discussed later on in this chapter. To create a file with the vi editor, follow these steps:

1. `vi` <filename> and press *Enter*
2. Press *I* to enter Insert Mode and add your text
3. Keep on adding the custom text to the file until you are done with it
4. Press the *Esc* key to enter Command Mode
5. Type `:wq` and press *Enter* to save and exit

The following screenshot displays a file being created in vi editor:

Besides this method, there are other ways of creating a text file, such as using `nano`, `ed`, `joe`, `emacs`, or `pico` editors. You can try your hand at using them too.

Editing files with the vi editor

The vi editor is the most popular editor used to edit or create new files from a shell prompt. It comes in text-based as well graphical interface form, with extended features. This text-based editor is used to write a script, edit system configuration files, or develop the source code of a programming language. The name vi is pronounced as vee-eye.

The **vim** (short for **vi improved**) version of the vi editor comes with many enhancements to make working with the vi editor easier. It supports extended features, such as syntax highlighting for many configuration files and programming languages. Whatever we learn about vi editor is applicable to vim also, so we will learn about the vi editor in this section.

There are three modes of operation of the vi editor, as follows:

- **Command Mode**
- **Insert Mode**
- **Line Mode**

The following diagram shows the different modes of vi editor, along with the keys used to switch between them:

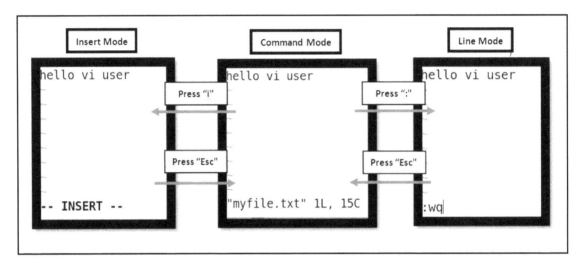

When working with the vi editor, it is essential to keep track of the mode you are working in. Many commands and keystrokes behave differently in different modes. The following table describes the different modes and their features in brief:

Mode	Feature
Command Mode	• By default, vi editor starts in Command Mode • Keystrokes in Command Mode are interpreted as commands to modify content • In this mode, you can give commands to perform cut, delete, copy, and paste operations, and also use keystrokes to navigate in the file • Editing and the insertion of text are not possible in this mode
Insert Mode	• Press the *I* key to switch to Insert Mode from Command Mode (pressing the *I* key to get into Insert Mode is the most commonly used option; however, there are other keys too that can be pressed to get into Insert Mode from Command Mode) • Insert Mode is used to modify or insert text into a file • Insert Mode is indicated by– – INSERT – – at the bottom of the screen • Press the *Esc* key to exit Insert Mode and return to Command Mode
Line Mode	• Press the *:* key to switch to Line Mode from Command Mode only (we cannot switch to Line Mode from Insert Mode directly) • Line Mode is indicated by the *:* colon key at the beginning of the last line of the vi editor and the cursor is placed immediately after this colon • We can use line editing commands inherited from older line editors, such as saving the contents of a file to disk, executing shell commands, and reading other files' contents, and so on • Requires pressing the *Enter* key after the command for execution • Press the *Esc* key to exit Line Mode and return to Command Mode

When you are in doubt and don't know your current working mode, press the *Esc* key twice and you will be back in Command Mode.

Working with files in vi editor

To start the `vi` editor and edit the file, use the following syntax:

```
$ vi <filename>
```

If the file exits with the specified filename, it will be opened and its contents are displayed in Command Mode. If the file does not exist, `vi` creates the file when it is saved on the disk for the first time. By default, `vi` uses an unnamed temporary buffer where the file is edited, until its contents are saved to disk. Now, let's understand the workings of `vi` in different modes in detail.

Insert Mode

This mode is used to enter new text in a file or modify the existing text in the file. There are multiple ways to get into Insert Mode, as described in the following table:

Key	Usage
a	Insert the text after the current cursor location, until the *Esc* key is pressed
A	Insert the text at the end of the line, until the *Esc* key is pressed
i	Insert the text before the current cursor location, until the *Esc* key is pressed
I	Insert the text at the beginning of the line, until the *Esc* key is pressed
o	Insert a new line following the current cursor location for entering text, until the *Esc* key is pressed
O	Insert a new line preceding the current cursor location for entering text, until the *Esc* key is pressed
s	Delete the character at the current cursor location and remain in Insert Mode, until the *Esc* key is pressed
S	Delete the line with the current cursor location and get into Insert Mode, until the *Esc* key is pressed
r	Replace the character at the current cursor position
R	Begin replacing text at the current cursor position until the *Esc* key is pressed

Line Mode

This mode is used to execute editing commands. The most popular operations performed in this mode include saving a file to disk, closing a file, and exiting vi editor without saving a file to disk. Line Mode operations require the *Enter* key to be pressed after the command is typed. Some of the most popular operations performed in Line Mode are described in the following table:

Operations	USAGE
Save and exit operations	
:q	Quits the vi editor only if no changes have been made to the file being edited
:q!	Quits the vi editor without saving the current changes in the opened file
:wq	Writes/saves the contents of the file to disk and exits the vi editor
:x	Writes/saves the contents of the file to disk and exits the vi editor
ZZ	Writes/saves the contents of the file to disk and exits the vi editor from Command Mode
Write/save to file operations	
:w	Writes/saves the contents of the file to disk
:w demo	Writes/saves the contents of the file to the disk with the filename demo
:w! demo2	Overwrites the file with the filename demo2
:f demo3	Renames the current file to the filename demo3
:w >> demo4	Appends the current file to the filename demo4
:5,10w demo5	Writes lines 5 through 10 to the filename demo5
:5,10w >>demo6	Appends lines 5 through 10 to the filename demo6
:r demo7	Reads the contents of the file with the filename demo7 at the current cursor position
:e demo8	Opens another file with the filename demo8
:e#	Switches between opened vi windows (note: this works only if you have saved the file once on disk using :w)
Search file contents	
/<pattern>	Searches the occurrence of specified patterns of text, inside buffers, in a forward direction.
?	Searches the occurrence of specified patterns of text, inside buffers, in a backward direction.
n	Repeats the last search command in a forward direction

| N | Repeats the search command in the opposite direction |

We can perform substitution in Line Mode. By default, it performs substitution on the current line only; however, we can prefix the substitution command `s` with the address option to perform substitution on multiple lines, as shown in the following table:

Line Mode command	Description
Substitution on current line	
`:s/file/book`	Substitutes the first occurrence of file with book on the current line
`:s/file/book/g`	Substitute all occurrences of file with book on the current line
Substitution between address range (x,y) specified	
`:1,5s/cat/dog/`	Substitutes the first occurrence of cat with dog between lines 1 and 5
`:1,5s/cat/dog/g`	Substitutes all occurrences of cat with dog between lines 1 and 5
Substitution in current file (%)	
`:%s/cat/dog/`	Substitutes the first occurrence of cat with dog throughout the file
`:%s/cat/dog/g`	Substitutes all occurrences of cat with dog in whole file
`:%s/cat/dog/gc`	Prompts before each substitution and substitutes all occurrences of cat with dog throughout the file

Determining line numbers in Line Mode of vi editor

Line Mode has the ability to determine the line number of the current line, or the total number of lines in a file being edited.

The following table lists the commands that are used to determine line numbers:

Command	Description
`:.=`	This returns the line number of the current line at the last line of the screen
`:=`	This returns the total number of lines at the last line of the screen

Ctrl + g	This tells the current line number, along with the total number of lines in the file at the last line of the screen (Command Mode keystroke combination)

How to execute external commands in Line Mode

Being able to execute shell commands from within the vi editor is sometimes quite useful. The following table lists some examples of shell command execution from Line Mode:

Line Mode command	Description
`:! <shell command>`	Executes a shell command (press *Enter* to return to vi editor)
`:!wc %`	Executes the `wc` command on the file opened in vi editor (`%` represents the file currently being edited)
`:sh`	Temporarily returns to the shell prompt (type *Exit* to return to vi editor)
`:r !<shell command>`	Reads the output from a shell command into the opened file at the current cursor position

Command Mode

This is the default mode of vi editor. In this mode, most navigation and browsing of file content is performed. Besides the navigation of file content, we also perform cut, delete, copy, and paste operations in Command Mode. The following table describes the popular navigation operations of Command Mode:

KEY	USAGE
Move by character	
Arrow keys	For moving the cursor up, down, left, and right
`j` or `<enter>`	For move the cursor one line down
`k`	For move the cursor one line up
`h` or Backspace	For move the cursor one character left
`l` or Space	For move the cursor one character right
Move by word	
`w`	For moving the cursor to the beginning of the next word

b	For moving the cursor to the previous word
e	For moving the cursor to the end of the current word
Move by line	
0 or ^	For moving the cursor to the beginning of the line
$	For moving the cursor to the end of the line
Move by sentence	
(	For moving the cursor to the beginning of the previous sentence
)	For moving the cursor to the end of the next sentence
Move by paragraph	
{	For moving the cursor to the beginning of the previous paragraph
}	For moving the cursor to the end of the next paragraph
Move by screen	
Ctrl + *F* or Page Down	For moving forward one screen
Ctrl + *B* or Page Up	For moving backward one screen
Ctrl + *D*	For moving down half a screen
Ctrl + *U*	For moving up half a screen
H	First line on screen
M	Middle line on screen
L	Last line on screen
Move inside whole document	
:0 or 1G or gg	For moving to the beginning of a file
:$ or G	For moving to the last line of a file
:n or nG	For moving to the nth line

Next, we will see how we to perform cut, delete, copy, and paste operations in Command Mode. The deletion of a character puts the text in an unnamed temporary buffer. The deleted character stored in a temporary buffer can be pasted at other places. Hence, we can say that a delete and paste operation is similar to a cut and paste operation.

The copying of character is known as yanking in context of vi editor. Copying (yanking) is performed using the yank y command. The following table describes various cut, copy, delete, and paste operations in vi editor:

KEY	USAGE
Deleting/cutting single characters	
x	Deletes a character at the current cursor position
Nx	Deletes the N-1 character on the right-hand side, starting at the current cursor position
3x	Deletes a total of three characters, starting with the character currently under the cursor position, followed by the next two on the right-hand side
X	Deletes a character to the left of the cursor
Deleting/cutting larger chunks	
dw	Deletes the word at the current position up to the next space or next punctuation
db	Deletes one word backward
d$	Deletes the line from the current cursor position to the end of the line
d^ or d0	Deletes the line from the current cursor position to the beginning of the line
dG	Deletes from the current line to the end of the file
dgg	Deletes from the current line to the beginning of the file
D	Deletes the rest of the current line
dd	Deletes the current line
Ndd or dNd	Deletes N lines from the current line
Copying/yanking text (puts text into a temporary buffer)	
yw	Yanks (copies) a word forward
yb	Yanks (copies) a word backward
y$	Yanks (copies) the line from the current cursor position to the end of the line
y^ or y0	Yanks (copies) the line from the current cursor position to the beginning of the line
yy	Yanks (copies) the current line and puts it in a buffer
Nyy or yNy	Yanks (copies) N lines and puts them in a buffer
p	Pastes the contents below the current line (the yanked line or lines from the buffer)
P	Pastes the contents above the current line
u	Undoes the previous operation
Ctrl + R	Redoes the last undo operation

Typing vimtutor at the prompt launches a concise, yet comprehensive, tutorial for beginners. This tutorial is short and to the point, to make beginners proficient in using vi editor.

Using text file manipulation tools

System administrators, developers, and users need to work with text files, configuration files, and log files when working on Linux. Some of these files are large; some of them are small or medium. The data contained in these files frequently needs to be viewed, updated, or extracted. In this section, we will learn how to manage and manipulate text files on Linux.

Different types of editor used to view file content

There are different types of editor used to view the content of files. Some editors, such as vim or nano, require the whole file to be loaded into memory first. These types of editors are not suitable for working on or viewing the contents of large log files, such as banking database log files, since as opening such large files can cause issues due to high memory utilization. However, in such scenarios, you can use the less command to view the contents of a large file, page by page, by scrolling up or down without the system having to place the entire file in memory at the beginning. This is much faster then a text editor, such as vi or nano.

less command

This is used to view larger files because it is a paging program; it displays the content page by page with scroll-back capabilities. We can also perform search operations and navigate inside the files:

- /<string>: To search for the <string> in a forward direction
- ?<string>: To search for the <string> in a backward direction
- q: To quit the less editor

Examples of the less command are as follows:

```
$ less /var/log/messages or
$ cat /var/log/messages | less
```

Main pages are displayed using the less utility.

more command

This program is also used to view larger files as it is also a paging program. It is an older utility with fewer options. The example of the `more` command is shown in the following screenshot:

```
[root@server ~]# more /var/log/messages
Aug 29 21:06:02 server rsyslogd: [origin software="rsyslogd" swVersion=
"8.24.0" x-pid="893" x-info="http://www.rsyslog.com"] rsyslogd was HUPe
d
```

cat command

Concatenate (**cat**) is one of the most frequently used Linux command-line utilities. It is most commonly used to view the contents of a single file or concatenate the contents of multiple files that are not very long. It does not provide scroll-back functionality.

The following screenshot demonstrates utilization of `cat` command with single file:

```
[root@server ~]# cat /etc/hosts
127.0.0.1    localhost localhost.localdomain localhost4 localhost4.local
domain4
::1          localhost localhost.localdomain localhost6 localhost6.local
domain6
```

The following screenshot demonstrates utilization of the `cat` command with multiple files:

```
[root@server ~]# cat /etc/hosts /etc/resolv.conf
127.0.0.1    localhost localhost.localdomain localhost4 localhost4.local
domain4
::1          localhost localhost.localdomain localhost6 localhost6.local
domain6
# Generated by NetworkManager
search example.com
nameserver 192.168.0.1
```

We can perform multiple tasks using the `cat` command, as listed in the following table:

Command	Description
cat file1 file2	Concatenate `file1` and `file2` and display the output. The entire contents of `file1` is followed by the contents of `file2`
cat file1 file2 > file3	Combine the contents of `file1` and `file2` and save the output into a new `file`, `file3`
cat demo1 >> demo2	Append the contents of the `demo1` file to the end of the existing file, `demo2`
cat > demo	Any subsequent lines typed in the Terminal will go into the `demo` file, until *Ctrl + D* is pressed
cat >> demo	Any subsequent lines typed are appended to the `demo` file, until *Ctrl + D* is pressed

tac command

The `tac` command is used to view the contents of a file backward from bottom to top, starting from the last line. The syntax of `tac` is exactly same as that of the `cat` command, as shown in the following screenshot:

```
[root@server ~]# tac /etc/resolv.conf
nameserver 192.168.0.1
search example.com
# Generated by NetworkManager
```

head command

The `head` command is used to print the first 10 lines of a file by default. However, it can be used with the `-n` option, or just `-<number>`, to display a different number of lines as specified. The filename whose contents are to be displayed is passed as an argument to the `head` command as shown in the following screenshot:

```
[root@server ~]# head /etc/passwd
root:x:0:0:root:/root:/bin/bash
bin:x:1:1:bin:/bin:/sbin/nologin
daemon:x:2:2:daemon:/sbin:/sbin/nologin
adm:x:3:4:adm:/var/adm:/sbin/nologin
lp:x:4:7:lp:/var/spool/lpd:/sbin/nologin
sync:x:5:0:sync:/sbin:/bin/sync
shutdown:x:6:0:shutdown:/sbin:/sbin/shutdown
halt:x:7:0:halt:/sbin:/sbin/halt
mail:x:8:12:mail:/var/spool/mail:/sbin/nologin
operator:x:11:0:operator:/root:/sbin/nologin
[root@server ~]#
[root@server ~]# head -n 2 /etc/passwd
root:x:0:0:root:/root:/bin/bash
bin:x:1:1:bin:/bin:/sbin/nologin
[root@server ~]#
[root@server ~]# head -1 /etc/passwd
root:x:0:0:root:/root:/bin/bash
```

tail command

The `tail` command is used to print last 10 lines of a file by default. However, like the `head` command, we can change the number number of lines to be displayed by using the `-n` option, or just `-<number>`, to display a different number of lines as specified. The filename whose contents are to be displayed is passed as an argument to the `tail` command, as shown in the following screenshot:

```
[root@server ~]# tail /etc/passwd
geoclue:x:991:985:User for geoclue:/var/lib/geoclue:/sbin/nologin
ntp:x:38:38::/etc/ntp:/sbin/nologin
sssd:x:990:984:User for sssd:/:/sbin/nologin
gdm:x:42:42::/var/lib/gdm:/sbin/nologin
gnome-initial-setup:x:989:983::/run/gnome-initial-setup/:/sbin/nologin
sshd:x:74:74:Privilege-separated SSH:/var/empty/sshd:/sbin/nologin
avahi:x:70:70:Avahi mDNS/DNS-SD Stack:/var/run/avahi-daemon:/sbin/nolog
in
postfix:x:89:89::/var/spool/postfix:/sbin/nologin
tcpdump:x:72:72::/:/sbin/nologin
student:x:1000:1000:student:/home/student:/bin/bash
[root@server ~]#
[root@server ~]# tail -n 2 /etc/passwd
tcpdump:x:72:72::/:/sbin/nologin
student:x:1000:1000:student:/home/student:/bin/bash
[root@server ~]#
[root@server ~]# tail -1 /etc/passwd
student:x:1000:1000:student:/home/student:/bin/bash
```

The `tail` command is more useful when we are troubleshooting issues using log files. It enables us to see the most recent lines of output by continuously displaying the addition of any new lines in the log file as soon as they appear. Thus, it enables us to monitor any current activity that is being reported or recorded, as shown in the following command line:

```
$ tail -f /var/log/messages
```

wc command

The `wc` command is used to count the lines, words, and characters in a file by default. It can accept `-l`, `-w`, or `-c` options to display only the lines, words, or characters respectively. The filename is passed as an argument to the `wc` command, as shown in the following screenshot:

```
[root@server ~]# wc /etc/passwd
  43    86 2246 /etc/passwd
[root@server ~]# wc -l /etc/passwd
43 /etc/passwd
[root@server ~]# wc -c /etc/group /etc/resolv.conf
 988 /etc/group
  72 /etc/resolv.conf
1060 total
[root@server ~]# wc -w /etc/hosts
10 /etc/hosts
```

file command

The `file` command scans the header of a file and tells us what kind of file it is. The file type to be identified is passed as an argument to the `file` command, as shown in the following screenshot:

```
[root@server ~]# file /etc/passwd
/etc/passwd: ASCII text
[root@server ~]#
[root@server ~]# file /bin/passwd
/bin/passwd: setuid ELF 64-bit LSB shared object, x86-64, version 1 (SY
SV), dynamically linked (uses shared libs), for GNU/Linux 2.6.32, Build
ID[sha1]=1e5735bf7b317e60bcb907f1989951f6abd50e8d, stripped
[root@server ~]#
[root@server ~]# file /home
/home: directory
```

Viewing compressed files

In Linux, we can view the contents of a compressed file without decompressing it. It is a good option to view large log files, which are compressed using this utility. There are multiple utilities that have the letter z prefixed to their name for working with `.gzip` compressed files.

This table lists some z family commands:

Command	Description
`zcat demo.gz`	To view a compressed `demo.gz` file
`zless demo.gz` or `zmore demo.gz`	To view a compressed `demo.gz` file page by page
`zgrep -i host demo.gz`	To search inside a compressed `demo.gz` file
`zdiff file1.gz file2.gz`	To compare two compressed files, `file1.gz`, and `file2.gz`, using the `diff` command
`zcmp file1.gz file2.gz`	To compare two compressed files, `file1.gz` and `file2.gz` using the `cmp` command

Similarly, for other text manipulation, utilities can also be clubbed with other compression methods, such as `bzip2` and `xz`. To display the contents of the file inside the `bzip2` compressed archive, we can use `bzcat`, `bzless` command and, to display the contents of the file inside the `xz` archive, we can use the `xzcat` and `xzless` respectively.

Utilization of the `zcat` command is shown in the following screenshot:

```
[root@server ~]# zcat /var/log/messages-20180805.gz
Aug 14 12:22:56 server nm-dispatcher: req:1 'dhcp4-change' [enp0s3]: start running ordered scripts...
Aug 14 12:22:56 server systemd: Started Network Manager Script Dispatcher Service.
Aug 14 12:23:41 server dbus[567]: [system] Activating via systemd: service name='net.reactivated.Fprint' unit='fprintd.service'
Aug 14 12:23:41 server systemd: Starting Fingerprint Authentication Daemon...
Aug 14 12:23:41 server dbus[567]: [system] Successfully activated service 'net.reactivated.Fprint'
Aug 14 12:23:41 server systemd: Started Fingerprint Authentication Daemon.
Aug 14 12:23:41 server journal: D-Bus service launched with name: net.reactivated.Fprint
Aug 14 12:23:41 server fprintd: Launching FprintObject
Aug 14 12:23:41 server journal: entering main loop
Aug 14 12:24:11 server journal: No devices in use, exit
```

Utilization of the `zgrep` command is shown in the following screenshot:

```
[root@server ~]# zgrep dbus /var/log/messages-20180805.gz
Aug 14 12:23:41 server dbus[567]: [system] Activating via systemd: service name='net.reactivated.Fprint' unit='fprintd.service'
Aug 14 12:23:41 server dbus[567]: [system] Successfully activated service 'net.reactivated.Fprint'
```

cut command

The `cut` command is used to display only specific columns or characters from a text file or from other command outputs. For example, in the following command, we display the login names from the `/etc/passwd` file:

```
$ cut -d: -f1 /etc/passwd
```

Output upon execution of the preceding command is shown in the following screenshot:

```
gnome-initial-setup
sshd
avahi
postfix
tcpdump
student
[root@server ~]#
```

The following command line displays the first and third fields from a colon-delimited file (extra lines stripped from output):

```
$ cut -d: -f1,3 /etc/passwd
```

Output upon execution of the preceding command is shown in the following screenshot:

```
gdm:42
gnome-initial-setup:989
sshd:74
avahi:70
postfix:89
tcpdump:72
student:1000
[root@server ~]# |
```

The following command line display only the first four characters of every line in the /etc/passwd file:

```
$ cut -c 1-4 /etc/passwd
```

sort command

The sort command is used to sort the lines of a text file in ascending or descending order, or sort as per a specified key. The following example illustrates the working of the sort command.

An example of the sort command to sort the /etc/passwd file in ascending order is shown in the following screenshot:

```
[root@server ~]# sort /etc/passwd
abrt:x:173:173::/etc/abrt:/sbin/nologin
adm:x:3:4:adm:/var/adm:/sbin/nologin
avahi:x:70:70:Avahi mDNS/DNS-SD Stack:/var/run/avahi-daemon:/sbin/nolog
in
bin:x:1:1:bin:/bin:/sbin/nologin
chrony:x:992:987::/var/lib/chrony:/sbin/nologin
colord:x:997:994:User for colord:/var/lib/colord:/sbin/nologin
daemon:x:2:2:daemon:/sbin:/sbin/nologin
dbus:x:81:81:System message bus:/:/sbin/nologin
ftp:x:14:50:FTP User:/var/ftp:/sbin/nologin
games:x:12:100:games:/usr/games:/sbin/nologin
gdm:x:42:42::/var/lib/gdm:/sbin/nologin
geoclue:x:991:985:User for geoclue:/var/lib/geoclue:/sbin/nologin
gluster:x:996:993:GlusterFS daemons:/var/run/gluster:/sbin/nologin
gnome-initial-setup:x:989:983::/run/gnome-initial-setup/:/sbin/nologin
halt:x:7:0:halt:/sbin:/sbin/halt
libstoragemgmt:x:998:995:daemon account for libstoragemgmt:/var/run/lsm
:/sbin/nologin
```

An example of the `sort` command to sort the `/etc/passwd` file by the third field numerically is shown in the following screenshot. Here, the `-t` option specifies a delimiter and the `-k` option specifies a field to be used for sorting:

```
[root@server ~]# sort -t: -k 3n /etc/passwd
root:x:0:0:root:/root:/bin/bash
bin:x:1:1:bin:/bin:/sbin/nologin
daemon:x:2:2:daemon:/sbin:/sbin/nologin
adm:x:3:4:adm:/var/adm:/sbin/nologin
lp:x:4:7:lp:/var/spool/lpd:/sbin/nologin
sync:x:5:0:sync:/sbin:/bin/sync
shutdown:x:6:0:shutdown:/sbin:/sbin/shutdown
halt:x:7:0:halt:/sbin:/sbin/halt
mail:x:8:12:mail:/var/spool/mail:/sbin/nologin
operator:x:11:0:operator:/root:/sbin/nologin
games:x:12:100:games:/usr/games:/sbin/nologin
ftp:x:14:50:FTP User:/var/ftp:/sbin/nologin
rpcuser:x:29:29:RPC Service User:/var/lib/nfs:/sbin/nologin
rpc:x:32:32:Rpcbind Daemon:/var/lib/rpcbind:/sbin/nologin
ntp:x:38:38::/etc/ntp:/sbin/nologin
```

uniq command

The `uniq` command is used to remove duplicate lines from a sorted file. It requires the duplicate entries to be in the adjacent lines and, hence, it is mostly used in combination with the `sort` command, which is used to sort the file contents first. The syntax of the `uniq` command is as follows:

```
$ sort <filename> | uniq
  or
$ sort -u <filename>
```

To count duplicate lines in the file, execute the command line, shown as follows :

```
$ sort <filename> | uniq -c
```

To display only the entries that are duplicates, execute the command line, shown as follows:

```
$ sort <filename> | uniq -cd
```

paste command

The `paste` command is used to combine fields from different files, or combine lines from multiple files. For example, we have two files, `f1` containing the employee name, and `f2` containing their employee ID and phone number.

To paste content from `f1` and `f2`, execute the steps in the command line, as shown in the following screenshot:

```
[root@server ~]# cat f1
Harjinder Walia
Sanjay Bandyopadhyay
Rahul baliyan
Ranvijay Singh
Rajneesh Pandey
[root@server ~]# cat f2
E001    831-666-1234
E002    831-777-1234
E003    832-666-1234
E004    833-888-1234
E005    832-777-1234
[root@server ~]# paste f1 f2
Harjinder Walia E001    831-666-1234
Sanjay Bandyopadhyay    E002    831-777-1234
Rahul baliyan   E003    832-666-1234
Ranvijay Singh  E004    833-888-1234
Rajneesh Pandey E005    832-777-1234
```

To paste the contents separated with a delimiter, execute the `paste` command, as shown in the following screenshot:

```
[root@server ~]# paste -d":" f1 f2
Harjinder Walia:E001    831-666-1234
Sanjay Bandyopadhyay:E002       831-777-1234
Rahul baliyan:E003      832-666-1234
Ranvijay Singh:E004     833-888-1234
Rajneesh Pandey:E005    832-777-1234
```

The commonly used delimiters with the `-d` option are space, Tab, |, :, and comma. An enhanced version of the `paste` command is `join`, which can work on files that have similar columns.

Redirecting output to files and programs

When we execute any program, by default, its output or error is displayed on the screen. We can redirect the text output of a program to a file using the input/output redirection operator or to another program using pipes. For this, when any command is executed, there are three standard file streams (file descriptors) created and opened by the operating system. The streams are known as standard input (stdin), standard output (stdout), and standard error (stderr).

The first stream is associated with stdin (numbered as 0) used to read input from keyboard. The second file stream is associated to stdout (numbered as 1) used by program to print output on screen, and the last file stream is stderr (numbered as 2), used by our program to print errors onscreen.

The following table list the different file descriptors (also known as channel) along with their numeric value, default connection and symbolic name:

Channel description	Channel symbolic name	Default connection	Descriptor value
Standard input	stdin	Keyboard	0
Standard output	stdout	Terminal	1
Standard error	stderr	Terminal	2
Other files	filename	Other files	3+

Redirecting stdout/stderr to a file prevents any process output from appearing on the Terminal. Linux has got a special file such as /dev/null which discards any channel output redirected to it. The less than symbol (<) is used for input redirection from a file, the greater than symbol (>) is used for output redirection to a file, and if we repeat the use of the output redirection symbol (>>) twice instead of once, then it appends the contents to the filename suffixed to it.

The following table explains the use of input/output redirection operators:

Operator usage	Explanation
`Cmd > file`	Redirects the command output to a file
`Cmd >> file`	Redirects and append the command output to the current file content
`Cmd 2> file`	Redirects the command standard error to a file
`Cmd 2>> file`	Appends the command standard error to the current file contents
`Cmd 2> /dev/null`	Discards standard error messages by redirecting them to `/dev/null`
`Cmd &> file` or `Cmd >file 2>&1`	Redirects both standard output and standard error messages to one file
`Cmd >>file 2>&1`	Appends both standard output and standard error messages to one file

Here are some examples of output redirection:

- Save the last 10 lines of `/var/log/messages` to `f1` by executing following command:

  - `$ tail -n 10 /var/log/message > f1`

- Append the `date` to the file named `f1` by executing following command:

  - `$ date >> f1`

- Save the errors in a file named `error` and display the output onscreen by executing following command:

  - `$ find /etc/ -name passwd 2> error`

- Save the output in a file named `result` and the error in a file named `error`:

  - `$ find /etc/ -name passwd > result 2> error`

- Save the output or error received upon execution of the `find` command in the common file named as `both`, as shown in the following command line:

  - `$ find /etc/ -name passwd &> both or`

  - `$ find /etc/ -name passwd > both 2>&1`

- Save the output in a file named `result` and discard the error messages by executing the following command:

  - `$ find /etc/ -name passwd > result 2> /dev/null`

- Read from a file using input redirection by executing the following command:

  - `$ wc -l < /etc/hosts`

Pipes

The Unix philosophy is to have simple and short programs (commands) used together to solve a complex problem, instead of having a complex program with several options. To accomplish this goal, pipes were created, which fetch the output of one command as input to another command. The symbol used for pipes is a vertical bar (|) between two or more commands, as follows:

```
$ command1 | command2 | command3 ..
```

Here are a few example showing the usage of pipes (redirecting the output from one program as an input to another program):

- Paginate the long output of any command using pipes, as shown in the following example:

  - `$ ls -l /bin | less`

- Pipe multiple commands together as shown in the following example:

  - `$ ls | head -3 | tail -1`

- Combine piping and redirection, as shown in the following example:

  - `$ ls | head -3 | tail -1 > output`

- Send standard output, as well as standard errors from the command, through a pipe to another process, as shown in the following example:

  - `find /etc -name passwd |& wc -l or find /etc -name passwd 2>&1 | wc -l`

tee command

The advantage of using pipes is that you don't have to save the output of a command in temporary files before passing it to another subsequent command for processing. This saves disk space and improves the time of execution, since reading and writing to disk are generally the slowest bottlenecks in the system. And, if you require the input to be saved in a file before passing it to a subsequent command, Linux has another beautiful command, known as `tee`. The syntax of the `tee` command is as follows:

```
$ command1 | tee <log_filename> | command2 ......
```

Here is an example of `tee` command usage:

- Send the output of the `ls` command to the `wc` command and to a file named `listoffile`:

  - `$ ls | tee listoffile | wc`

- Send standard output, as well as standard errors from the command, through a pipe-through tee to another file and then to a subsequent command:

  - `$ find /etc -name passwd |& tee logfile | wc -l`

Using grep for text matching

Grep (short for **Global Regular Expression Print**) is a command that is used extensively to as a text search tool in text files. It searches for a pattern in a file and prints the corresponding line, which contains the matching pattern. It scans files for specified patterns and can be used with regular expressions, as well as text strings. Its syntax is as follows:

```
$ grep [options] pattern [files]
```

The following table demonstrates when the `grep` command is used:

Command	Usage
grep 'student' /etc/passwd	Search for a string, student, in a file, /etc/passwd, and print all matching lines
grep -v 'student' /etc/passwd	Print all lines that do not contain the string student
grep -i 'STUDENT' /etc/passwd	Search for a string, STUDENT, in a case-insensitive manner and print all matching lines (-i ignore case)
grep -c 'student' /etc/passwd	Print the total number of lines that contain the text student in the /etc/passwd file
grep -rl 'student' /etc/	Search the directory recursively and print the filenames that have the string student
grep -rL 'student' /etc/	Search the directory recursively and print the filenames that don't have the string student
grep -n 'student' /etc/passwd	Print the line number, along with the line containing the pattern student
grep -A1 'student' /etc/passwd	Print an additional one line after the match
grep -B1 'student' /etc/passwd	Print an additional one line before the match
grep -C1 'student' /etc/passwd	Print an additional one line after, and one line before, the match
grep -a 'dir' /bin/mkdir	Search inside the /bin/mkdir binary file and print the line containing the string dir
grep 'root' /etc/passwd	Print the line containing the string root anywhere on a line
grep '^root' /etc/passwd	Print the line that begins with the string root
grep 'bash$' /etc/passwd	Print the line that ends with the string bash

`grep '^$' <filename>`	Print the empty lines from the file
`grep -v '^$' <filename>`	Print only non-empty lines from the file
`grep '[br]oot' /etc/passwd`	Print the lines that contain either string beginning with the characters b or r, and followed by the string oot, anywhere on a line in the /etc/passwd file
`who | grep 'student'`	Print the line containing the string student by reading input from stdin

An example of matching a string in a file using grep is shown in the following screenshot:

```
[root@server ~]# grep 'root' /etc/passwd
root:x:0:0:root:/root:/bin/bash
operator:x:11:0:operator:/root:/sbin/nologin
```

An example of printing those lines that do not contain the specified string using grep is shown in the following screenshot (some output stripped):

```
[root@server ~]# grep -v 'root' /etc/passwd
bin:x:1:1:bin:/bin:/sbin/nologin
daemon:x:2:2:daemon:/sbin:/sbin/nologin
adm:x:3:4:adm:/var/adm:/sbin/nologin
lp:x:4:7:lp:/var/spool/lpd:/sbin/nologin
sync:x:5:0:sync:/sbin:/bin/sync
shutdown:x:6:0:shutdown:/sbin:/sbin/shutdown
```

The grep command can be used with the -c option to count the occurrence of a specified pattern. The following example shows how to count the number of CPU cores in a system using grep command:

```
$ grep -c name /proc/cpuinfo (count the number of cpu cores in
system)
```

The following screenshot shows how to use grep command to count the occurrence of root string in the /etc/passwd file:

```
[root@server ~]# grep -c 'root' /etc/passwd
2
```

An example of printing the line number, along with the matching lines using the `grep`, is shown in the following screenshot:

```
[root@server ~]# grep -n 'root' /etc/passwd
1:root:x:0:0:root:/root:/bin/bash
10:operator:x:11:0:operator:/root:/sbin/nologin
```

An example of printing the lines that begin with a specified string is shown in the following screenshot:

```
[root@server ~]# grep '^root' /etc/passwd
root:x:0:0:root:/root:/bin/bash
```

Text extraction using sed and awk

It is very often necessary to extract the same text repeatedly from a file. For such an operation, where we need to edit a file at the same place, or extract the same text from multiple files, we use `sed` and `awk`. There are multiple text extraction utilities. However, these utilities use fewer system resources, execute faster, and are simpler to use.

sed

This is one of the oldest and most popular Unix text processing tools. It is a non-interactive stream editor. It is typically used for filtering text, as well as performing text substitution and the non-interactive editing of text files. There are two main ways of invoking the `sed` command, as follows:

- `sed -e command <filename>`: Specify editing commands at the command line, operate on the filename specified, and display the output on the Terminal. Here, the `-e` command option allows us to specify multiple editing commands simultaneously at the command line.
- `sed -f scriptfile <filename>`: Specify a script file containing `sed` commands to operate on a specified filename and display the output on the Terminal.

Now, we discuss the most popular operations performed using sed, for example, substitution. The following table lists the basic syntax for substitution operations:

Command	Usage
sed 's/original_string/new_string/s file	Substitute the first occurrence of the original string in each line with a new string
sed 's/original_string/new_string/g' file	Substitute all occurrences of the original string in each line with a new string specified
sed '1,3s/original_string/new_string/g' file	Substitute all occurrences of the original string in each line with a new string from line one to line three in the same file
sed -i 's/original_string/new_string/g' file	Substitute all occurrences of the original string with a new string in each line in the same file

Using the sed **utility with the print command**:

The p command will print the matching lines and the -n option suppresses standard output so that only matching lines are displayed, as shown in the following example:

```
$ sed -n '1,3' /etc/passwd
$ sed -n '/^root/' /etc/passwd
```

Using the sed **utility with the substitute command**:

The s command will replace the matching string with a new string. The s option can be prefixed with a range to restrict the replacement to a specified number of lines, as shown in the following example:

```
$ sed '/^student/s/bash/sh/' /etc/passwd
```

Using the sed **utility with delete command**:

In the following example, the sed d command will delete the empty and commented lines from ntp.conf and create a backup file of ntp.conf with the extension backup as ntp.conf.backup, as shown in the following command line:

```
$ sed -i.backup '/^#/d;/^$/d' /etc/ntp.conf
```

Use the -i option with caution, because the changes, once made inside the file, are not reversible. It is always a better way to first use sed without the -i option and then redirect the output to a new file.

awk

The `awk` command is used to extract data from a file and print specific contents. It is quite often used to restructure the data and construct reports. Its name is derived from the last names of its creators: Alfred Aho, Peter Weinberger, and Brian Kernighan. Its main features include the following:

- It is an interpreted programming language similar to C
- It is used for data manipulation in files, and for retrieving and processing text from files
- It views files as records and fields
- It has arithmetic and string operators
- It has variables, conditional statements, and loops
- It reads from a file or from a standard input device and outputs to a standard output device such as a Terminal

Its general invoking syntax is as follows:

```
$ awk   '/pattern/{command}'   <filename>
```

The printing of a selected column or row from a file is the basic task generally performed using `awk`.

In the following example, the `awk` command is used to print the contents of a file line by line until the end of the file is reached:

```
$ awk '{ print $0}' /etc/passwd
```

In the following example, `awk` command is used to print the first field (column) of the line containing the username `student`. Here `-F` option is used to set the field separator as `:`.

```
$ awk -F: '/student/{ print $1}' /etc/passwd
```

In the following example, the `awk` command is used to print selective fields from the line containing the matching pattern in file `/etc/passwd`:

```
$ awk -F: '/student/{print "Username :", $1, "Shell :", $7}' /etc/passwd
```

Finding a file (locate and find commands)

If we can quickly find the files we are looking for, it will definitely make us happier Linux users. We can search any directory or multiple directories for a file in a Linux system as and when needed. CentOS 7 has two popular utilities that are used to search for files:

- The `locate` command
- The `find` command

Locate

This utility performs a search through a previously created database of files and directories available on our system. It matches all entries that contain a specified character string. This sometimes returns a very long list of matching results, which can be further filtered using the `grep` command, as shown in the following command line:

```
$ locate zip | grep bin
$ locate iproute2
```

The `locate` command uses a database created by another program, `updatedb`. Most Linux systems run this program automatically once a day using a scheduler. However, we can update the `locate` command database any time by running the `updatedb` command on a Terminal.

Find

Find is the most useful and often used utility in a Linux system. It traverses through the filesystem directory tree from any location to search for a file on a specified condition. Its general syntax is as follows:

```
$ find  [pathnames]    [conditions]
```

We can search for a file in the `/var` directory containing a specific string in its name, as shown in the following command line:

```
$ find /var -name "*.log"
```

When no argument (path) is given, it searches for a file in the current directory and its sub-directories only.

We can use the `find` command to search a file or directory in the /usr directory having the name gcc, as shown in the following command line:

```
$ find /usr -name gcc
```

We can narrow down our search by specifying the type of file to search for, such as by using d for directories and f for files, as shown in the following command line:

```
$ find /usr -type f -name gcc
$ find /usr -type d -name gcc
```

Search for files above a particular size:

- The following `find` command line is used to list the files with a size of 0 KB in the /var directory:

  ```
  $ find /var -type f -size 0
  ```

- The following `find` command line is used to list files with a size of more than 2 MB in the /var/log directory:

  ```
  $ find /var/log -type f -size +2M
  ```

- The following `find` command line is used to find a file with the name messages, and then compress it using the gzip utility with xargs:

  ```
  $ find /var/log -type f -name messages | xargs gzip
  ```

- Find all the .jpg images and archive them with xargs and tar, as shown in the following command line:

  ```
  $ find / -name *.jpg -type f -print | xargs tar -cvzf images.tar.gz
  ```

Summary

In this chapter, we began with learning various methods for creating a text file. This was followed by taking a walk through the different text manipulation utilities that are helpful in performing daily operations. These utilities mainly included tools such as head, tail, wc, sort, less and more. Then, we learned the various techniques of input-output redirection into files and programs. After that, we had a quick tour of text filtering and extraction tools, such as grep, sed, and awk. Finally, we saw how to search files in CentOS 7 using the find and locate commands.

In our next chapter, we will learn about managing users and groups in CentOS 7.

User and Group Management

4

Linux is a multiuser OS, so it is essential to have a basic understanding of user management. In this chapter, you will learn how to add, delete, modify, and suspend user accounts and grant them permissions to perform essential tasks. You will also learn how to apply password policies in a Linux environment.

In this chapter, we will cover the following:

- Understanding different types of users and groups in CentOS 7
- Executing commands as a superuser in CentOS 7
- Creating, modifying, and deleting local user accounts
- Creating, modifying, and deleting local group accounts
- Managing user passwords and aging policies

Understanding users and groups in CentOS 7

Managing different types of users and groups is one of the primary roles of system administration. Using different types of user and group account as a role-based access control is configured into the system. Depending upon the privileges of user, we can restrict user access to various system resources.

Defining a user

Each process running on our system is started by a user, to whom it belongs. Access to different files and directories by running processes is determined by the user associated with that process. Similarly, every file in our system is owned by some user and access to different files and directories on the system is restricted by user privileges. By default, new files created are owned by the user creating the file.

There are generally three types of user account in Linux systems:

- Root user (administrator)
- System users (used by various services)
- Regular users (normal users who carry out daily operations)

Identifying the current user

Since Linux is a multiuser OS, we can have multiple users logged in at the same time. The following table lists the different commands that are used to find information about the logged-in user and other information associated with users:

Command	Description
$ who	Display currently logged in users
$ w	Display detailed information of currently logged in users
$ whoami	Display current user
$ id	Display information about current logged in user (such as User ID, primary group and secondary group, and SELinux context)
$ id <username>	Display information about the username passed as the first argument to the id command

Examples of the id command, who command and the w command usage are shown in the following screenshot:

```
[root@server ~]# id
uid=0(root) gid=0(root) groups=0(root) context=unconfined_u:unconfined_r:unconfined_t:s0-s0:c0.c1023
[root@server ~]# whoami
root
[root@server ~]# who -a
           system boot  2018-09-13 15:51
           run-level 5  2018-09-13 15:52
student   ? :0           2018-09-13 15:52   ?          1629 (:0)
           pts/0         2018-09-13 15:53              0 id=/0    term=0 exit=0
root      + pts/0        2018-09-13 15:53   .          2559 (192.168.56.1)
[root@server ~]# w
 17:46:19 up  1:54,  2 users,  load average: 0.00, 0.01, 0.05
USER     TTY      FROM            LOGIN@   IDLE   JCPU   PCPU WHAT
student  :0       :0              15:52    ?xdm?  34.11s 0.22s /usr/libexec/gnome-session-binary --session gnome-classic
root     pts/0    192.168.56.1    15:53    3.00s  0.14s  0.03s w
```

To show the user associated with the file, use the long-listing (ls -l) command, which displays user associations in the third column as shown in the following command line:

```
$ ls -l /tmp
```

To view the user associated with a process, use the `ps` command with the `u` option. Most of the time, the `a` option is also clubbed with the `ps` command to display all the processes associated with the Terminal as shown in the following command:

```
$ ps –au
```

All Linux users are assigned a unique integer number known as a **User ID** (**UID**). Specific UID numbers and ranges of numbers are used for particular purposes by Linux systems.

The following table that lists the various UID ranges and their description:

UID	Description
UID 0	Root user is always assigned UID as 0.
UID 1-999	UID 1-999 are assigned to system user accounts. Of this, UID 1-200 are statically assigned to system processes and UID 201–999 are reserved for the system. UID 201-999 are dynamically allocated in the system to an application upon its installation in CentOS 7.
UID 1000+	Regular user accounts have UID 1000 onward by default.

The mapping of user information, such as `username`, `UID`, `GID`, and the `home` directory of the user, is defined in a plain text file, `/etc/passwd`. The `/etc/passwd` file contains seven colon-separated fields, as follows:

```
username : password : UID : GID: Gecos : /home/dir : Default shell
```

The following table describes the various fields of the `/etc/passwd` file:

Field	Description
username	It is the user login name associated with the UID for human readability (should be between 1 and 32 characters).
password	In this field, passwords were originally stored in encrypted format. Now, they are stored in the `/etc/shadow` file.
UID	It is the UID that system uses to identify a user: UID 0: reserved for root UID 1-200: reserved for predefined system accounts (static) UID 201-999: reserved for system accounts (dynamic) UID 1000+: reserved for regular user accounts
GID	It is the primary GID of the user, used by the system to associate the user to its primary group

Gecos	This field is optional and contains user-related extra information, such as user's full name, address, contact details, and so on
/home/dir	This field contains the absolute path of the user's home directory
Default shell	It is the absolute path of the user's default shell (this program runs when the user logs in to the system), which provides the users command prompt

The contents of last two lines in /etc/passwd file is shown in the following the screenshot:

```
[root@server ~]# tail -2 /etc/passwd
student:x:1000:1000:student:/home/student:/bin/bash
jack:x:1001:1001::/home/jack:/bin/bash
```

Understanding groups in Linux

Linux uses groups to organize users in the system. Groups are collections of accounts with certain shared features and access controls. Like users, a group also have a name, which is associated to a number known as the **Group ID (GID)**, and is generally the same as the UID. Local group information is stored in the /etc/group file. There are two types of group associated with user accounts:

- **Primary groups**:
    - Every user has only one primary group.
    - It is the default group of a user to which he belongs.
    - Each local user's primary group is defined by the GID number of the group listed in the third field of the /etc/passwd file.
    - By default, the primary group owns the new files created by the user.
    - Generally, the primary group of a newly created user will have the same name as the user. Each user is the only member of this private primary group of the user.
- **Supplementary groups**:
    - Each can be associated with 0 or more supplementary groups.
    - Each local user's secondary group entry is defined in the last field of the /etc/group file. This file contains a comma-separated list of users in the last field, which determines the group membership of users for a group.

- Supplementary group membership helps in implementing access rights, privileges, and security considerations to files and other resources in the system. The various fields of the /etc/group file are as follows:

  ```
  groupname : password : GID : <comma separated list of
  users who belong to this group>
  ```

The following screenshot displays the contents of the last two line of the /etc/group file:

```
[root@server ~]# tail -2 /etc/group
HR:x:1005:student
jack:x:1001:
```

Executing commands as superuser in CentOS 7

Every operating system has an account to administer the resources of that system. In the case of CentOS Linux, this user account is known as **root**, very often called the **superuser**. The root account is the most privileged account in a Linux/Unix system. This account is used to carry out system administration tasks, such as managing user accounts and their passwords, managing software packages, modifying system files, and restarting system services. Extra caution must be taken while working as the root user as it has no security restrictions imposed on it. If the root account is compromised, then another person will have full administrative control of the system. The root account on Linux is equivalent to the local administrator account on Windows.

When you are logged in as the root user, the shell prompt displays the hash # symbol by convention to make the user aware that you are working as most the privileged user in the system.

In Linux, there are two commands, su and sudo, which are used to temporarily grant root access to a normal user. We will discuss these commands one by one.

Switching users with the su command

The **su** (short for **switch user** or **substitute user**) command is used to switch into other user accounts. If a username is not specified as an argument to the su command, it takes the root account into consideration. There are two ways of invoking this command, as follows:

- `$ su - <username>`: This method starts a new **login shell** as another username specified. It sets up the shell environment as if this was a proper login as that user in the system.

- `$ su <username>`: This method starts a **non-login shell** as the username specified. It just launches the new shell with the current user environment settings, without invoking other username shell variables.

  In the absence of any username, su – invokes the root shell and asks for root credentials to be given at the prompt as shown in the following screenshot:

```
[student@server ~]$ su -
Password:
Last login: Thu Sep 13 17:56:06 IST 2018 on pts/0
[root@server ~]# |
```

Disadvantages of using the su command to grant root access to a normal user

Once the user has logged in as the root account using su, they can do anything for as long as they want, without being asked again for a root password. This command also has limited logging features.

Using sudo to run commands as the root user

In the previous method, the standard user temporarily becomes the root using the su command; all the privileges of root are granted by specifying the root password. This method is not suitable for running some programs as root as it gives unlimited privileges to the normal user. Granting privileges using sudo is less dangerous and is the preferred method.

The `sudo` feature is used to assign more limited privileges to user accounts, based on the settings in the `/etc/sudoers` file. In this method, `sudo` requires the user to enter their own password for authentication and not the password of the account they are trying to access. This method allows them to delegate system administration tasks, without giving them access to the root password. We can also restrict the privileges of the user to a specific subset of commands; that is, he can execute only a limited number of specified commands as root. Any command executed using `sudo` is logged by default into the `/var/log/secure` log file.

To execute just one command with root privilege, type `sudo <command>`. After the execution of the command, you will return to being a normal unprivileged user. An example of using `sudo` to execute just the `iptables` command with root privileges is shown in the following screenshot:

```
[student@server ~]$ sudo iptables -nvL
[sudo] password for student:
Chain INPUT (policy ACCEPT 226 packets, 15808 bytes)
 pkts bytes target     prot opt in      out      source             destination

Chain FORWARD (policy ACCEPT 0 packets, 0 bytes)
 pkts bytes target     prot opt in      out      source             destination

Chain OUTPUT (policy ACCEPT 118 packets, 13384 bytes)
 pkts bytes target     prot opt in      out      source             destination
```

The log of commands executed using `sudo` is stored in `/var/log/secure` as shown in the following screenshot:

```
[student@server ~]$ sudo tail /var/log/secure
Sep 13 18:00:49 server sudo: student : TTY=pts/0 ; PWD=/home/student ; USER=root ; COMMAND=/sbin/iptables -nvL
Sep 13 18:00:55 server sudo: student : TTY=pts/0 ; PWD=/home/student ; USER=root ; COMMAND=/bin/tail /var/log/secure
```

An example of granting a user rights to execute an admin command using `sudo` by making the required entry in the `/etc/sudoers` file is shown in the following screenshot:

```
[root@server ~]# tail  /etc/sudoers
# %users  ALL=/sbin/mount /mnt/cdrom, /sbin/umount /mnt/cdrom

## Allows members of the users group to shutdown this system
# %users  localhost=/sbin/shutdown -h now

## Read drop-in files from /etc/sudoers.d (the # here does not mean a comment)
#includedir /etc/sudoers.d
#
student ALL=/sbin/iptables -nvL
student ALL=/usr/bin/tail /var/log/secure
```

In CentOS 7, all members of group wheel can use `sudo` to run any command as root by specifying their own password. This was not set as the default rule in the `/etc/sudoers` file in CentOS 7.

Creating, modifying, or deleting local user accounts

There are multiple commands that can be used to manage local user accounts in CentOS 7. This section covers only the most popular commands available in CentOS 7 to manage local user accounts.

Creating a user with the useradd command

The `useradd` command, when run without options, creates a user account with default parameters. The default parameters are read from the `/etc/login.defs` file and include parameters such as valid UID, GID number, default password aging rules, and so on. Values from this file are used while creating a new user only. The syntax of `useradd` is as follows:

```
$ useradd    <username>
```

`useradd --help` will display options that can be used with the `useradd` command to override the default parameters.

An example of using the `useradd` command to create a user account is shown in the following screenshot:

```
[root@server ~]# useradd sam
[root@server ~]# passwd sam
Changing password for user sam.
New password:
BAD PASSWORD: The password is shorter than 8 characters
Retype new password:
passwd: all authentication tokens updated successfully.
```

Apart from `useradd`, we can also use the `adduser` command to create a local user account in Linux. You can read more about `adduser` in the man page, using the man `adduser` command.

Modifying a user with the usermod command

The `usermod` command is used with various options to modify the existing user account parameters. The `usermod --help` command will display the various options that can be used. The syntax of `usermod` is as follows:

```
$ usermod    -<option>    <username>
```

The following table lists the common options used with `usermod` and their descriptions:

Options	Description
usermod -c "Comments" <username>	Add comments, such as the user's full name, address, phone number, and so on, in the GECOS field.
usermod -g <gid> <username>	Modify the user's primary group.
usermod -G <groupname> <username>	Modify the user's secondary group.
usermod -a -G <groupname> <user>	Used with the -G option only. It appends the user to the secondary group mentioned, without removing the user from other groups.
usermod -s <shell> <username>	Modify the login shell of the user account.
usermod -L <username>	Lock a user account.
usermod -U <username>	Unlock a user account.

An example of using the `usermod` command to modify the user's login shell is shown in the following screenshot:

```
[root@server ~]# tail -1 /etc/passwd
sam:x:1002:1002::/home/sam:/bin/bash
[root@server ~]# usermod -s /bin/sh sam
[root@server ~]# tail -1 /etc/passwd
sam:x:1002:1002::/home/sam:/bin/sh
```

The following command is used to view the associated `groups` of a user:

```
$ groups <username>
$ groups sam
```

The `usermod` command can be used to add a new secondary group in the existing secondary groups of a user. The following command will add a new secondary group wheel in the existing secondary groups of user `sam` as shown in the following screenshot:

```
[root@server ~]# groups sam
sam : sam
[root@server ~]# usermod -aG wheel sam
[root@server ~]# groups sam
sam : sam wheel
```

Deleting a user account with the userdel command

The `userdel` command is used to delete the existing user account. The `userdel` command can be used in two ways as mentioned follows:

- `userdel <username>`: This removes the user entry from the `/etc/passwd` file, but leaves the user's home directory and mail intact. This way of deleting a user account is not recommended.
- `userdel -r <username>`: This removes the user and the user's home directory, along with the user's mail box. This will remove the files owned by the user along with the user's account from his home directory. An example of `userdel` command with option `-r` is shown in the following screenshot:

```
[root@server ~]# tail -1 /etc/passwd
sam:x:1002:1002::/home/sam:/bin/sh
[root@server ~]# userdel -r sam
[root@server ~]# tail -1 /etc/passwd
jack:x:1001:1001::/home/jack:/bin/bash
```

Creating, modifying, or deleting local group accounts

Groups are used for organizing users. A group is a collection of accounts with shared permissions. However, a group must exist before a user is added to that group. There are multiple commands that can be used to manage group accounts in CentOS 7. This section covers only the most popular commands available in CentOS 7 to manage local group accounts.

Control of group membership is managed with the `/etc/group` file. It lists the group, along with its members.

Creating supplementary groups with groupadd

The `groupadd` command can be used with multiple options to create a supplementary group for user accounts, or a system user group.

The following table list the `groupadd` command with various options along with their description:

Command	Description
groupadd <groupname>	Creates a user private groups (GID 1000+) from the next available GID from the range given in the `/etc/login.defs` file
groupadd -g GID <groupname>	Creates a user private group using the given GID
groupadd -r <groupname>	Creates a system group using a GID from the default system group's range (1-999), or as given in the `/etc/login.defs` file.

An example of `groupadd` command usage is shown in the following screenshot:

```
[root@server ~]# groupadd -g 3000 HR
[root@server ~]# groupadd -r sysusers
[root@server ~]# tail -3 /etc/group
jack:x:1001:
HR:x:3000:
sysusers:x:982:
```

Modifying existing groups with the groupmod command

The `groupmod` command is used to modify group properties such as the group's GID, group name, and so on. The example in following image shows how to use the `groupmod` command with the `-n` option to modify the `groupname` of a specified group:

```
[root@server ~]# tail -1 /etc/group
sysusers:x:982:
[root@server ~]# groupmod -n  appusers sysusers
[root@server ~]# tail -1 /etc/group
appusers:x:982:
```

The `-g` option is used to assign a new GID to an existing `groupname` as shown in the following screenshot:

```
[root@server ~]# tail -2 /etc/group
HR:x:3000:
appusers:x:982:
[root@server ~]# groupmod -g 9000 HR
[root@server ~]# tail -2 /etc/group
HR:x:9000:
appusers:x:982:
```

Deleting a group with the groupdel command

The `groupdel` command is generally used to delete a group from the system if it is not the primary group of any existing user. The following command line shows how to delete a group named `appusers` from the system using the `groupdel` command:

```
$ groupdel appusers
$ tail -2 /etc/group
```

Managing user passwords and aging policies

This section covers commands that are used to manage passwords and password aging parameters in the shadow password file available in CentOS 7.

Setting a user password using the passwd command

The `passwd` command is used to either set the user's initial password or modify the user's existing password. The syntax of the `passwd` command is as follows:

```
$ passwd    <username>
```

The root user can set the password for any user to any value without knowing his current password. For a regular user, the default policy is to use at least an eight-character password, and it should not be a dictionary word, or the username, or a previous password. An example updating a user's password using the `passwd` command is shown in the following screenshot:

```
[root@server ~]# passwd jack
Changing password for user jack.
New password:
BAD PASSWORD: The password is shorter than 8 characters
Retype new password:
passwd: all authentication tokens updated successfully.
```

Understanding the shadow password file

In the early days of Linux's evolution, encrypted passwords were stored in a human-readable file, `/etc/passwd`. This was considered a safe mechanism for keeping passwords until dictionary attacks on encrypted passwords became more prevalent. Now, to harden Linux security, the encrypted passwords (salted password hashes) are stored in the `/etc/shadow` file. This file also contains password aging policy parameters. Only those with root access can modify or read this file. We can view the last line of this file by executing the command line given as follows:

```
# tail -1 /etc/shadow
```

On execution of the preceding command, we get the following output, which displays the encrypted password along with the salt and various password aging parameters:

```
jack:$6$cKc/hj8V$JZPyiz6TMpz/YpPtSPdNARPd/gXxLqm3c0qHZinNmweXEpM/IMBYGiBYXZ
w7OuzLnr0YkFdZZifPvywkJYuqv0:17783:0:99999:7:::
```

In the preceding output, the second field of the `/etc/shadow` file is the password field and contains the following three pieces of information, separated by a `$` symbol, in the `/etc/shadow` file:

- `6`: It represents the hashing algorithm used to encrypt the password. The number 1 indicates MD5 hashing, number 5 indicates SHA-256 hashing, and number 6 indicates the SHA-512 hashing algorithm.
- `cKc/hj8V`: It represents the randomly chosen salt used to encrypt the hash. This salt and the unencrypted password are combined and encrypted to create the password hash. Use of the salt prevents two or more users with the same password from having identical entries in the `/etc/shadow` file.
- `JZPyiz6TMpz/YpPtSPdNARPd/gXxLqm3cOqHZinNmweXEpM/IMBYGiBYXZw7Ouz LnrOYkFdZZifPvywkJYuqv0`: It is the encrypted hash.

When the user enters his password at the login prompt, the system looks up the entry for the user in `/etc/shadow`, then combines the salt of the user with the unencrypted password and generates a hash value using the specified hashing algorithm. If the password matches, the user gets logged in; otherwise, the login attempt fails.

Understanding password aging parameters

The `chage` command is used to list the existing password aging policy or to modify the policy. The `/etc/shadow` file contains nine colon-separated fields, which include both the encrypted password and the password aging policy. The following is the format of the information contained in the `/etc/shadow` file:

```
name : password : lastchange : minage : maxage : warning : inactive :
expire : blank
```

The following table lists the `/etc/shadow` file fields and their descriptions:

Field	Description
Login name	It is the user account login name on the local system.
Password	It is an encrypted password. If this field contains the ! symbol, then it means the password is locked.
Lastchange	It is the date of the last password change, represented by the number of days since `01.01.1970`.
Minimum age	It is the minimum number of days before which a password cannot be changed.`0` in this field means no minimum day requirement.

Maximum age	It is the maximum number of days after which the password must be changed.
Warning Period	It is the number of days before password expiry, when the user starts getting a warning to change his password.0 in this field means no warning would be given.
Inactive	It is the number of days an account remains active after a password has expired. A user can still log in during this inactive period and change his password. After the specified number of days, the account will get locked and become inactive.
Expiry date	It is the account expiration date, represented as the number of days since 01.01.1970.
Blank	A blank field reserved for future use.

By default, passwords are set to not expire. Forcing passwords to expire is part of a strong security policy. We can modify the default expiration settings by making changes in the /etc/login.defs file. We can change the password aging policy using the chage command. The syntax of the chage command is given follows:

```
$ chage    [option]    <username>
```

An example of the chage command to list all existing password aging policy parameters for a user is shown in the following screenshot:

```
[root@server ~]# chage -l jack
Last password change                                    : Sep 13, 2018
Password expires                                        : never
Password inactive                                       : never
Account expires                                         : never
Minimum number of days between password change          : 0
Maximum number of days between password change          : 99999
Number of days of warning before password expires       : 7
```

The following table lists the various options that are used with the chage command and their descriptions:

Option	Description
Chage -l <username>	Lists all the user's current aging parameter settings
Chage -d 0 <username>	Forces password change on next login
Chage -m 3 <username>	Sets the minimum number of days a user can keep a password

`Chage -M 30 <username>`	Sets the maximum number of days a user can keep a password (`-1` here means unlimited)
`Chage -W 7 <username>`	Sets the number of days at which the user starts getting warnings before a password change
`Chage -d YYY-MM-DD <username>`	Sets the last change date for a password (the `/etc/shadow` file stores the number of days starting from 1 Jan 1970)
`Chage -E YYYY-MM-DD <username>`	Sets the password expiration date for the user (the `/etc/shadow` file stores the number of days starting from 1 Jan 1970)

An example of the `chage` command to modify various parameters is shown in the following screenshot:

```
[root@server ~]# chage -m 0 -M 30 -W 7 -I 5 jack
[root@server ~]# chage -l jack
Last password change                                    : Sep 13, 2018
Password expires                                        : Oct 13, 2018
Password inactive                                       : Oct 18, 2018
Account expires                                         : never
Minimum number of days between password change          : 0
Maximum number of days between password change          : 30
Number of days of warning before password expires       : 7
```

Restricting user access

Once the account expiration date set using the `chage` command is reached, the user cannot log in to the system interactively. Some parameters of the `chage` command can be set using `useradd` and `usermod`. The `usermod` command can be used to lock an account with the `-L` option as shown in follows command line:

```
# usermod -L jack
# su - jack
```

We can also unlock the user account using the `-U` option as shown in the following command line:

```
# usermod -U jack
```

Fake shell or nologin shell

At times, we may need a user account with a password for authentication with a system, but do not require an interactive shell with that username. This helps in preventing the user account being used for logging in to the system with that password. In those scenarios, we can set the user's shell to /sbin/nologin. If the user tries to log in to system, the nologin shell closes the connection of the user as shown in the following screenshot:

```
[root@server ~]# usermod -s /sbin/nologin jack
[root@server ~]# su - jack
Last login: Thu Sep 13 18:58:57 IST 2018 on pts/1
This account is currently not available.
```

An example of such a situation could be a mail server, where a user account is needed to store mail and passwords for the user to authenticate with the mail client and retrieve their mail; however, if the /sbin/nologin shell is assigned, then the user cannot log in to the system using that account.

Summary

In this chapter, we began by learning about the different types of users and groups on CentOS 7. This was followed by understanding the difference between su and sudo for temporarily granting root privileges to the user. Then, we learned about the management of local user accounts and local user groups. Finally, we looked at how passwords are set and stored in Linux and how password aging policies are implemented in CentOS 7.

In the next chapter, we will learn about managing file permissions in CentOS 7.

5
Managing File Permissions

Permissions are one of several good features that make Linux more secure when applied properly. Since Linux is a multi-user OS, different users will be working with multiple programs and files, and so on. Permissions help keep things secure and organized. In this chapter, you will learn how to manage access controls on files using basic read, write, and execute permissions and user or group ownership. You will also learn to apply special permissions and the **access control list** (**ACL**).

In this chapter, we will cover the following topics:

- Understanding Linux filesystem permissions
- Managing file permissions
- Managing file ownership
- Special permissions
- Managing default permissions
- Managing ACL on files

Understanding Linux filesystem permissions

On Linux/Unix-based operating systems, every file belongs to a user and to a group. By default, the user who creates the file is the owner of that file and the file belongs to that user's primary group. Access to the file via the Linux filesystem is controlled by permissions applied to that file. These permissions are classified for the owner (also known as the **user**) of the file, group (also known as the **group owner**) of that file, and for everybody else (also known as **others**) in the Linux system.

There are three types of standard permissions that are applied to files:

- Read, represented by the letter r
- Write, represented by the letter w
- Execute, represented by the letter x

These are generally grouped in triplets (such as rwx or r-w) to represent a class of permissions. Each file has three classes of permissions; that is, these permissions affect access to three categories in the system:

- **User/owner (u)**: Describes permissions applicable to the user who is the owner of that file. By default, it is the user who creates the file.
- **Group (g)**: Describes permissions applicable to the group that owns the file.
- **Others/everyone else (o)**: Describes permissions for everybody else in the system.

Effect of permissions on files and directories

The permissions control access to files and directories. The same permissions have different effects on files and directories.

Here is a table listing the permissions and the corresponding effect of permissions on the file and directories:

Permission	Effect on files	Effect on directories
Read (r)	Contents of file can be read	Contents of directory can be listed using the ls command
Write (w)	Contents of file can be modified	We can create or delete files and modify permissions on the files or directory
Execute (x)	We can execute files as commands	Contents of directory can be accessed (we can use the cd command on that directory)

If a user has read permission on a directory, it means they can list the names of files in it using the ls command only. If a user has only execute permission on a directory, then they cannot list the contents of the directory with the ls command; however, if a user knows the contents of the directory, they can access the contents explicitly by accessing the filename.

Any user can delete a file or sub-directory if they have write permission to the directory in which the file resides, irrespective of the ownership or permission on the file itself. Root has full control of permissions; it can access or delete any file in the filesystem. However, there are some advance permissions such as `chattr` and **Security-Enhanced Linux** (**SELinux**) controls, which can be used to create access controls for root. SELinux is a mandatory access control, which is discussed in `Chapter 9`, *Overview and Essential Advance Utilities*.

Viewing applied permissions and ownership

The `ls` command with the `-l` option is used to get detailed information on the directory contents, which includes permissions and ownership. It will list the detailed information of all the files that reside in the directory. To prevent the descent into the directory and view the information of the directory itself, use the `-d` option with the `ls` command, as shown in the following screenshot:

```
[root@server ~]# ls -l /opt/
total 0
drwxr-xr-x. 2 root root 6 Sep  7  2017 rh
[root@server ~]# ls -ld /opt/
drwxr-xr-x. 3 root root 16 Jul 13 19:39 /opt/
```

The first character in a long listing tells us the type of file. A hyphen (–) sign here represents a regular file that can contain data or text, or it can be a binary file. The following table lists various types of files and their identifiers used as the first character in a long-listing format.

Here is a table listing file types and their descriptions:

Type	Description
–	File
d	Directory
l	Link (symbolic link similar to shortcuts on Windows)
c	Character-type device files
b	Block-type device files
s	Socket-type files
p	Named pipes

Managing file permissions

The `chmod` command is used to modify the permissions on a file. **Change mode** (**chmod**) permissions are also known as **modes** of a file. Using `chmod`, we can modify permissions separately for the owner, group, and the rest of the world (others) in the system. There are two ways in which we can modify permissions with `chmod`: one is by using numbers and the other is by using symbolic notations.

Modifying file permissions with chmod using symbols

The `chmod` command is used to change the permission or mode of a file or directories. It takes the new set of permissions as the first argument, followed by the list of files and directories, to apply those new permissions. The symbolic method has the following syntax:

```
$ chmod    whowhatwhich    file  |  directory
```

Here is a table listing the keywords used with `chmod` and their descriptions:

Keyword	Description
Who	It represents whose permission you want to change: u: User permissions g: Group permissions o: Other permissions a: All user permissions If nothing is specified in this field, it takes (a) as the default value.
What	It represents what you want to do with permissions: +: Add some permissions in the existing set of permissions −: Remove some permissions from the existing set of permissions =: Set exactly the specified permissions, irrespective of the existing set of permissions
Which	It represents which permissions you are using: r: Read w: Write x: Execute

The following are some examples to illustrate the usage of the chmod command, using symbols:

List the existing permissions of the file named myfile,as shown in the following screenshot:

```
[root@server demo]# touch myfile
[root@server demo]# ls -l myfile
-rw-r--r--. 1 root root 0 Sep 30 07:40 myfile
```

Add execute permission for the user to the file named myfile, as shown in the following screenshot:

```
[root@server demo]# chmod u+x myfile
[root@server demo]# ls -l myfile
-rwxr--r--. 1 root root 0 Sep 30 07:40 myfile
```

Remove the write permission from the group and add the execute permission for others to the file named myfile, as shown in the following screenshot:

```
[root@server demo]# chmod g-w,o+x myfile
[root@server demo]# ls -l myfile
-rwxr--r-x. 1 root root 0 Sep 30 07:40 myfile
```

Set the read permission exactly and remove any existing permissions for all to the file named myfile, as shown in the following screenshot:

```
[root@server demo]# chmod a=r myfile
[root@server demo]# ls -l myfile
-r--r--r--. 1 root root 0 Sep 30 07:40 myfile
```

Set the execute permission exactly and remove any existing permissions for all from the file named myfile, as shown in the following screenshot:

```
[root@server demo]# chmod +x myfile
[root@server demo]# ls -l myfile
-r-xr-xr-x. 1 root root 0 Sep 30 07:40 myfile
```

Managing file permissions with chmod using numbers

The `chmod` command can also be used to modify file or directory permissions, using the numeric method. This method sets exactly the new permissions specified, using numbers with the `chmod` command, irrespective of the existing permissions of the file or directory. In the numeric method, permissions are represented by three-digit (or four-digit when setting special permissions) octal numbers. Each octal number represents a number between zero and seven, which is the sum of permissions for an access level—either a user, group, or others. The syntax to apply permissions using numbers is as follows:

```
$ chmod    ###    file  |   directory
```

Here, each # represents permissions for a user, group, and other access levels, starting from left to right. It is the sum of all the permissions (read, write, and execute) of that access level, where each permission has a certain numeric weightage, as follows:

Here is a table listing the numeric weightage of permissions:

Permission	Numeric weightage
Read (r)	4
Write (w)	2
Execute (x)	1

When setting permissions using the numeric method, we calculate the total sum of permissions we need for the user, group, or others; for example, if you want to use `set-rwx-r-xr--` as the new permission for `file1`, you do the following:

$$user \rightarrow rwx \rightarrow 4+2+1=7$$

$$group \rightarrow r\text{-}x \rightarrow 4+1=5$$

$$others \rightarrow r\text{-}\text{-} \rightarrow 4=4$$

The following example of the chmod command shows the usage of the chmod to set permissions using numbers and the usage of chmod to set the same permissions using symbols:

```
$ chmod 754 file1
$ chmod u=rwx,g=rx,o=r file1
```

The following are some examples to illustrate the usage of the chmod command using numbers:

Set the read permission for the user, the write permission for the group, and no permission for others on the file named file1, as shown in the following screenshot:

```
[root@server demo]# ls -l
total 0
-r-xr-xr-x. 1 root root 0 Sep 30 07:40 file1
[root@server demo]# chmod 420 file1
[root@server demo]# ls -l
total 0
-r---w----. 1 root root 0 Sep 30 07:40 file1
```

Use chmod with the -R option to recursive set permissions on all files and sub-directories within a directory. With the X option, you can add or remove execute permissions for directories only and not files. Although not used much, it is a useful option sometimes; you can use chmod -R +rX /data to set execute permissions for directories in the /data folder, but not for any file within it.

Managing file ownership

Every file or directory created on a Linux system belongs to a user and a group, which are also known as the owner of the file or the group owner of the file. Ownership of the file or the directory can be modified by the root user, or the owner of the file. Group ownership again can only be modified by the root user or the owner of the file, for the groups only to which he is a member. This section covers how to manage the ownership of files and directories.

Understanding default ownership

When we create a file or directory, it gets certain default ownership and group ownership. The user who creates the file becomes the user (owner) of that file, and the primary group of that user becomes the group of that file. To find out whether a user or a group has the permissions to access a file or a directory, a shell checks the ownership of that file in the following order:

1. When accessing a file, a shell checks whether you are the owner of a file. If a user is the owner of a file, then the user gets access to the file with the permissions that are set for the owner of the file.
2. If the user is not the owner of the file, a shell checks for the group of the file. If the user is a member of a group assigned to the file, then he gets access to the file with the permissions that are set for the group of the file.
3. If the user is neither the owner of the file and doesn't belong to the group assigned to the file, then the user gets access to the file with other permissions.

The long-listing `ls -l` command is used to view the current ownership of the file. The third and fourth fields of output of the long-listing command display the owner and group of the file, as shown in the following screenshot:

```
[root@server demo]# ls -l /home/
total 4
drwx------.  5 jack     jack      107 Sep 13 18:57 jack
drwx------. 18 student  student  4096 Sep 30 00:42 student
```

Modifying user ownership with chown

The `chown` command can be used to change the user ownership as well as the group ownership of a file or directory. Initially, we will see how the `chown` command can be used to change file ownership. The syntax of the `chown` command is as follows:

```
$ chown     <user_name_to_set_as_owner>     <file_or_foldername>
```

The following are some the examples to illustrate the usage of the `chown` command:

List current ownership of file named `myfile` using the `ls` command is shown as follows:

```
$ ls -l myfile
```

Grant user ownership of the file named `myfile` to `jack`, as shown in the following screenshot:

```
[root@server demo]# ls -l
total 0
-r---w----. 1 root root 0 Sep 30 07:40 myfile
[root@server demo]# chown jack myfile
[root@server demo]# ls -l
total 0
-r---w----. 1 jack root 0 Sep 30 07:40 myfile
```

The chown command is very often used with the -R option to recursively modify the ownership of a complete directory tree. The following command is used to grant ownership of a directory named mydir and all files and sub-directories within it to the user jack, as shown in the following screenshot:

```
[root@server demo]# mkdir mydir
[root@server demo]# ls -l
total 0
drwxr-xr-x. 2 root root 6 Sep 30 09:51 mydir
-r---w----. 1 jack root 0 Sep 30 07:40 myfile
[root@server demo]# chown -R jack mydir/
[root@server demo]# ls -l
total 0
drwxr-xr-x. 2 jack root 6 Sep 30 09:51 mydir
-r---w----. 1 jack root 0 Sep 30 07:40 myfile
```

Modifying group ownership with chown

The chown command can also be used to modify group ownership of a file or directory by prefixing a group name with a colon (:) sign or period (.) sign, as shown in the following command:

```
$ chown :group <filename_or_directoryname>
```

The following screenshot shows the usage of the chown command to change the group of myfile to jack:

```
[root@server demo]# ls -l
total 0
drwxr-xr-x. 2 jack root 6 Sep 30 09:51 mydir
-r---w----. 1 jack root 0 Sep 30 07:40 myfile
[root@server demo]# chown .jack myfile
[root@server demo]# ls -l
total 0
drwxr-xr-x. 2 jack root 6 Sep 30 09:51 mydir
-r---w----. 1 jack jack 0 Sep 30 07:40 myfile
[root@server demo]# chown :jack mydir/
[root@server demo]# ls -l
total 0
drwxr-xr-x. 2 jack jack 6 Sep 30 09:51 mydir
-r---w----. 1 jack jack 0 Sep 30 07:40 myfile
```

Modifying both user and group ownership with chown

The chown command can also be used to modify both the owner and group of the file simultaneously by using either of the following syntax:

```
$ chown     owner:group     <filename_or_dirname>

$ chown     owner.group     <filename_or_dirname>
```

The chown command can be used to change the owner of the file named myfile to root and the group of the file to wheel, as shown in the following screenshot:

```
[root@server demo]# ls -l myfile
-r---w----. 1 jack jack 0 Sep 30 07:40 myfile
[root@server demo]# chown root:wheel myfile
[root@server demo]# ls -l myfile
-r---w----. 1 root wheel 0 Sep 30 07:40 myfile
```

Modifying group ownership with chgrp

The chgrp command is also used to modify the group of a file or directory. This can only modify the group owner, unlike the previous command, chown,which could be used to modify user ownership and group ownership. The syntax of this command is as follows:

```
$ chgrp     <new_groupname>     <filename_dirname>
```

The chgrp command can be used to change the group of the myfile file to the group jack,as shown in the following screenshot:

```
[root@server demo]# ls -l myfile
-r---w----. 1 root wheel 0 Sep 30 07:40 myfile
[root@server demo]# chgrp jack myfile
[root@server demo]# ls -l myfile
-r---w----. 1 root jack 0 Sep 30 07:40 myfile
```

Special permissions

Besides the basic permissions set, which is applicable by default, Linux also has some special/advanced permission sets, which are used sometimes to enhance some functionalities. These permissions are applicable to files (mainly executable files) and directories. These are `setuid`, `setgid`, and `sticky bit`.

Modifying special permissions for files

`Setuid` and `setgid` are two special permissions that are applied to executable files.

If `setuid` is applied to an executable file, it means that if that file is executed as a program, then it will run as the user of the file and not as the user who ran the program.

Similarly, when `setgid` is applied to the file, it runs as the group of the file and not as the group that ran the program.

The `passwd` command has `setuid` applied by default in Linux systems, as shown in the following screenshot:

```
[root@server demo]# ls -l /usr/bin/passwd
-rwSr-xr-x. 1 root root 27832 Jun 10  2014 /usr/bin/passwd
```

The `chmod` command can be used to add `setuid` to a script file named `myscript`, as shown in the following command line:

```
$ ls -l myscript
$ chmod u+s myscript

or

$ chmod 4755 myscript
$ ls -l myscript
```

The `chmod` command can be used to add `setgid` on a script file named `myscript` as shown in the following command line:

```
$ ls -l myscript
$ chmod g+s myscript
```

or

```
$ chmod 2755 myscript
$ ls -l myscript
```

Modifying special permission, for directories

The `sticky bit` and `setgid` are special permissions that are applied to special directories.

Using sticky bit

The `sticky bit` special permission is used to put a restriction on the deletion of files. When sticky bit is set on a directory, then only the owner of the file and the root user can delete the files within that directory, for example:

The `/tmp` folder has got sticky bit applied by default in Linux systems, as shown in the following screenshot:

```
[root@server demo]# ls -ld /tmp/
drwxrwxrwt. 13 root root 4096 Sep 30 10:05 /tmp/
```

The following example illustrates the usage of the `chmod` command to add sticky bit to a directory:

```
$ ls -ld mydir
$ chmod o+t mydir
```

or

```
$ chmod 1775 mydir
$ ls -ld mydir
```

Using setgid

The setgid special permission is used to enable group inheritance from the parent directory. When setgid is set on a directory, then files created in that directory will inherit the group affiliation from the parent directory, instead of inheriting it from the user who creates the file. It is generally used on collaborative (shared) directories to automatically change a file from the default user private group to the shared group.

The following command line is used to view the existing permission of a directory:

```
$ ls -ld mydir
```

The following example illustrates the usage of the chmod command to add the setgid permission to a directory:

```
$ chmod g+s mydir
or
$ chmod 2770 mydir
$ ls -ld mydir
```

Here is a table listing special permissions and their effect on files and directories:

Special permission	Numerically fourth-digit weightage	Effects on files	Effects on directories
setuid (u+s)	Setuid= 4	Files are executed as the user that owns the file, not the user running that file	No effect
setgid (g+s)	Setgid = 2	Files are executed as the group that owns the file	Enables group inheritance. Files created in the directory have their group owner set as the group owner of the directory
sticky bit (o+t)	Sticky bit = 1	No effect	Only the root or the owner of the files can delete the files from the directory with a sticky bit set

 Extra care is to be taken when setting these special permissions, as incorrect setting (usage) of the setuid and setgid on binaries can lead to privilege escalation. Such scenarios can help an attacker gain access to the root account via a regular user account.

Managing default permissions

The files get their default permissions from the users or processes that create them. If a file is created using text editors, it will have read and write permissions and no executable permissions for everyone. Similarly, a binary executable created using compilers generally has executable permission sets, since they are meant for execution.

Understanding umask

Default file and folder permissions are set by the umask program. The umask command without any argument will display the existing value of umask. The same command, when followed by a new octal value as an argument, will set the new value of umask. The following command line is used to view the existing umask of a user:

```
$ umask
```

Normal users have a different umask,and the root has a different umask value, to decide the default permissions for files and directories. The following examples illustrate the different umask values the exit in system for a regular user and a root user:

- Execute the umask command on Terminal as a root user to view the umask value for the root account, as shown in the following screenshot:

```
[root@server demo]# umask
0022
```

- To view the umask value of student user, first switch to student user account and then execute the umask command as shown in the following screenshot:

```
[root@server demo]# su - student
Last login: Sun Sep 30 00:42:09 IST 2018 on :0
[student@server ~]$ umask
0002
```

For files, the maximum default value is generally 666 (normal files do not require execute permissions to be set by default), and for directories the maximum default value is 777 (since directories require execute permissions to be set using the cd command). The umask values are taken off from the maximum default octal values to decide the default permissions for files and directories.

For example, let's understand the `umask` value `0022` that is the default value of the root account. It means remove write permissions for the group and others from the maximum permissions of files and directories. Hence, the default permission for the file will be `644`, and for the directory it will be `755`. Similarly, a `umask` value of `0002` that is the default value of the normal user account, means remove write permissions for others from the maximum permissions of files and directories. Hence, the default permission for the file will be `664`, and for the directory it will be `775`.

> While setting a new `umask` value of user, if the argument of `umask` command contains fewer than three octal digits, then leading zeros are assumed in the argument part.

Managing ACL on files

Standard Linux file permissions are applicable for file owners, groups of files, or everyone else in the system. Using standard permissions, we cannot give multiple users or multiple groups different permissions for a single file. This kind of delicate control is provided using ACLs in Linux. We can give permissions to more than one user or one group for the same file.

File owners or root can set ACLs on individual files or on directories if the filesystem is mounted with ACL support enabled. CentOS 7's default filesystem is `XFS`, which has built-in ACL support. Although not all applications (such as `tar`) support ACL, it is still a great functionality available in the Linux system.

Viewing ACL permissions

Using the `ls -l` command, we can view standard permission and tell whether a file or a directory has ACL applied to it. If the tenth character in the permission is the + symbol, then it indicates that ACL is applied on that file or directory.

If the plus (+) symbol is present on a file, it means the user permission represents the user ACL setting, the group permission represents the ACL mask (and not the group owner setting), and other permissions are other ACL settings. An example to find out whether the ACL permissions are applied on file is shown in the following screenshot:

```
[root@server demo]# ls -l file1
-rw-r-xr--+ 1 root root 0 Sep 30 10:21 file1
```

If ACL is applied on a file, then modifying its group permissions with `chmod` will change the ACL mask and not the group owner permissions.

Using getfacl

To view the ACLs on a file or directory, the `getfacl` command is used. Its syntax is shown in the following screenshot:

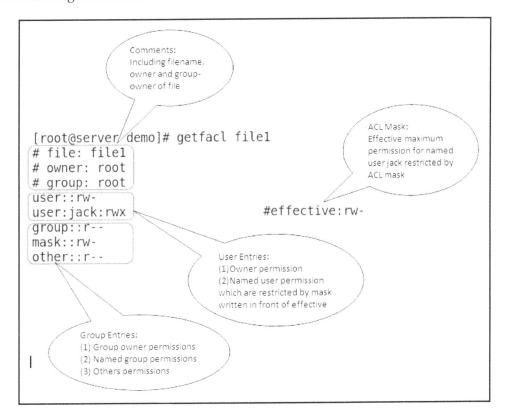

The `getfacl` command can also be used to export the ACL applied to a file or directory into a file, as shown in the following command line:

```
$ getfacl -R /data > file.acl
```

The exported ACL can be imported from the file and applied using the `setfacl` command, as shown in the following command line:

```
$ setfacl --set-file=file.acl
```

ACL mask

The ACL mask is used to set the maximum effective permissions for the group owner of a file, named users of a file, and named groups of a file. The maximum permissions of the owner or others are the ones that are set using `chmod` and not controlled by the ACL mask.

The ACL mask is set on a file using the `setfacl` command as follows:

```
$ setfacl   -m    m::r    filename
```

The ACL mask is viewed using the `getfacl` command as follows:

```
$ getfacl      filename
```

The `getfacl` command displays a string `#effective:` in front of the entries that are restricted by the mask. It gets updated automatically whenever group permissions are updated with `chmod`.

The following table lists the user types and corresponding ACL precedence in Linux systems:

User type	ACL precedence
Owner user	ACL permissions apply
Named user	ACL permissions apply (should be equal to or less than ACL mask)
Group	ACL permissions apply (should be equal to or less than ACL mask)
Named group	ACL permissions apply (should be equal to or less than ACL mask)
Others	ACL permissions apply

Modifying ACL permissions

ACLs use the same standard filesystem permission representation, which is used with `chmod`.

The following table list the symbols and their corresponding permission representation in ACL:

Symbol	Permission
r	Read
w	Write
x	Execute
–	That permission is absent
X	Indicates the execute permission should be set on directories and not on regular files

Using setfacl

The setfacl command is used with the –m option to modify or add new ACLs to a file or directory. For example, file owner permissions can be set using chmod or using setfacl. If no named user is specified in the user part of setfacl, then that permission applies to the file owner, as shown in the following command:

```
$ ls -l file1
$ setfacl -m u::rwx file1
```

Named user ACLs are set on a file using the username or UID, as shown in the following command:

```
$ setfacl -m u:jack:rwx file1
```

If no named group is specified in ACL, then that ACL applies to the group owner, as shown in the following command:

```
$ setfacl -m g::rw file1
```

We can modify or add a named group ACL to a file using the group name or GID, as shown in the following command:

```
$ setfacl -m g:sam:rw  file1
```

We can set the ACL using output from getfacl command and giving it as input to setfacl command. In the following example, the --set-file option enables the setfacl command to read the input from a file or stdin (–), as shown in the following command:

```
$ getfacl file1 | setfacl  --set-file=- file2
```

We can set the ACL recursively using the `-R` option on directories. The `X` option is also generally used with recursion, so that directories will get executable permissions set, and this prevents adding executable permissions to files accidentally when setting ACL permission recursively:

```
$ setfacl -R -m u:jack:rX dir1
```

We can set default ACLs on directories to enable ACL inheritance on all new files and sub-directories using the `-d` option or by prefixing the `setfacl` command with `d:`, as shown in the following command line:

```
$ setfacl -m d:u:jack:rwX directory
```

To remove default ACLs, use the `-x` option with `d:`, as shown in the following command line:

```
$ setfacl -x d:u:jack:rwX directory
```

Removing an ACL

The `setfacl` command is also used with the `-x` option to remove the applied ACL for any user or group. The only difference when removing ACL from setting ACL is that we don't specify the permission while removing. The following example illustrates the usage of the `setfacl` command to remove the ACL applied to a file named as `file1` for the user jack and the group sam:

```
$ setfacl -x  u:jack,g:sam  file1
```

To remove all ACLs from a file or directory, we can use the `-b` option, as shown in the following command:

```
$ setfacl -b file1
```

Summary

In this chapter, we began with learning about different types of permissions in Linux systems and how to manage them using numbers as well as using symbols. Then we learned about the managing of file ownership using the `chown` and `chgrp` commands. This was followed by understanding special permissions for executable and directories. Then we learned how to manage default permissions. Finally, we looked at how to view, set, and delete ACLs on files and directories in CentOS 7.

In the next chapter, we will learn about process management in CentOS 7. Process management is an essential skill that is required to manage your system resources. It will lay the solid foundation for optimizing system performance.

6
Process Management

Processes access multiple resources in a running system. Process management is essential to manage these resources effectively and keep your system up and running smoothly. In this chapter, you will learn how to view processes running on a Linux system and how to employ interactive management from the command line. Then, you will learn how to control different programs running on a Linux system using the command line. You will also learn how to communicate with different processes using signals and how to modify their priority level on a running system.

In this chapter, we will cover the following topics:

- Understanding processes
- Viewing current processes
- Communicating with processes using signals
- Monitoring processes and load averages
- Managing a processes' priority levels with nice and renice
- Controlling jobs on the command line

Understanding processes

This section deals with various concepts related to processes, such as their types, states, attributes, and so on. Process management is an essential skill that all types of users of Linux systems should master.

Defining a process

A process is an instance of a program in execution. It differs from a program or command in the sense that a single program can start several processes simultaneously. Each process uses several resources, as mentioned in the following list:

- An address space in memory
- Each process has some security properties, such as ownership, privileges, and so on
- Each process has a state
- Each process has local and global environment variables
- Each process has a scheduling context
- Each process has allocated resources, such as file descriptors, network ports, and so on
- A kernel keeps tracks of each process by assigning each process a unique **process ID (PID)** number
- A user's program accesses the information for each process through a directory called /proc/PID, which is maintained by a kernel

Process creation on a Linux system

All processes on CentOS 7 are descendants of the first system process, known as **systemd**. An existing process (parent) duplicates its own address space using a fork system call to create a new process (child) structure. Each new process is assigned a unique PID for tracking process state, CPU usage, memory usage, and other characteristics. PIDs are generally assigned in ascending order when a new process is created. The PID 1 is assigned to the systemd process. The PID and **PPID** (short for **Parent Process ID**) are the attributes of each process running on a Linux system.

PPID is the PID of a parent process that starts the child process. If a parent dies, that process is known as an **orphan** process. For a long time, the orphan process has been adopted by the init (PID=1) process. However, nowadays, in recent kernels, kthread (PID=2) is the adoptive process for orphan child processes.

A **thread ID (TID)** number is the same as PID for single-threaded processes. For multi-threaded processes, each thread shares the same PID, but a different TID.

Processes types

There are different types of processes, based on the task they are performing. Some of the common types of processes that exist on a Linux system are described in the following subsections.

Interactive processes

This type of process is started by a user, either on the command line or a through graphical user interface, such as Bash shell, Firefox, `top` command, and so on.

Batch processes

These kind of processes are scheduled to run from the Terminal and disconnect themselves from the Terminal at a later stage. An example of this is `updatedb`.

Daemons

These processes are automatically started on system boot up and continue to run until shutdown or until stopped in-between manually. They continuously wait for a user or system request in the background. By convention, the names of most daemon programs end with the letter d, such as `httpd`, `named`, `mysqld`, and so on.

Threads

Threads are also known as **lightweight processes** (**LWPs**). Each thread has a main process whose memory and other resources are shared by a thread. Each thread is scheduled and runs independently by the kernel. A thread can end at any time without terminating the whole process, and a process can also create new threads at any time. For example, when we open multiple tabs in a Firefox browser, it creates multiple threads, and each thread runs independently.

Kernel threads

These are kernel tasks that are started and used by the kernel, and users do not have much control over them, such as `kthreadd`.

Process states

Linux is a multitasking operating system, where each CPU core executes one process at any single point in time. This process of scheduling (constantly shifting processes on and off the CPU), and allocating CPU time as per priority, is one of the key functions of a kernel. Based on this, processes are assigned a state such as running, sleeping, stopped, and so on, which keeps changing with the circumstances.

The following table lists Linux process states with their flags and descriptions:

Name of process state	Flag	Kernel defined name	Description
Running	R	TASK_RUNNING	In this state, a process is either currently executing on a CPU or waiting to run in a queue. This state is also known as **runnable** when a process is ready to run and is waiting in a queue.
Sleeping	S	TASK_INTERRUPTIBLE	In this state, a process is waiting for an event to complete. On receiving a signal, the process returns to the running state.
	D	TASK_UNINTERRUPTIBLE	In this state, a process will not respond to a signal. It is used only in specific conditions, usually associated with I/O, when interruptions are not desirable.
	K	TASK_KILLABLE	In this state, a process is in the sleeping state and will only respond to a kill signal to exit.
Stopped	T	TASK_STOPPED	This state is reached when a process is stopped by a job control signal.
Zombie	Z	EXIT_ZOMBIE	A zombie or defunct process state is one where a process has terminated but its entry is not removed from the process table by the respective parent.

Viewing current processes

Each process running on a Linux system has various attributes, such as PID, PPID, the CPU time consumed by the process, the physical and virtual memory consumption of the process, and so on. All of this information can be found in the process table of the operating system. When working in a multi-user environment, it might happen that a process started by a user consumes the CPU cycle excessively. Hence, it is essential to manage processes and to manage computer resources efficiently. For this, we need to identify the types of processes and change their priority levels, or even terminate them if required. This section describes the use of various commands that are helpful for viewing processes and their attributes.

Listing running processes

The **ps** (short for **process status**) is used to list the current processes information that's available in the process table. It's similar to the `tasklist` command of Windows, which also used to list the running tasks of Windows in the command prompt.

The ps command

The Linux version of the `ps` command supports three types of format, as follows:

- **Unix (POSIX) standard**: In this format, options may be grouped and prefixed with a hyphen
- **BSD standard**: In this format, various options can be grouped, but they are not prefixed with a hyphen symbol
- **GNU standard**: In this format, long options are used, which are prefixed with two hyphen symbols

Various uses for the `ps` command, are described in the following subsections.

Displaying processes running from the current shell

Use the `ps` command, as shown in the following screenshot to list the process running from the current shell:

```
[root@server ~]# ps
  PID TTY          TIME CMD
 1898 pts/0    00:00:00 bash
 2816 pts/0    00:00:00 ps
```

The output shows rows of data with the following columns:

Command	Description
PID	The process ID of the running process
TTY	The Terminal type from which the process is running
TIME	The cumulative CPU time consumed by the process and the child processes started by the process
CMD	The command that runs as the current process

Displaying all processes by their user

The `ps` command can be used with the `-u` option to filter processes by user, as shown in the following command line:

```
$ ps -u student
```

Displaying all processes in different formats

The `ps` command can be used display all running processes on a system in different formats, as follows:

Display all the processes running in the system in Unix format.

The `ps` command can be used to display all running processes in a simple Unix format with either the `-A` option or the `-e` option, as shown in the following command line:

```
$ ps -A
or
$ ps -e
```

The `ps` command can be used to display a detailed listing of all the running processes by using the `-e` option to show all the processes and the `-f` option to show full details of each process in Unix format, as shown in the following command line:

```
$ ps -ef
```

The output on execution of preceding command is shown in the following screenshot:

```
[root@server ~]# ps -ef | head -5
UID        PID  PPID  C STIME TTY          TIME CMD
root         1     0  0 Oct19 ?        00:00:02 /usr/lib/systemd/systemd --switched-root --system --deserialize 22
root         2     0  0 Oct19 ?        00:00:00 [kthreadd]
root         3     2  0 Oct19 ?        00:00:00 [ksoftirqd/0]
root         5     2  0 Oct19 ?        00:00:00 [kworker/0:0H]
[root@server ~]# ps -eF | head -5
UID        PID  PPID  C    SZ   RSS PSR STIME TTY          TIME CMD
root         1     0  0 48438  6740   1 Oct19 ?        00:00:02 /usr/lib/systemd/systemd --switched-root --system --deserialize 22
root         2     0  0     0     0   0 Oct19 ?        00:00:00 [kthreadd]
root         3     2  0     0     0   0 Oct19 ?        00:00:00 [ksoftirqd/0]
root         5     2  0     0     0   0 Oct19 ?        00:00:00 [kworker/0:0H]
```

In the preceding example, we have limited the output of the `ps` command to display only the top five lines using the head command. In subsequent examples, we have used the same technique to limit the output of `ps` command for demonstration purposes.

The output shows rows of data with the following columns:

Command	Description
UID	User ID of the person who ran the command
PID	Process ID of the command
PPID	Parent process that started the command
C	Number of children a process has
STIME	Start time for the process
TTY	Terminal associated with the process; you will see a question mark ? if a process is not attached to a Terminal
TIME	Cumulative CPU time consumed by the process and the child processes started by the process
CMD	The command that was run to start the process
Using the -F option with -e ($ ps -eF) will list further columns:	
PSR	Processor number to which the process is assigned
SZ	Total amount of memory size in physical pages for the given process
RSS	Resident set size is the actual physical memory size consumed by a process

Display all the processes running in system using BSD syntax.

The ps command can be used with the aux option to display all running processes in BSD syntax, as shown in the following command line. Here, option a lists all of the processes attached to Terminals, option u lists the users of processes, and option x lists all processes that are not associated with a Terminal:

```
$ ps aux
```

The output on execution of the preceding command is shown in the following screenshot:

```
[root@server ~]# ps aux | head -5
USER       PID %CPU %MEM    VSZ    RSS TTY      STAT START   TIME COMMAND
root         1  0.0  0.1 193752   6740 ?        Ss   Oct19   0:02 /usr/lib/systemd/systemd --switched-root --system --deserialize 22
root         2  0.0  0.0      0      0 ?        S    Oct19   0:00 [kthreadd]
root         3  0.0  0.0      0      0 ?        S    Oct19   0:00 [ksoftirqd/0]
root         5  0.0  0.0      0      0 ?        S<   Oct19   0:00 [kworker/0:0H]
```

The output shows rows of data with the following columns:

Command	Description
USER	The name of the user associated with the process
PID	The unique numeric process ID assigned to the process

%CPU	Percentage of the CPU used by a process (the length of time the process has been running for, divided by the total CPU time used by the process)
%MEM	Percentage of the RAM memory used by the process (memory used divided by the total memory available)
VSZ	Virtual memory size expressed in KiB
RSS	Resident set size is the actual physical memory size consumed by the process
TTY	The Terminal controlling the process; you will see ? if the process is not attached to a Terminal
STAT	Displays the following process states: R: Running S: Sleep interruptible D: Sleep uninterruptible T: Stopped Z: Zombie <: High priority N: Low priority L: Has pages locked into memory s: Session leader l: Multithreaded +: Foreground process
START	Date or time when the process was started
TIME	Cumulative CPU time consumed by the process and the child processes started by the process
CMD	Command used to start the process

Sorting processes based on different parameters

In this section, we will cover different examples to show you how the sorting of processes can be done with the ps command based on different parameters. The output of each example is shown in the subsequent screenshots.

- Sort processes in ascending order by the highest CPU utilization:

```
[root@server ~]# ps aux --sort -pcpu| head -5
USER        PID %CPU %MEM     VSZ   RSS TTY      STAT START   TIME COMMAND
gdm        1382  0.2  3.3 3218228 131592 ?       Sl   22:49   0:04 /usr/bin/gnome-shell
root          1  0.1  0.1 193752  6740 ?         Ss   22:48   0:02 /usr/lib/systemd/systemd --switched-root --system --deserialize 22
root          2  0.0  0.0      0     0 ?         S    22:48   0:00 [kthreadd]
root          3  0.0  0.0      0     0 ?         S    22:48   0:00 [ksoftirqd/0]
```

- Sort processes in ascending order by the highest memory utilization:

```
[root@server ~]# ps aux --sort -pmem| head -5
USER       PID %CPU %MEM    VSZ   RSS TTY     STAT START   TIME COMMAND
gdm       1382  0.2  3.3 3218228 131592 ?     Sl   22:49   0:04 /usr/bin/gnome-shell
root      1014  0.0  0.4 320912 18592 tty1    Ssl+ 22:49   0:00 /usr/bin/X :0 -background none -noreset -audit 4 -verbose -auth /run/gdm/auth-f
or-gdm-uSmgU3/database -seat seat0 -nolisten tcp vt1
gdm       1488  0.0  0.4 1099444 17368 ?      Sl   22:49   0:00 /usr/libexec/gsd-media-keys
root       880  0.0  0.4 573820 17184 ?       Ssl  22:49   0:00 /usr/bin/python -Es /usr/sbin/tuned -l -P
```

- Combine both the CPU and memory utilization for sorting by a single command:

```
[root@server ~]# ps aux --sort -pcpu,+pmem| head -5
USER        PID %CPU %MEM     VSZ     RSS TTY       STAT START    TIME COMMAND
gdm        1382  0.1  3.3 3218228 131592 ?         Sl   22:49    0:04 /usr/bin/gnome-shell
root          2  0.0  0.0       0       0 ?         S    22:48    0:00 [kthreadd]
root          3  0.0  0.0       0       0 ?         S    22:48    0:00 [ksoftirqd/0]
root          5  0.0  0.0       0       0 ?         S<   22:48    0:00 [kworker/0:0H]
```

If a zombie process entry is available in the process table, it will appear as exiting or defunct.

Displaying processes by user

To filter processes by user, the −u option is followed by the username. Multiple usernames can be provided, separated by a comma. In the following example, the ps command is used to list the processes started by user Apache only, as shown in the following screenshot:

```
[root@server ~]# ps -f -u apache
UID        PID  PPID  C STIME TTY          TIME CMD
apache    7477  7476  0 00:39 ?        00:00:00 /usr/sbin/httpd -DFOREG
apache    7478  7476  0 00:39 ?        00:00:00 /usr/sbin/httpd -DFOREG
apache    7479  7476  0 00:39 ?        00:00:00 /usr/sbin/httpd -DFOREG
apache    7480  7476  0 00:39 ?        00:00:00 /usr/sbin/httpd -DFOREG
apache    7481  7476  0 00:39 ?        00:00:00 /usr/sbin/httpd -DFOREG
```

Displaying process information by name

To list process information by process name, use the -C option, followed by the exact process name, as shown in the following screenshot:

```
[root@server ~]# ps -C httpd
  PID TTY          TIME CMD
 7476 ?        00:00:00 httpd
 7477 ?        00:00:00 httpd
 7478 ?        00:00:00 httpd
 7479 ?        00:00:00 httpd
 7480 ?        00:00:00 httpd
 7481 ?        00:00:00 httpd
```

Displaying process details by PID

To display process information using PID, use the -p option, followed by the PID of processes, separated by a comma, as shown in the following screenshot:

```
[root@server ~]# ps -f -p 7476,2512,904
UID        PID  PPID  C STIME TTY          TIME CMD
root       904     1  0 Oct04 ?        00:00:00 /usr/sbin/crond -n
root      2512   880  0 Oct04 ?        00:00:00 sshd: root@pts/0
root      7476     1  0 00:39 ?        00:00:00 /usr/sbin/httpd -DFOREG
```

Displaying a process hierarchy in a tree style

To display the parent-child relationship between processes, the --forest option is used, as shown in the following screenshot:

```
[root@server ~]# ps -f --forest -C httpd
UID        PID  PPID  C STIME TTY          TIME CMD
root      7476     1  0 00:39 ?        00:00:00 /usr/sbin/httpd -DFOREG
apache    7477  7476  0 00:39 ?        00:00:00  \_ /usr/sbin/httpd -DF
apache    7478  7476  0 00:39 ?        00:00:00  \_ /usr/sbin/httpd -DF
apache    7479  7476  0 00:39 ?        00:00:00  \_ /usr/sbin/httpd -DF
apache    7480  7476  0 00:39 ?        00:00:00  \_ /usr/sbin/httpd -DF
apache    7481  7476  0 00:39 ?        00:00:00  \_ /usr/sbin/httpd -DF
```

Displaying the child processes of a parent

To display the child processes of a parent using the PID of the main process, we can use the `--ppid` option. The main parent process is owned by the root, and child processes are forked and owned by the parent. The example of the `ps` command to display the child of a specified parent `PID` is shown in the following screenshot:

```
[root@server ~]# ps --ppid 7476
  PID TTY          TIME CMD
 7477 ?        00:00:00 httpd
 7478 ?        00:00:00 httpd
 7479 ?        00:00:00 httpd
 7480 ?        00:00:00 httpd
 7481 ?        00:00:00 httpd
```

Displaying the thread of a process

To display the thread of a process, the `-L` option is used with the `ps` command, as shown in the following screenshot:

```
[root@server ~]# ps -e -f -L | head
UID        PID  PPID   LWP  C NLWP STIME TTY          TIME CMD
root         1     0     1  0    1 22:48 ?        00:00:02 /usr/lib/systemd/systemd --switched-root --system --deserialize 22
root         2     0     2  0    1 22:48 ?        00:00:00 [kthreadd]
root         3     2     3  0    1 22:48 ?        00:00:00 [ksoftirqd/0]
root         5     2     5  0    1 22:48 ?        00:00:00 [kworker/0:0H]
root         6     2     6  0    1 22:48 ?        00:00:00 [kworker/u4:0]
root         7     2     7  0    1 22:48 ?        00:00:00 [migration/0]
root         8     2     8  0    1 22:48 ?        00:00:00 [rcu_bh]
root         9     2     9  0    1 22:48 ?        00:00:00 [rcu_sched]
root        10     2    10  0    1 22:48 ?        00:00:00 [lru-add-drain]
```

The output shows rows of data with several columns, all of which have been covered in previous examples, except the `LWP` column, which represents the TID, and **NLWP** (short for **Number of Lightweight Processes**), which represents the number of threads in a process here.

Displaying the pid of a process if the process name is known

To print only the PIDs of processes whose names are known, we use the -C option, followed by the exact process name and the -o option, followed by pid=, as shown in the following screenshot:

```
[root@server ~]# ps -C httpd -o pid=
 7476
 7477
 7478
 7479
 7480
 7481
```

You can look up the meaning of all the labels and the various process state descriptions in the Unix standard and BSD standard from the man page of the ps command.

Using the pstree command

This command is used to display the parent-child relationship in hierarchical format. The output of this command is quite similar to the output of the ps axjf command and the ps -ef --forest command, as shown in the following command line:

```
$ pstree
```

The following screenshot displays the tree hierarchy of a single process with PID using the pstree command:

```
[root@server ~]# pstree -p 7476
httpd(7476)─┬─httpd(7477)
            ├─httpd(7478)
            ├─httpd(7479)
            ├─httpd(7480)
            └─httpd(7481)
```

Display the tree hierarchy of a user's processes by executing the command line given:

```
$ pstree -p student
```

On execution of the preceding command, the PIDs assigned to each process are shown in parentheses after each process name.

Finding the PID of a running process

Very often, we need to identify a PID to manage it, for example, if you need to stop the execution of a process. Sometimes, you may need to change the priority level of a process. Hence, to communicate with a process, the most commonly used method is using its PID. This section covers multiple commands that are used to find the PID of a running process.

Using the pgrep command

The `pgrep` command is used to look up currently running processes based on their name and other attributes, and displays the matching process PID. Its syntax is as follows:

```
$ pgrep    [options]    pattern
```

The following are examples to explain the use of the `pgrep` command:

To list processes with the `sshd` command name, which is also owned by root, execute the command line as follows:

```
$ pgrep -u root sshd
```

To list processes owned by the user `root` or `daemon`, execute the command line as follows:

```
$ pgrep -u root,daemon
```

The `pgrep` command can be used to list processes by specifying a pattern containing the process name. The following command line will find the PID of process that has the name of Firefox:

```
$ pgrep firef
```

The following example shows the usage of the `pgrep` command to list all the processes of the user student:

```
$ pgrep -U student
```

pidof

The `pidof` command can be used to find the process ID of a running program, if the argument provided to the `pidof` command is the exact process name, as shown in the following command line:

```
$ pidof bash
$ pidof firefox
```

The ps command with grep

Practically, it is difficult to remember the exact name of processes running on a Linux system. In scenarios where you do not remember the exact name of a process, the `pidof` command will not return the PID in the output. In such cases, the `ps` command output can be given as input to the grep filter to find the desired process name, as shown in the following command line:

```
$ ps aux | grep <process_name>
$ ps aux | grep sshd
```

The second column of output contains the PID of the filtered process.

Communicating with processes using signals

Processes communicate with each other using signals. We can also communicate with processes using `kill`, `pkill`, or the `killall` command to pass different signals.

Defining a signal and its types

A signal is a kind of software interrupt to a process. A signal can also be considered as a notification that needs to be processed for a specific event. `Kill`, `pkill`, and `killall` are programs that are used to deliver these signals to processes. On Linux, every signal name begins with the characters SIG. The signal numbers described in the following table may vary on different Linux hardware platforms, however, in any case, the signal name and meaning will remain the same.

The following table lists the popular signals used for process management, along with their descriptions:

Signal no.	Signal name	Meaning	Description
1	SIGHUP	Hangup	Given when controlling Terminal hangup (closed when user is away).
2	SIGINT	Keyboard interrupt	Used to terminate a program using the keyboard key combination *Ctrl + C*.
3	SIGQUIT	Keyboard quit	Used to terminate a program using the keyboard key combination *Ctrl + D*.

9	SIGKILL	Terminate forcefully	Causes the forceful, abrupt termination of a program by the user. Cannot be blocked, ignored, or handled.
15 (default)	SIGTERM	Terminate gracefully	Terminates the program gracefully. This signal can be blocked, ignored, or handled. It is the default signal sent by the `kill` command.
18	SIGCONT	Continue	Tells a stopped process to resume.
19	SIGSTOP	Stop	Suspends a process. This signal can't be blocked or handled.
20	SIGTSTP	Keyboard Stop	Used to suspend a process using the keyboard key combination *Ctrl + Z*. This signal can be blocked, ignored, or handled.

The `kill` command is used to list all of the signals supported by your Linux, system as shown in the following screenshot:

```
[root@server ~]# kill -l
 1) SIGHUP       2) SIGINT       3) SIGQUIT      4) SIGILL       5) SIGTRAP
 6) SIGABRT      7) SIGBUS       8) SIGFPE       9) SIGKILL     10) SIGUSR1
11) SIGSEGV     12) SIGUSR2     13) SIGPIPE     14) SIGALRM     15) SIGTERM
16) SIGSTKFLT   17) SIGCHLD     18) SIGCONT     19) SIGSTOP     20) SIGTSTP
21) SIGTTIN     22) SIGTTOU     23) SIGURG      24) SIGXCPU     25) SIGXFSZ
26) SIGVTALRM   27) SIGPROF     28) SIGWINCH    29) SIGIO       30) SIGPWR
31) SIGSYS      34) SIGRTMIN    35) SIGRTMIN+1  36) SIGRTMIN+2  37) SIGRTMIN+3
38) SIGRTMIN+4  39) SIGRTMIN+5  40) SIGRTMIN+6  41) SIGRTMIN+7  42) SIGRTMIN+8
43) SIGRTMIN+9  44) SIGRTMIN+10 45) SIGRTMIN+11 46) SIGRTMIN+12 47) SIGRTMIN+13
48) SIGRTMIN+14 49) SIGRTMIN+15 50) SIGRTMAX-14 51) SIGRTMAX-13 52) SIGRTMAX-12
53) SIGRTMAX-11 54) SIGRTMAX-10 55) SIGRTMAX-9  56) SIGRTMAX-8  57) SIGRTMAX-7
58) SIGRTMAX-6  59) SIGRTMAX-5  60) SIGRTMAX-4  61) SIGRTMAX-3  62) SIGRTMAX-2
63) SIGRTMAX-1  64) SIGRTMAX
```

Each signal has a default action associated with it, such as the termination of a process, stopping a process, continuing a stopped process, and so on.

Sending signals to processes

There are multiple methods for sending signals to a process. One of the most common is using a keyboard interrupt such as *Ctrl + C*, *Ctrl + D*, and so on. Another method is using the `kill`, `killall`, and `pkill` commands.

Sending signals to processes by PID using the kill command

The `kill` command sends a signal to a process by PID. Contrary to its name, the `kill` command can be used to send any signal to processes. The default signal sent by the `kill` command is SIGTERM, for example, signal number 15. The syntax of the kill command is as follows:

```
$ kill   -<signal_name_or_signal_number>    PID_OF_PROCESS
```

The following are examples to explain the usage of `kill` command:

- For sending a default signal to a process to terminate it gracefully, use the following command:

    ```
    $ kill PID
    ```

- To terminate a process using the signal name, use the following command:

    ```
    $ kill -SIGTERM PID
    ```

- To terminate a process using the signal number, use the following command:

    ```
    $ kill -15 PID
    ```

- To terminate a process forcefully, use either of the following commands:

    ```
    $ kill -SIGKILL PID
    or
    $ kill -9 PID
    ```

This is similar to the operation that we perform using the Task Manager in Windows when we right-click on the process name in the Task Manager and pass the end process command:

- The `kill` command can be used to suspend/stop a process and send it to the background if it is running in the foreground. This can be done by using either of the following commands:

    ```
    $ kill -SIGTSTP  PID
    or
    $ kill -20 PID
    ```

- To resume a process if it has been stopped, use either of the following commands:

```
$ kill -SIGCONT PID
or
$ kill -18 PID
```

Sending signals to multiple processes by name

We can also send signals to a process or multiple processes using by their name with the help of the `killall` command and the `pkill` command, as discussed in the following subsections.

killall

The `killall` command is used to send a signal to one or more processes on matching one of the following conditions:

- **Command**: Match exact process name
- **Owner**: Match exact name of the owner of the process
- **All system**: System-wide processes

Its syntax is as follows:

```
$ killall    <process_name>
$ killall   -<signal>      <process_name>
$ killall   -<signal>    -u   <username>      <process_name>
```

pkill

The `pkill` command is also used to send a signal to multiple processes on matching a combination of the criteria, which is explained in following examples:

- Using `pkill` with the command pattern: The `pkill` command can be used to send a signal to the matching processes name, as shown here:

```
$ pkill    <command_name_pattern>
 $ pkill    -<signal_name_or_signal_number>    <command_name_pattern>
```

The example of sending a signal to multiple sleep processes using a single `pkill` command is shown in the following screenshot:

```
[root@server ~]# sleep 3000&
[1] 1661
[root@server ~]# sleep 4000&
[2] 1662
[root@server ~]# pkill -SIGTERM sleep
[1]-  Terminated              sleep 3000
[2]+  Terminated              sleep 4000
```

- Using the `pkill` command with UID: The `pkill` command can be used to send a signal to processes owned by the specified Linux user account by specifying its UID, as shown in the following syntax:

      $ pkill   -u   <username_or_uid>   <command_pattern>

- Using the `pkill` command with GID: The `pkill` command can be used to send a signal to processes owned by the specified Linux group account by specifying its GID, as shown in the following syntax:

      $ pkill   -g   <groupname_or_gid>   <command_pattern>

- Using the `pkill` command with Parent PID: The `pkill` command can be used to send a signal to all of the child processes of the specified parent process, as shown in the following syntax:

      $ pkill   -P   PPID   <command_pattern>

- Using the `pkill` command with Terminal name: The `pkill` command can be used to send a signal to processes running from a specific controlling Terminal, as shown in the following syntax:

      $ pkill   -t   <terminal_name>   -U   UID   <command_pattern>

Monitoring processes and load averages

The load average is the average of the load for a given period of time on each CPU. It takes into account the following:

- Actively running processes (including each thread as an individual, separate task) on a CPU core.

- Runnable processes, waiting for a CPU to become available.

- Sleeping processes, for example, waiting for some kind of resource (generally disk I/O or network I/O) to become available.

- Linux counts each physical CPU core and microprocessor hyper-thread as separate execution units, and refers to them as individual CPUs. Each CPU has an independent request queue. We can count the total number of system CPUs using by the following command:

  - `$ grep "model name" /proc/cpuinfo | wc -l`

Understanding load averages on Linux

The load average of processes are viewed using the w, uptime, or top command, or with gnome-system-monitor in GUI mode. These commands display the load averages by using a combined representation of all CPUs for the last 1, 5, and 15 minutes.

uptime

The uptime command tells you how long your system has been up and running. However, at the same time, it provides other useful information, such as the number of users currently logged in and the system load average for the past 1, 5, and 15 minutes:

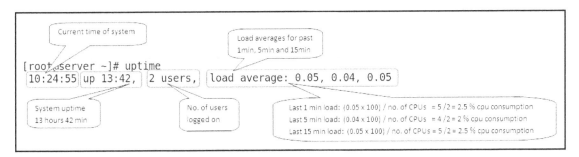

When we have more than one CPU, the load average will be divided by the number of CPUs as explained in the preceding screenshot. The increase in load for a short duration is not a problem, however, a continuous spike in the last 5 or 15 minute load averages may be a cause for concern.

w

The w command is used to display information about the users that are currently logged onto the machine and their running processes. The first line (header) in the output is the same as what we saw in the uptime output. An example of the w command is shown in the following screenshot:

```
[root@server ~]# w
 00:06:39 up  1:17,  1 user,  load average: 0.00, 0.01, 0.05
 USER     TTY      FROM             LOGIN@   IDLE   JCPU   PCPU WHAT
 root     pts/0    192.168.56.1     23:08    7.00s  0.23s  0.01s w
```

The output shows rows of data with the following columns:

Command	Description
USER	User login name
TTY	The controlling Terminal type, listed as pts/N (pseudo-terminal) in GUI, or ttyN on the system console or other directly connected device
FROM	Remote hostname from which the user has logged in
LOGIN@	Login time of the user
IDLE	How long it has been since the user typed any input on that Terminal
JCPU	CPU time consumption of all the processes attached to tty, including jobs currently running in the background
PCPU	CPU time consumption of the current processes named in the WHAT field
WHAT	The command line of the process currently executing

Real-time interactive process monitoring

The ps command gives static snapshots of processes running on a system. Sometimes, real-time monitoring of a system is also required. The top command is used to perform real-time monitoring of a system.

top

The top program provides a continuously updated real-time view of the processes running on a system after every 2 seconds, until its execution is stopped by pressing *q*. It displays multiple pieces of information, including system uptime, a list of the running tasks, the CPU status, and a memory status summary, followed by the different resources consumed by each process. The top command is executed as follows:

```
$ top
```

The output on execution of the preceding command is shown in the following screenshot:

```
top - 00:19:09 up  1:30,  1 user,  load average: 0.00, 0.01, 0.05
Tasks: 160 total,   1 running, 159 sleeping,   0 stopped,   0 zombie
%Cpu(s):  0.2 us,  0.2 sy,  0.0 ni, 99.7 id,  0.0 wa,  0.0 hi,  0.0 si,  0.0 st
KiB Mem :  3881008 total,  3196192 free,   344080 used,   340736 buff/cache
KiB Swap:  1023996 total,  1023996 free,        0 used.  3277228 avail Mem

  PID USER      PR  NI    VIRT    RES    SHR S  %CPU %MEM     TIME+ COMMAND
 2982 root      20   0  161972   2288   1576 R   0.3  0.1   0:00.07 top
    1 root      20   0  193752   6740   4152 S   0.0  0.2   0:02.56 systemd
    2 root      20   0       0      0      0 S   0.0  0.0   0:00.00 kthreadd
    3 root      20   0       0      0      0 S   0.0  0.0   0:00.05 ksoftirqd/0
    5 root       0 -20       0      0      0 S   0.0  0.0   0:00.00 kworker/0:0H
    7 root      rt   0       0      0      0 S   0.0  0.0   0:00.02 migration/0
    8 root      20   0       0      0      0 S   0.0  0.0   0:00.00 rcu_bh
    9 root      20   0       0      0      0 S   0.0  0.0   0:00.32 rcu_sched
   10 root       0 -20       0      0      0 S   0.0  0.0   0:00.00 lru-add-drain
   11 root      rt   0       0      0      0 S   0.0  0.0   0:00.06 watchdog/0
```

The output shows a system information summary, followed by each different processes' information in rows, with the descending order of CPU usage in the following columns:

System Information Summary	
1) The first line displays how long the system has been up, how many users are logged on, and what the load average is.	
2) The second line displays the total number of processes followed by the number of running, sleeping, stopped, and zombie processes.	
3) The third line displays the various CPU usage parameters:	
us	Percentage of CPU time used running un-niced user processes
sy	Percentage of CPU time used running kernel processes
ni	Percentage of CPU time used running user-niced processes
id	Percentage of CPU time spent when the kernel handler was idle
wa	Percentage of CPU time spent waiting for I/O completion
hi	Percentage of CPU time spent serving hardware interrupts
si	Percentage of CPU time spent serving software interrupts
st	Steal time is the percentage of a CPU's idle time used by the virtual machine's hypervisor

4) The fourth and fifth lines display memory usage. Line number four displays physical memory and line number five displays virtual memory.	
5) The sixth line contains the heading for the process information list in descending order of CPU usage. It has the following fields:	
PID	Process ID number.
USER	Username of the owner of the process.
PR	System priority of the process.
NI	User priority value for a process, also known as the nice value.
VIRT	Total memory a process is using. Virtual memory is a combination of resident set, shared memory, and swapped memory.
RES	Physical memory used by a process.
SHR	Shared memory used by a process.
S	Process status codes are displayed here (D,R, S, T, and Z).
%CPU	Percentage of CPU used since the process started.
%MEM	Percentage of memory used by a process.
TIME+	Execution time.
COMMAND	Command name used to start the process.

The `top` command is like command line Task Manager in Linux. Using top, we can perform interactive monitoring and manage running processes. There are quite a few single-key shortcuts to manage the different attributes of a running process.

The following table lists various keyboard shortcuts that are used to manage the `top` command, as well as their descriptions:

Keyboard shortcut (on top)	Description
t	Toggle display of summary information
m	Toggle display of memory information
l	Toggle display of uptime information
1	Toggle display of all CPUs' summary or individual CPU's summary
H	Toggle threads display in summary information of tasks
s	Change the refresh rate of the screen in seconds
A	Sort the process list by the top resource consumers
r	Renice (change the priority) a selected process, by providing PID and then the nice value

k	Send a signal to a specific process (the default signal is to terminate), by providing PID and then a signal number
f	Open the configuration screen of the top command
M	Sort processes by memory usage, in descending order
P	Sort processes by CPU utilization in descending order
? or h	Display help for interactive keystrokes
U	Filter display for usernames
q	Quit
Enter, Space key	Immediately refreshes the displayed information

The following are examples to explain the usage of the `top` command:

- Display the process status of only the specified `pid` with the following command:

    ```
    $ top -p pid
    ```

- Specify a delay between consecutive screen refreshes while running `top` commands with the following command:

    ```
    $ top -d 2
    ```

- Display the `top` command's output for specified iterations only by using the following command:

    ```
    $ top n <number>
    ```

You can read more about sophisticated utilities, such as `htop` for process monitoring, which gives you the ability to scroll down vertically and horizontally to view more processes.

Managing a processes' priority with nice and renice

Linux is a multi-program system. At any given point of time, several processes are running or waiting in a queue on the system, however, a single CPU can actually execute one task at a time. If we have more long process queue, then it might happen that some more important processes spend more time waiting than executing. So, to overcome this problem, Linux allows us to set and modify a processes' priority. Lower-priority processes get less CPU time and higher-priority processes get more CPU time. Using the `nice` and `renice` command, we can manage the priority of processes.

Understanding priority

The priority of a process is known as its **nice** value (or **niceness**). It tells you how much nice (number of CPU cycles used) a process is on CPU. Its value varies from –20 to 19. A lower nice value represents a higherpriority process, which will take more CPU cycles, while a higher nice value represents a lowpriority process that can wait longer and consumes less CPU cycles. So, a nice value of –20 represents the highest priority and a nice value of 19 represents the lowest priority. The default value for new processes is generally 0, which is inherited from their parent.

Modifying priority

Assigning a low nice value, that is, a higher priority, to a CPU-hungry process will impact the performance of other processes running on the same Linux system. Hence, only root is allowed to give a higher priority to a process, for example, setting negative nice values on running processes.

Normal users can only lower the priority of their processes, that is, they can set only a higher positive value than the existing nice value for a given process.

Viewing the priority of a process

The priority of a process can be viewed using different commands in CentOS 7, as follows:

- Using gnome-system-monitor to display the nice level in GUI mode. This is the GUI Task Manager in CentOS 7. It is invoked by pressing **Application | System Tools | System Monitor**:

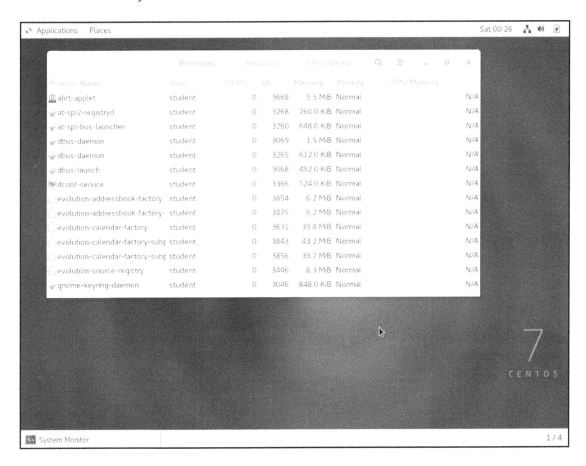

- The `top` command can also be used to display the priority of processes. It shows two columns, named `NI` (displaying the `nice` level mapping of processes) and `PR` (displaying the priority value mapping in a kernel to a larger priority queue).

- The `ps` command can also be used to display the `nice` level by using `o` option to print selected columns, which will also include the nice field, as shown in the following screenshot:

```
[root@server ~]# ps axo pid,comm,nice --sort=-nice | head
  PID COMMAND          NI
   36 khugepaged       19
  554 alsactl          19
 3719 tracker-extract  19
 3764 tracker-miner-a   -
 3776 tracker-miner-f  19
 3785 tracker-miner-u   -
   35 ksmd              5
  571 rtkit-daemon      1
    1 systemd           0
```

If a minus (–) symbol is displayed in the output of the `ps` command, then it means that a process is running with a different scheduling policy with a higher priority.

Modifying the priority of a new process (nice value)

Normally, when a process is started, it gets the default priority value of `0`. The `nice` command is used to start a process with a different priority. Its syntax is as follows:

```
$ nice  -n  <NICELEVEL>  <command>
```

An example of changing priority of a process using the `nice` command is shown in the following screenshot:

```
[root@server ~]# ps -axo ni,comm,pid | grep sleep
  0 sleep            4424
[root@server ~]# nice -n 10 sleep 1000 &
[1] 4430
[root@server ~]# ps -axo ni,comm,pid | grep sleep
  0 sleep            4424
 10 sleep            4430
```

Root can set a nice value between (–20 to 19), and an unprivileged, normal user can set a nice value between (0 to 19).

Modifying the priority of a running process (renice)

The `renice` command is used to change the nice level of an existing process. Its syntax is as follows:

```
$ renice    -n    <NICELEVEL>    <PID's>
```

In the following screenshot, a standard user is trying to increase the priority of a process by assigning a negative value, hence they are getting Permission denied, as shown in the following screenshot:

```
[student@server ~]$ sleep 800&
[1] 8342
[student@server ~]$ renice -n -10 8342
renice: failed to set priority for 8342 (process ID): Permission denied
```

Now, when a standard user lowers the priority of a process by assigning a positive value, it is set immediately, as shown in the following screenshot:

```
root@server ~]# ps -axo ni,comm,pid | grep sleep
 0 sleep            4424
10 sleep            4430
root@server ~]# renice -n 5 4430
430 (process ID) old priority 10, new priority 5
root@server ~]# ps -axo ni,comm,pid | grep sleep
 5 sleep            4430
 0 sleep            4448
```

Apart from the `renice` command, the `top` command can also be used to modify the nice value of a running process. The following steps are used to modify a process priority using the `top` command:

1. Invoke the `top` command
2. Press *r* key on the keyboard to bring up the option for specifying a new nice value on the `top` command's current interactive session
3. Enter the new `nice` value and PID, followed by pressing the *Enter* key

Controlling jobs on the command line

Linux supports executing programs in the foreground as well as in the background. This feature allows you to run multiple programs from a single instance of a shell. This feature is known as job control or job management.

Understanding different terms related to job management

This section describes various terms related to job management on a Terminal.

Jobs management with its associated controlling Terminal

A job is a command that's launched from a Terminal window. Each job can run as an independent background program or as an attached program from a Terminal (also known as the controlling Terminal here). The TTY field of the ps command is used to display the controlling Terminal name associated with a program.

Some programs, such as daemons (system services), are started by the system and do not have any controlling Terminal. Hence, these programs are not considered a member of a job and cannot be run in the foreground. Such programs have ? in the TTY field of the ps aux command.

When a program is started as a foreground process from a Terminal, then that Terminal cannot be used for anything else, as it is executing that particular foreground process. Take the following command, for example:

```
$ sleep 1000
```

After execution of the preceding command, the Terminal will not respond to any other program, as it is controlling the sleep program in the frontend for 1000 seconds.

Foreground processes or jobs

A foreground process or job is a process that is directly executed from the shell (also known as the **controlling** Terminal here). As long as that foreground job is running, other processes have to wait until it has completed for shell access.

This method of launching programs is fine, as long as a program is short and gets completed in a short period of time. If a program that requires a long time (say, many hours to complete) is launched from the shell in the foreground, it will make that shell unavailable for that number of hours. Such a practice is not suitable for command execution.

A foreground process will have + appended to its status when its details are viewed using the ps command. The plus + symbol means that it is in a foreground process group.

Start a sleep command in the foreground in one Terminal, as shown in the following command line:

```
$ sleep 1000
```

The following image list all the processes with specified columns and filter them using the grep command to display the a list of processes with sleep in their command name:

```
[root@server ~]# ps -eo pid,tid,ni,pri,stat,cmd | grep sleep
 4488  4488   0  19 S     sleep 60
 4540  4540   0  19 S+    sleep 1000
 4542  4542   0  19 R+    grep --color=auto sleep
```

If you want to terminate a foreground program in-between, then use *Ctrl* + *C* (interrupt from the keyboard).

Background processes or jobs

For a program that takes a long time to complete, launching it as a background process (job) is the ideal practice. This frees up the shell, making it available for other tasks. We can execute other commands in the Terminal while a program is running as a background job from the controlling Terminal.

By default, all programs are executed as a foreground job from the Terminal. To start a job in the background from the Terminal, add an and at the end of the command. For example, start a sleep command in the background from a Terminal, as shown in the following screenshot:

```
[root@server ~]# sleep 2000 &
[1] 4660
```

Suspending a foreground process to the background

We can move a foreground process to the background by following these two steps:

1. First, press *Ctrl* + *Z*, which moves the process to the background in a Stopped state
2. Second, enter the `bg` command to change state of the last background process to Running from `Stoppedas`, as shown in the following screenshot:

```
[root@server ~]# sleep 5000

^Z[1]    Terminated                  sleep 2000

[2]+  Stopped                        sleep 5000
[root@server ~]# jobs
[2]+  Stopped                        sleep 5000
[root@server ~]# bg
[2]+ sleep 5000 &
[root@server ~]# jobs
[2]+  Running                        sleep 5000 &
```

Managing jobs in the background

A program is started in the background by appending an ampersand (&) to the end of a command. On launching the program in the background, it displays a job ID (unique for the running session) and the PID of the background process, as shown in the following screenshot:

```
[root@server ~]# jobs
[root@server ~]# sleep 5000&
[1] 4766
```

Use the `jobs` command to display the background jobs associated with the shell. The jobs command displays the job ID, state, and command name. If there is more the one background job, the default selection will have + in front of it, as shown in the following screenshot:

```
[root@server ~]# sleep 5000&
[1] 8632
[root@server ~]# sleep 6000&
[2] 8634
[root@server ~]# sleep 7000&
[3] 8635
[root@server ~]# jobs
[1]   Running                 sleep 5000 &
[2]-  Running                 sleep 6000 &
[3]+  Running                 sleep 7000 &
```

The `fg` command is used to bring a background job to the foreground using its job ID. The job ID and the `%` of the program is followed by the job number displayed in square brackets, as shown in the following screenshot:

```
[root@server ~]# jobs
[1]   Running                 sleep 5000 &
[2]-  Running                 sleep 6000 &
[3]+  Running                 sleep 7000 &
[root@server ~]# fg %2
sleep 6000
|
```

Send a foreground program to the background by first suspending it using *Ctrl* + *Z* on the Terminal, as shown in the following screenshot:

```
[root@server ~]# jobs
[1]   Running                 sleep 5000 &
[2]-  Running                 sleep 6000 &
[3]+  Running                 sleep 7000 &
[root@server ~]# fg %2
sleep 6000
^Z
[2]+  Stopped                 sleep 6000
[root@server ~]# jobs
[1]   Running                 sleep 5000 &
[2]+  Stopped                 sleep 6000
[3]-  Running                 sleep 7000 &
```

The `jobs` command, when used with the `-l` option, will also list the program ID. To get some more information, we can use the `ps` command with the `j` option, as shown in the following screenshot:

```
[root@server ~]# jobs -l
[1]   8632 Running                 sleep 5000 &
[2]+  8634 Stopped                 sleep 6000
[3]-  8635 Running                 sleep 7000 &
[root@server ~]# ps j
 PPID   PID  PGID   SID TTY      TPGID STAT   UID   TIME COMMAND
  891  1014  1014  1014 tty1      1014 Ssl+     0   0:47 /usr/bin/X :0
 1890  1898  1898  1898 pts/0     8912 Ss       0   0:00 -bash
 4489  4500  4500  4500 pts/1     4500 Ss+      0   0:00 -bash
 1898  8632  8632  1898 pts/0     8912 S        0   0:00 sleep 5000
 1898  8634  8634  1898 pts/0     8912 T        0   0:00 sleep 6000
 1898  8635  8635  1898 pts/0     8912 S        0   0:00 sleep 7000
 1898  8912  8912  1898 pts/0     8912 R+       0   0:00 ps j
```

The `bg` command followed by `%` and the job ID is used to start a stopped program in the background, as shown in the following screenshot:

```
[root@server ~]# jobs
[1]   Running                 sleep 5000 &
[2]+  Stopped                 sleep 6000
[3]-  Running                 sleep 7000 &
[root@server ~]# bg %2
[2]+ sleep 6000 &
[root@server ~]# jobs
[1]   Running                 sleep 5000 &
[2]-  Running                 sleep 6000 &
[3]+  Running                 sleep 7000 &
```

Summary

In this chapter, we began by learning what a process is, and what different states and types of processes are in a Linux system. Then, we looked at different methods that exist in CentOS 7 to view running processes. This was followed by understanding how processes communicate with each other and how we can communicate with processes using signals. Thereafter, we learned how to monitor running processes and how to manage their priority using nice values. Finally, we looked at how `jobs` (commands) are managed on the command line by launching some applications in the background and switching an application from the background to the foreground, and vice versa.

In the next chapter, we will learn about networking concepts and networking commands in CentOS 7. We will also learn how to perform secure remote logins and backups over a network.

Managing Networking in CentOS

7

A standalone system is often not of much use. Networking enables us to exchange information and share resources with other network devices and connected computers. In this chapter, you will learn essential skills required for managing network connections from the command line. Then you will learn how to access the remote system using **SSH** (short for **Secure Shell**) and the secure transfer of files with **SCP** (short for **Secure Copy**) and `rsync` utilities.

In this chapter, we will cover the following:

- Linux networking concepts
- Using Linux networking commands
- Managing networks with nmcli
- Editing network configuration files
- Configuring hostname and **DNS** (short for **Domain Name System**) resolution
- Accessing remote logins with SSH
- Transferring files in Linux

Linux networking concepts

A network is a group of two or more computers or computing devices connected using any communication media, such as cables or wireless media. These devices may be located in the same geographical location or spread across the world. A network environment provides these three services:

- Enables connected devices to communicate with each other
- Enables multiple users to share devices such as printers, copiers, scanners, and so on over the network
- Enables the sharing of files and managing of information across computers

Most organizations use two types of network: one for communication with internal staff and another for the outside world. **Intranet** is the term used to define communication within the internal network of an organization and **internet** is used for external communication. The internet is also the largest network in the world and is popularly known as a network of networks.

Common terms used in Linux networking

This section describes the various terms that are used to define computing devices and networking terminologies used in Linux.

IP address

Each device connected to a network must have at least one unique address that is used to identify that device on the network. This address is known as the IP address and it is essential for routing the packet from the source to the destination through the network. Information or data over the network is transferred in the form of packets. Each packet has a header attached to it containing the information required to route the packet from the source to the destination. There are two different types of IP address schemes available, called IPv4 and IPv6.

IPv4

IPv4 is a 32-bit logical address used by computing devices to communicate with each other using the TCP/IP protocol stack. It is generally expressed in the decimal notation of four octets, with each octet containing 8 bits separated by a dot. The value of each octet can vary from 0 to 255. This address can further be broken down into two parts; for example, a network part and host part:

- **Host part**: The host part is used to identify a host on a subnet. No two hosts on the same subnet can have the same host part.
- **Network part**: The network part is used to identify a subnet. Hosts on the same subnet can communicate to each other without needing a router.

By using 32 bits for addresses, we can have a maximum of 4.3 billion unique addresses, many of which are reserved and cannot be used. Hence, to meet future requirements, IPv6 with an 128-bit address was created.

IPv6

IPv6 uses 128 bits for addressing. It is expressed in eight octets, containing 16 bits each, separated by colon. The use of 128 bits provides the 3.4×10^{38} unique addresses. The shifting of networked equipment and addresses from IPv4 to IPv6 requires a lot of understanding and effort. IPv6 does not have a broadcast address.

We will be restricting our discussion in this chapter to IPv4, as it is still more widely used and you will encounter it the most while performing networking.

Different classes of IP addressing

IPv4 addresses are divided into **five public** classes named A, B, C, D, and E, and **three private** IP address classes.

Public classes

There are five different public IP address classes from A to E. Here, classes A, B, and C are divided into two parts: **network address** (short for **Net ID**) and **host address** (short for **Host ID**). Net ID identifies the network and Host ID identifies the host on the network as shown in table here:

Public class	Octet 1	Octet 2	Octet 3	Octet 4	Range
Class A	Net ID	Host ID	Host ID	Host ID	1.0.0.0 to 127.255.255.255
Class B	Net ID	Net ID	Host ID	Host ID	128.0.0.0 to 191.255.255.255
Class C	Net ID	Net ID	Net ID	Host ID	192.0.0.0 to 223.255.255.255
Class D	Multicast address				224.0.0.0 to 239.255.255.255
Class E	Reserved for the future				240.0.0.0 to 255.255.255.254

Private classes

The following three IP address ranges are reserved for private use within the internal network of an organization. These IPv4 addresses can be used within a network, campus, and so on, and are not routable on the internet. Hence, if any packet contains any of these private IP addresses, it is dropped by the routers. Generally, the NAT mechanism is used for communicating with the public IPv4 address space when machines are working on private IPv4. The following table lists the private IPv4 address classes along with their address ranges and some special IPv4 addresses, such as link-local address and loopback address:

Private class	Address range	Subnet mask	Address block
Class A	10.0.0.0 to 10.255.255.255	255.0.0.0	10.0.0.0 /8
Class B	172.16.0.0 to 172.31.255.255	255.240.0.0	172.16.0.0 /12
Class C	192.168.0.0 to 192.168.0.255	255.255.0.0	192.168.0.0 /16
Loopback address	127.0.0.0 to 127.255.255.255	255.0.0.0	127.0.0.0 /8
Link-local address (APIPA)	169.254.0.0 to 169.254.255.255	255.255.0.0	169.254.0.0 /16

Loopback address

`127.0.0.1` is a special address that always points to local system (localhost) and is used for the testing of various services. The network `127.0.0.0/8` is a loopback network of the local system. It enables server-client communication on a single system.

Link-local address or APIPA

The link-local address or **Automatic Private IP Addressing** (**APIPA**) is used if a machine connected in a DHCP environment is unable to acquire an IP address from the DHCP sever. This also helps in establishing communication between machines on the same network by allocating them IP addresses in the range of `169.254.0.0/16`, if the DHCP server is not connected or down.

Netmask

Netmask is used to identify a subnet. Binary AND operations of the 32-bit Host IP address with 32-bit netmask yields the network part of the address. The lowest possible address on a subnet is all zeros in the host part; it represents the network address. The highest possible address on a subnet is all ones in the host part; it represents the broadcast address for all hosts on a subnet. It is expressed in two forms. The conventional syntax uses a decimal representation of the network part while the new syntax uses CIDR notation to represent the network prefix (number of ones in the network address). For example, we can represent a 24-bit netmask in both these forms as shown below:

- **Conventional form**: `255.255.255.0`
- **CIDR notation**: `/24`

Let us assume that we are having following IP address and netmask information with us:

- `10.1.1.212 / 8`
- `192.168.1.100 / 24`

Now, using the above limited information we can find other related network information such as network address and broadcast address as given in the next table:

Network information for system having these details : `10.1.1.212 / 8`

Information description	Values
IP address (host address)	`10.1.1.212`
Netmask (network prefix)	`255.0.0.0/8`

Network address	10.0.0.0
Broadcast address	10.0.0.255

Network Information for system having these details : 192.168.1.100 / 24

Information description	Values
IP address (host address)	192.168.1.100
Netmask (network prefix)	255.255.255.0/24
Network address	192.168.1.0
Broadcast address	192.168.1.255

Gateway

A gateway is generally a router device or computer that is used to connect two or more dissimilar networks. In the case of Linux, it is the entry in the kernel routing table that is used when none of the route entries are matched.

Hostname

Hostname is a human-readable name associated with a machine IP address. A DNS server is used to map the hostname to the IP address and vice versa. We can view the hostname of any machine by typing `hostname` command without any argument as shown below:

```
$ hostname
```

 Every machine has got a special hostname that is, localhost associated with the loopback IP address 127.0.0.1. This address is used for testing various services on the system.

Nameserver

Nameserver is also known as the **DNS server**. The purpose of the DNS server is to convert the hostname to an IP address and vice versa. There is a default fixed order of files, which are looked up when doing DNS lookup in CentOS 7. This order is managed by the rules written in the `nsswitch.conf` file and can be altered by an administrator. The following two files are looked up when resolving a DNS query in system:

- `/etc/hosts`: The entries made in this file are first looked up before forwarding the query to the DNS server. It is a kind of local database of hostnames and IP address mappings. It is also quite useful for small isolated networks.
- `/etc/resolv.conf`: If the answer of DNS query is not found in the `/etc/hosts` file, then the query is passed to the DNS server mentioned in `/etc/resolv.conf`. This file can be updated using dhclient or manually.

Following command is used to display the current settings of nameserver:

```
$ cat /etc/resolv.conf
```

After configuring the nameserver, verify the DNS connectivity using host command as shown here:

```
$ host www.google.com
```

NetworkManager

The NetworkManager is a GUI application used for the management of network settings. It comes with a daemon and Gnome applet to provide the network status and quick access for modification. The changes made using NetworkManager are stored in the `/etc/sysconfig/network-scripts` directory and thus it overrides any manual changes made there. If you want to configure the network connections manually by modifying the network scripts file, then NetworkManager should be disabled. NetworkManager provides a user-friendly method for manager network connections and is ideal for beginners.

Network interface naming conventions

Conventionally, network interfaces in Linux are enumerated sequentially as `eth0`, `eth1`, `eth2`, and so on.

The following table list the traditional names of interfaces with their descriptions:

Interface name	Description
`eth0`, `eth1`, and so on	Ethernet interfaces
`wlan0`, `wlan1`, and so on	Wireless interfaces
`eth0:1`, `eth0:2`, and so on	Alias interfaces
`ppp0`, `ppp1`, and so on	Dial-up interface
`bond0`	First-bonded network device
`virbr0`	Internal bridge for virtual hosts
`lo`	Loopback interface

Now, CentOS 7 has new default naming conventions. The interface name is based on hardware, topology, and device type.

The following table illustrates the network interface naming convention in CentOS 7:

Character in naming convention	Description
First two characters represent type of interface	• `en`: Ethernet interface • `wl`: Wlan interface • `ww`: WWAN interface
Next characters represent type of adapter	• `o`: Onboard adapter • `s`: Hotplug slot • `p`: PCI card • `x`: MAC address
Last character is a number `N`, to represent an index, ID, or port	• `N`: 0, 1, 2, and so on

If a fixed name could not be determined using new interface naming scheme then the old conventional naming scheme such as `eth0` or `eth1` is used. The example of new interface naming scheme is given here:

- `eno1`: First embedded network interface
- `enp1s0`: The first PCI card network interface with hotplug slot index 0

If the biosdevname feature is enabled in the server, then this naming scheme is overridden with a different naming scheme.

Using Linux networking commands

This section discuss the various networking commands and basic utilities that are used to display or modify the existing network configurations.

Viewing IP address details

In CentOS 7, we have three major utilities to display the device and address information:

- Newer IP command (/sbin/ip)
- Almost obsolete ifconfig command from net-tools package (/sbin/ifconfig)
- Versatile netstat command (/usr/bin/netstat)

Using the IP command

The ip is a very powerful utility that is used to perform many tasks. Multiple older utilities such as ifconfig and route command were earlier used to perform these functions. The absolute path of the ip command is /sbin/ip.

Following are the examples to illustrate the usage of ip command:

- The following ip command is used to display the IP address:

```
$ /sbin/ip addr show
```

- The ip command can also be used to display statistics of the network performance (received and transmitted packets, errors, dropped counters, and so on) as shown in command line here:

```
$ ip -s link show enp0s3
```

- The ip command can also be used to display the routing information as shown in command line here:

```
$ /sbin/ip route show
```

The /sbin/ip command can also be used to assign multiple IP addresses to a single device using aliases. Binding multiple IP addresses to a single NIC with a different label is useful in many cases (for example, in virtual hosting). Aliases are treated as separate interfaces and are generally configured when NetworkManager is turned off. The command to create an alias is as follows:
```
$ ip addr add 10.1.1.250/24 dev enp0s8 label enp0s8:0.
```

Using ifconfig command

This is an older command used to display or modify the current configuration of network interfaces. The usage of ifconfig command is now obsolete and it is replaced with the newer ip utility. Now, the ip addr and ip link commands are preferred to display network interface information in place of ifconfig.

The following table lists the popular options of ifconfig with their descriptions:

Command	Description
$ ifconfig	Display the current configuration of active interfaces only
$ ifconfig -a	Display all interfaces information which are available in system, whether they are active or inactive
$ ifconfig eth0	Display the configuration of the specified interface eth0
$ ifconfig eth0 up	Activate the network adapter eth0, if it is down.
$ ifconfig eth0 down	Deactivate the network adapter eth0, if it is up.

The ifconfig command can be used to assign an IP address and netmask to a network adapter. These are runtime changes and are lost after reboot. Following command line shows how to use ifconfig for making runtime assignment of IP address and netmask to an interface:
```
$ ifconfig eth0 192.168.1.51/24
or
$ ifconfig eth0 192.168.1.51 netmask 255.255.255.0
```

Some naive users still find, the older ifconfig command easier to use, in comparison to the new and more versatile ip command.

The ifconfig utility is a part of the net-tools package. If this package is not installed on the system, then you may not get access to this utility on CentOS 7.

Netstat

The `netstat` command can also be used to print interface details. To display kernel interface information for all the interfaces, the `-i` option is used with the `-e` option to display the extended information for the interfaces as shown in command line here:

```
$ netstat -ie
```

Viewing the routing information

Irrespective of the underlying IP addressing scheme, while communicating, the information needs to travel from a host on one network to a host on another network. Each host can have multiple routing tables, which decide how to route the traffic to a particular network from the host. The routing table makes sure the correct network interface is used for sending the packets to a destination network. We can also define the IP address of any intermediate router that is required to reach the destination network in routing table.

Using the ip route command

The `ip route` command is one of the many features of the newer `ip` utility. This command can be used to display or modify the existing IP routing table. We can add, delete, or modify specific static routes to specific hosts or networks using `ip route` command.

Following are the examples to illustrate the usage of ip route command:

- We can use `ip route` command to display the current routing table as follows:

  ```
  $ ip route
  ```

- The `ip route` command can be used to add static routes in routing table. In the following example we **add network routing** information for `25.25.25.0/24` network, to route it through `eth0` interface, as shown here:

  ```
  $ ip route add 25.25.25.0/24  dev  eth0
  ```

- The `ip route` command can also be used to **add host routing** information. In the following example we add information to route IPv4 address `15.15.15.15` through `eth1` interface:

  ```
  $ ip route add 15.15.15.15 dev eth1
  ```

- The `ip route` command can also be used to delete the static route from the routing table. In the following example we **delete network routing** information for `25.25.25.0/24` network as shown here:

  ```
  $ ip route del 25.25.25.0/24 dev eth0
  ```

- The `ip route` command can also be used to **delete host routing** information. In the following example we delete information to route IPv4 address `15.15.15.15` through `eth1` interface:

  ```
  $ ip route del 15.15.15.15 dev eth0
  ```

Using route command

The `route` command is also used to modify the routing table.

Following are the examples to illustrate the usage of route command:

- Use the `route` command as shown here to display the current routing table:

  ```
  $ route -n
  ```

- The `route` command can also be used to add a static route in the routing table. The following route command syntax is used to add a network routing information in the routing table:

  ```
  $ route add -net x.x.x.x/prefix dev <devname>
  ```

- The following route command syntax is used to add a host routing information in the routing table:

  ```
  $ route add -host x.x.x.x dev <devname>
  ```

- The `route` command can also be used to delete a static route in the routing table. The following `route` command syntax is used to delete a network routing information in the routing table:

  ```
  $ route del -net x.x.x.x/prefix dev <devname>
  ```

- The following `route` command syntax is used to delete a host routing information in the routing table:

  ```
  $ route del -host x.x.x.x dev <devname>
  ```

Using netstat command

The `netstat` command, which is known as network statistics, is a versatile command with lots of features. This command is used to print network connections details, kernel routing table information, interface statistics, open ports, and so on. In this section, we restrict ourselves to the usage of the `netstat` command to fetch the routing table information only.

Following are the examples to illustrate the usage of netstat command.

- Use the `netstat` command to display the kernel routing table information with the `-r` option as shown here:

    ```
    $ netstat -r
    ```

- Use the `netstat` command to display the kernel routing table information without resolving the hostname or port names as shown here:

    ```
    $ netstat -anr
    ```

`netstat` is one of the few commands that is available by default on Unix-like operating systems and Windows operating systems as well.

Gateway

We can add or delete the default gateway at run-time using the `route` command. The default gateway tells us where to send the packet if none of the network or host entry in routing table matches with the destination IP address of packet.

The following command line is used to delete the default gateway from the routing table:

```
$ route del default gw <ip_address_of_default_gateway>
```

The following command line is used to add the default gateway in the routing table:

```
$ route add default gw <ip_address_of_default_gateway>
```

To add same permanent gateway for all the interfaces, we can modify the `/etc/sysconfig/network` file and add the following entry:

```
GATEWAY=<ip_address_of_new_default_gateway>
```

To assign different gateway entries for each interface, we modify the `/etc/sysconfig/network-scripts/ifcfg-<interfacename>` configuration file as follows:

```
GATEWAY=<ip_address_of_new_default_gateway>
```

Viewing nameserver details

The nameserver or DNS server information is stored in the `/etc/resolv.conf` file. This file can be updated using dhclient or NetworkManager or by an administrator, manually. In this file, we can specify a maximum of three nameserver directives in their order of precedence from top to bottom.

The contents of nameserver configuration file can be viewed as shown here:

```
[root@server ~]# cat /etc/resolv.conf
nameserver 1.1.1.1
nameserver 8.8.8.8
```

Network troubleshooting utilities

In this section, we will learn about some networking tools/troubleshooting utilities. Networking tools are quite useful for monitoring and debugging network issues such as network connectivity and network traffic.

Using ethtool command

The `ethtool` is a utility for displaying and configuring Ethernet card driver and hardware settings. Changes made using `ethtool` are runtime changes and not persistence changes.

Following are the examples to illustrate the usage of ethtool command:

- Display the Ethernet interface's current settings using `ethtool` command as shown here:

  ```
  $ ethtool enp0s3
  ```

- Display the Ethernet interface driver settings using `ethtool` command as shown here:

  ```
  $ ethtool -i enp0s3
  ```

- Modifying the Ethernet interface settings using `ethtool` command as shown h:

```
$ ethtool --change enp0s3 speed 10 duplex half autoneg off
```

- Blink the Ethernet interface port light for 10 seconds for identification using `ethtool` command as shown here:

```
$ ethtool --identify enp0s3 10
```

Using ping command

The `ping` command is used to verify the network connectivity of a remote host. It can tell you whether the machine connected to the network is online and responding. It also provides stats for network packet loss and latency measurement.

Following are the examples to illustrate the usage of ping command:

- The ping command can be used to identify the status of a remote host (if it's alive or not) as shown here:

```
$ ping <hostname_or_host_ipaddress>
$ ping 8.8.8.8
```

- The ping command can be used send the `ping` request through a specific interface as shown here:

```
$ ping -I eth0 8.8.8.8
```

- The `ping` command can be used to troubleshoot DNS issues by sending ping request to a specified URL. If we are able to `ping` a URL using its IP address, but we are not getting reply of ping by specifying name of same URL, it means our DNS server is not set up properly or not working properly. An example of `ping` command with URL is shown here:

```
$ ping www.google.com
```

- The `ping` command can also be used to send the fixed number of packets using the `-c` option as shown here:

```
$ ping -c 4 8.8.8.8
```

In the case of Windows, by default, the `ping` command sends only four packets, whereas in the case of Linux, the `ping` command will continue to send the packets by default unless its execution is aborted by pressing *Ctrl* + *C*. ICMP ping cannot be considered a durable diagnostic tool, just one of many. The network diagnostic depends on many factors in a network. At the same time, ICMP ping is the most basic and default utility, which every system user should know how to use.

Using tracepath command

The `tracepath` command is used to trace the path from the origin to the destination. Each line in the `tracepath` output represents a router (hop) that the packet passes through.

The example of `tracepath` command is shown in image here:

```
[root@server ~]# tracepath www.google.com
 1?: [LOCALHOST]                                  pmtu 1500
 1:  gateway                                       0.285ms
 1:  gateway                                       0.635ms
 2:  192.168.0.1                                   2.054ms asymm 64
 3:  192.168.1.1                                   2.293ms asymm 63
 4:  192.168.1.1                                   2.336ms pmtu 1492
 4:  172.31.34.18                                 11.719ms asymm 62
 5:  no reply
 6:  172.31.210.142                               18.869ms asymm 60
 7:  172.31.210.98                                15.146ms asymm 59
 8:  10.10.10.10                                  12.970ms asymm 58
 9:  ws82-230-252-122.rcil.gov.in                 11.040ms asymm 57
10:  ws81-230-252-122.rcil.gov.in                 23.002ms asymm 56
11:  172.31.210.113                               31.713ms asymm 55
```

Using traceroute command

This command is used to display or inspect the network path taken to reach the destination by a packet. It is quite useful in troubleshooting network delays and errors.

By default, the `traceroute` and `tracepath` commands use UDP packets for probing the path to a destination. The `traceroute` command has options to inspect the path using ICMP (`-I`) or TCP (`-T`) packets, if IDS or IPS blocks the UDP traffic.

Following is an example to illustrate the usage of traceroute command:

- The `traceroute` command can be used to display the route taken by the packet to reach the network host as shown in image here:

```
[root@server ~]# traceroute www.google.com
traceroute to www.google.com (74.125.130.99), 30 hops max, 60 byte packets
 1  gateway (10.0.3.2)  0.292 ms  0.223 ms  0.214 ms
 2  192.168.0.1 (192.168.0.1)  5.099 ms  5.656 ms  5.518 ms
 3  192.168.1.1 (192.168.1.1)  6.322 ms  6.197 ms  6.012 ms
 4  172.31.34.18 (172.31.34.18)  11.812 ms  16.129 ms  16.077 ms
 5  * * *
 6  172.31.210.142 (172.31.210.142)  15.510 ms  21.915 ms  23.210 ms
 7  172.31.210.98 (172.31.210.98)  23.035 ms  14.547 ms  15.010 ms
 8  10.10.10.10 (10.10.10.10)  13.248 ms  13.728 ms  13.712 ms
 9  ws82-230-252-122.rcil.gov.in (122.252.230.82)  10.481 ms  12.842 ms  12.110 ms
10  ws81-230-252-122.rcil.gov.in (122.252.230.81)  12.802 ms  13.188 ms  12.911 ms
11  172.31.210.113 (172.31.210.113)  12.855 ms  12.592 ms  10.977 ms
```

Using mtr command

This command combines the functionalities of `ping` and `traceroute`. It constantly polls a remote server and fetches the latency and performance changes over time. The example for usage of mtr command is shown here:

```
$ mtr www.google.com
```

Output on execution of preceding command is shown here:

```
                        My traceroute  [v0.85]
server.example.com (0.0.0.0)                      Sun Oct 21 04:45:28 2018
Keys:  Help   Display mode   Restart statistics   Order of fields   quit
                                         Packets              Pings
 Host                                   Loss%   Snt   Last   Avg  Best  Wrst StDev
 1. 10.0.3.2                            0.0%     5    0.3   0.3   0.2   0.3   0.0
 2. 192.168.0.1                         0.0%     5    1.8   2.8   1.7   6.7   2.1
 3. 192.168.1.1                         0.0%     5    2.0   4.4   2.0  12.8   4.6
 4. 172.31.34.18                        0.0%     5    8.2  15.8   8.2  27.5   7.5
 5. ???
 6. 172.31.210.142                      0.0%     5   20.3  26.3  11.6  73.5  26.6
 7. 172.31.210.98                       0.0%     5   17.2  18.7  10.7  32.8   8.4
 8. 10.10.10.10                         0.0%     5   12.1  18.0  12.1  23.9   5.1
 9. 172.31.210.113                      0.0%     5   16.6  21.0  10.2  39.1  11.4
10. 172.31.110.120                      0.0%     5   20.4  14.9  12.0  20.4   3.2
11. 72.14.195.18                        0.0%     5   13.2  24.7  12.3  60.2  20.3
12. 108.170.251.117                     0.0%     5   11.3  27.0  11.3  56.0  18.0
13. 216.239.41.235                      0.0%     5   47.3  63.7  47.3  89.7  19.9
14. 209.85.242.157                      0.0%     5   92.7  99.9  92.7 114.4  10.1
15. 209.85.242.12                       0.0%     4   97.0 103.1  97.0 112.4   6.9
16. 74.125.37.249                       0.0%     4   99.3  99.1  94.8 103.0   3.3
17. ???
```

Verifying DNS connectivity

There are multiple tools that are available in CentOS 7 to verify DNS connectivity.

Using nslookup command

This is a network administration tool for querying the DNS to obtain the domain name or IP address mapping or any other specific DNS record. It can be used in non-interactive mode as well as in interactive mode in CLI by a user.

Following are the examples to illustrate the usage of nslookup command:

- The usage of `nslookup` command to find the IP address of domain name is shown here:

```
$ nslookup www.centos.org
```

- The usage of `nslookup` command to find the authoritative nameserver of a domain is shown here:

```
$ nslookup –type=ns centos.org
```

- The `nslookup` command can be used to make a non-authoritative query of an MX record from a DNS server specified in `/etc/resolv.conf` file is shown here:

```
$ nslookup –query=mx centos.org
```

- The `nslookup` command can be used to make an authoritative query of an MX record from the DNS server. We can specify the authoritative nameserver for the zone as an argument as shown here:

```
$ nslookup –query=mx centos.org ns1.centos.org
```

Using host command

Host is one of the simplest DNS lookup utilities. If the `host` command is used without any option, it prints the short summary for its argument DNS lookup.

The example of `host` command are shown in command line here:

```
$ host www.centos.org
$ host 8.8.8.8
```

Using dig command

DIG (short for **Domain Information Groper**) is the most flexible and versatile DNS lookup utility for DNS troubleshooting.

Following are the examples to illustrate the usage of dig **command:**

- The usage of `dig` command to find the IP address of a domain name is shown in command line here:

```
$ dig centos.org
```

- The `dig` command can be use to return only an IP address by making a short DNS lookup as shown in command line here:

```
$ dig centos.org +short
```

- The `dig` command can be used with an option to turn off extra information and display only the required answer as shown in command line here:

```
$ dig centos.org MX +noall +answer
$ dig centos.org NS +noall +answer
$ dig centos.org ANY +noall +answer
```

- The `dig` command can be used to perform the reverse lookup (find out the hostname of the specified IP address) by using the `-x` option as shown in command line here:

```
$ dig -x 8.8.8.8 +short
```

DIG is a flexible and versatile tool. It is recommended to refer the manual of the `dig` utility (`$ man dig`).

Finding local ports and services information

There are multiple services running on standard logical ports in the Linux system. Well-known ports and their related service entries are available in the `/etc/services` file. It's vital to identify the status of running services in the system. There are multiple commands such as `netstat`, `ss`, and so on that are used to find out the status of running services in localhost.

Using the ss command

The `ss` command is another utility used to view socket statistics, similar to the `netstat` command. The advantage of using `ss` is that it can display more TCP and connection state information than other tools that exist by default.

An example of `ss` command usage is shown here:

```
[root@server ~]# ss -ant
State      Recv-Q Send-Q    Local Address:Port              Peer Address:Port
LISTEN     0      128                  *:111                        *:*
LISTEN     0      128                  *:22                         *:*
LISTEN     0      128          127.0.0.1:631                        *:*
LISTEN     0      100          127.0.0.1:25                         *:*
ESTAB      0      0       192.168.56.100:22               192.168.56.1:51444
LISTEN     0      128                :::111                       :::*
LISTEN     0      128                :::80                        :::*
LISTEN     0      128                :::22                        :::*
LISTEN     0      128               ::1:631                       :::*
LISTEN     0      100               ::1:25                        :::*
```

Using the netstat command

As discussed earlier, the `netstat` command is used to display all the active connections and routing tables information. This command is useful for monitoring performance and troubleshooting.

An example of `netstat` command usage is shown here:

```
[root@server ~]# netstat -ant
Active Internet connections (servers and established)
Proto Recv-Q Send-Q Local Address          Foreign Address        State
tcp        0      0 0.0.0.0:111            0.0.0.0:*              LISTEN
tcp        0      0 0.0.0.0:22             0.0.0.0:*              LISTEN
tcp        0      0 127.0.0.1:631          0.0.0.0:*              LISTEN
tcp        0      0 127.0.0.1:25           0.0.0.0:*              LISTEN
tcp        0      0 192.168.56.100:22      192.168.56.1:51444    ESTABLISHED
tcp6       0      0 :::111                 :::*                  LISTEN
tcp6       0      0 :::80                  :::*                  LISTEN
tcp6       0      0 :::22                  :::*                  LISTEN
tcp6       0      0 ::1:631                :::*                  LISTEN
tcp6       0      0 ::1:25                 :::*                  LISTEN
```

Here is a table listing the popular options used with the `ss` and `netstat` commands:

Option	Description
-a	Display all listening and non-listening sockets
-n	Display numbers instead of services name
-t	Display TCP sockets
-u	Display UDP sockets
-l	Display only listening sockets
-p	Display the process ID information of sockets

Web utilities

This section discusses the various command-line-based web utilities such as command-line downloaders, command-line web browsers, and so on.

Graphical and non-graphical web browsers

Web browsers are application software used to retrieve, transmit, or process information using the **World Wide Web** (**WWW**) protocol. In simple words, they send requests to web servers and display the response received from the web server.

Most of the time, we use graphical web browsers such as Firefox, Google Chrome, Opera, and so on, however, sometimes we do not have graphical environment and we still need to access websites. In those situations, we can use non-graphical browsers such as Lynx, elinks, W3M, and so on.

Command-line file downloader (wget)

The `wget` command is one of the most popular non-interactive command-line file downloaders in Linux. It can download multiple files/directories and can work in the background as well. The downloaded web page can be opened with any graphical or non-graphical browser.

Some of its popular features are as follows:

- Support of HTTP, HTTPS, and FTP protocols, as well as retrieval through HTTP proxies
- Resume partial downloads
- Large file downloads

- Recursive downloads for mirroring a website
- Password-required downloads

The syntax of `wget` command is shown here:

```
$ wget    <url>
```

An example of `wget` command usage is shown here:

```
[root@server ~]# wget https://ftp.mozilla.org/pub/firefox/releases/60.2.2esr/linux-x86_64/en-US
firefox-60.2.2esr.tar.bz2
--2018-10-21 06:16:39--  https://ftp.mozilla.org/pub/firefox/releases/60.2.2esr/linux-x86_64/en
US/firefox-60.2.2esr.tar.bz2
Resolving ftp.mozilla.org (ftp.mozilla.org)... 52.84.224.6
Connecting to ftp.mozilla.org (ftp.mozilla.org)|52.84.224.6|:443... connected.
HTTP request sent, awaiting response... 200 OK
Length: 53261895 (51M) [application/x-tar]
Saving to: 'firefox-60.2.2esr.tar.bz2'

36% [====================>                           ] 19,576,644   453KB/s  eta 67s  |
```

Command-line download and upload using curl

Curl (short for **Client URL Library**) is a non-interactive command-line tool to automate HTTP jobs done using web browsers and many more functions. Using curl, one can download multiple files or upload files to a URL using URL-based syntax.

An example of `curl` command usage is shown here:

```
[root@server Documents]# ls
[root@server Documents]# curl -o centos.html https://www.centos.org
  % Total    % Received % Xferd  Average Speed   Time    Time     Time  Current
                                 Dload  Upload   Total   Spent    Left  Speed
100 20976  100 20976    0     0  18415      0  0:00:01  0:00:01 --:--:-- 18432
[root@server Documents]# ls
centos.html
```

Managing a network with nmcli

There are several tools available in Linux for the management of a network, however in CentOS 7, the additional nmcli utility has simplified and speeded up the setup of networking. nmcli is an acronym for the NetworkManager command line and is used to control the network-manager utility from the command line. The nmtui utility used to be a favorite of system administrators, however nmcli saves a lot of time and its capability to be used in script has make it one of the best networking tools in Linux.

Defining basic terms

Following are the few basic terms which are used with nmcli and hence an overview of these will help us in understanding it better.

Device or interface

A device is a network interface such as eno1, eno2, enp0s1, eth0, and so on.

Connection

A connection in the context of nmcli is a collection of settings or configurations used to store a state of device. A single device can have multiple connections, however only one connection may be active at one time.

For example, a DHCP configuration of the network interface can be stored in one connection and a static configuration of the network interface can be stored in another state. This helps in switching connections rapidly, without changing the configuration manually every time. Connection is also popularly known as **connection profile.**

Displaying network information using nmcli

We can display the list of active connections or all saved connections using the nmcli command.

Following are the examples to illustrate the usage of nmcli **command for displaying network information:**

- Display the list of all connections using nmcli command as follows:

    ```
    $ nmcli con show
    ```

- Display only the active connections using nmcli command as follows:

    ```
    $ nmcli con show --active
    ```

- Display the details of a connection by specifying the connection ID (NAME) using nmcli command as follows:

    ```
    $ nmcli con show "enp0s3"
    ```

An example of nmcli command usage to display connection state is shown here:

```
[root@server ~]# nmcli con show
NAME    UUID                                      TYPE      DEVICE
enp0s3  79da4c5b-6d53-40eb-873c-edb25f60c7cc      ethernet  enp0s3
nat     45f7ceaf-9d2b-3eb9-a091-215f4d878300      ethernet  enp0s8
[root@server ~]#
[root@server ~]# nmcli con show --active
NAME    UUID                                      TYPE      DEVICE
enp0s3  79da4c5b-6d53-40eb-873c-edb25f60c7cc      ethernet  enp0s3
nat     45f7ceaf-9d2b-3eb9-a091-215f4d878300      ethernet  enp0s8
[root@server ~]#
[root@server ~]# nmcli con show enp0s3
connection.id:                          enp0s3
connection.uuid:                        79da4c5b-6d53-40eb-873c-edb25f6
connection.stable-id:                   --
connection.type:                        802-3-ethernet
connection.interface-name:              enp0s3
connection.autoconnect:                 yes
connection.autoconnect-priority:        0
connection.autoconnect-retries:         -1 (default)
connection.auth-retries:                -1
connection.timestamp:                   1540102478
connection.read-only:                   no
connection.permissions:                 --
connection.zone:                        --
connection.master:                      --
connection.slave-type:                  --
connection.autoconnect-slaves:          -1 (default)
```

- Display the device (interface) status as connected or disconnected using `nmcli` command as follows:

  ```
  $ nmcli dev status
  ```

- Display the device details using `nmcli` command as follows:

  ```
  $ nmcli dev show enp0s3
  ```

An example of `nmcli` command to display the device details is shown here:

```
[root@server ~]# nmcli dev status
DEVICE   TYPE       STATE        CONNECTION
enp0s8   ethernet   connected    nat
enp0s3   ethernet   connected    enp0s3
lo       loopback   unmanaged    --
[root@server ~]# nmcli dev show enp0s3
GENERAL.DEVICE:                        enp0s3
GENERAL.TYPE:                          ethernet
GENERAL.HWADDR:                        08:00:27:48:25:F5
GENERAL.MTU:                           1500
GENERAL.STATE:                         100 (connected)
GENERAL.CONNECTION:                    enp0s3
GENERAL.CON-PATH:                      /org/freedesktop/NetworkManager
WIRED-PROPERTIES.CARRIER:              on
IP4.ADDRESS[1]:                        192.168.56.100/24
IP4.GATEWAY:                           --
IP4.ROUTE[1]:                          dst = 192.168.56.0/24, nh = 0.0
IP6.ADDRESS[1]:                        fe80::ff14:181f:3b44:e69a/64
IP6.GATEWAY:                           --
IP6.ROUTE[1]:                          dst = ff00::/8, nh = ::, mt = 2
IP6.ROUTE[2]:                          dst = fe80::/64, nh = ::, mt =
IP6.ROUTE[3]:                          dst = fe80::/64, nh = ::, mt =
lines 1-16/16 (END)
```

Creating network connections using nmcli

We can create new connections or a connection profile using the `nmcli` command. While creating a connection profile, the order of arguments plays an important role. We can specify IP address, gateway, and so on. The connection argument must include the connection type, interface name, and connection name argument to create a connection profile. The additional details such as DNS server are set after the creation of a connection profile by modifying it (connection profile) later on.

Following are the examples to illustrate the usage of nmcli command for creating a new connection profile:

- Create a new connection profile named dhcp which will autoconnect as an Ethernet connection on the enp0s8 device using DHCP connectivity as shown here:

```
[root@server ~]# nmcli con add con-name "dhcp" type ethernet ifname enp0s8
Connection 'dhcp' (07e638e8-655b-41a7-9a5f-14a16798a1d8) successfully added.
[root@server ~]#
[root@server ~]# nmcli con show
NAME    UUID                                   TYPE      DEVICE
enp0s3  79da4c5b-6d53-40eb-873c-edb25f60c7cc   ethernet  enp0s3
nat     45f7ceaf-9d2b-3eb9-a091-215f4d878300   ethernet  enp0s8
dhcp    07e638e8-655b-41a7-9a5f-14a16798a1d8   ethernet  --
```

- Create another new connection profile named static and specify an IP address and gateway nmcli command. Also set the auto connect off on booting as shown here:

```
[root@server ~]# nmcli con add con-name "static" ifname enp0s8 autoconnect no type
ethernet ip4 25.25.25.25/24 gw4 25.25.25.254
Connection 'static' (1fe9cb38-3af7-44f2-b940-c884a7e60f87) successfully added.
```

- Display the connection profiles that exist in the system using nmcli command as shown here:

```
[root@server ~]# nmcli con show
NAME    UUID                                   TYPE      DEVICE
enp0s3  79da4c5b-6d53-40eb-873c-edb25f60c7cc   ethernet  enp0s3
nat     45f7ceaf-9d2b-3eb9-a091-215f4d878300   ethernet  enp0s8
dhcp    07e638e8-655b-41a7-9a5f-14a16798a1d8   ethernet  --
static  1fe9cb38-3af7-44f2-b940-c884a7e60f87   ethernet  --
```

- Change the connection profile of the existing device enp0s8 to static using nmcli command, as shown here:

```
[root@server ~]# nmcli con show
NAME    UUID                                    TYPE      DEVICE
enp0s3  79da4c5b-6d53-40eb-873c-edb25f60c7cc    ethernet  enp0s3
nat     45f7ceaf-9d2b-3eb9-a091-215f4d878300    ethernet  enp0s8
dhcp    07e638e8-655b-41a7-9a5f-14a16798a1d8    ethernet  --
static  1fe9cb38-3af7-44f2-b940-c884a7e60f87    ethernet  --
[root@server ~]#
[root@server ~]# nmcli con up static
Connection successfully activated (D-Bus active path: /org/freedesktop/NetworkManag
er/ActiveConnection/3)
[root@server ~]#
[root@server ~]# nmcli con show
NAME    UUID                                    TYPE      DEVICE
enp0s3  79da4c5b-6d53-40eb-873c-edb25f60c7cc    ethernet  enp0s3
static  1fe9cb38-3af7-44f2-b940-c884a7e60f87    ethernet  enp0s8
dhcp    07e638e8-655b-41a7-9a5f-14a16798a1d8    ethernet  --
nat     45f7ceaf-9d2b-3eb9-a091-215f4d878300    ethernet  --
```

• Switch the connection profile of the device `enp0s8` again to `dhcp` using `nmcli` command as shown here:

```
[root@server ~]# nmcli con up dhcp
Connection successfully activated (D-Bus active path: /org/freedesktop/NetworkManag
er/ActiveConnection/4)
[root@server ~]#
[root@server ~]# nmcli con show
NAME    UUID                                    TYPE      DEVICE
dhcp    07e638e8-655b-41a7-9a5f-14a16798a1d8    ethernet  enp0s8
enp0s3  79da4c5b-6d53-40eb-873c-edb25f60c7cc    ethernet  enp0s3
nat     45f7ceaf-9d2b-3eb9-a091-215f4d878300    ethernet  --
static  1fe9cb38-3af7-44f2-b940-c884a7e60f87    ethernet  --
```

The option we have to give as an argument while creating the nmcli connection profile depends on the type used. To view all the options available, we can type `nmcli con add help` in the command line.

Modifying network interfaces using nmcli

An existing connection profile can be modified using the `nmcli con mod` command. Additional settings such as DNS servers can be specified here. Some properties, such as IP addresses and gateways, have different names to the name which was used while creating the connection profile.

The command `nmcli con mod` is followed by arguments which are a set of key/value pairs. The `nmcli con show <connection_profile_name>` command is used to list the current key values for a connection.

When modifying a DHCP connection profile to static, the profile `ipv4.method` property key should be set as `manual`:

Property name while creating	Property name while modifying
`ip4`	`ipv4`
`gw4`	`gwv4`

Following are the examples to illustrate the usage of nmcli con mod command to modify network interface settings:

- Turn off auto connect for a connection profile as shown in command line here:

  ```
  $ nmcli con mod "static" connection.autoconnect no
  ```

- Specify a DNS server using `nmcli con mod` command as shown here:

  ```
  $ nmcli con mod "static" ipv4.dns "1.1.1.1"
  ```

- We can further add more values to a key by using the + or – symbol in front of the argument. We can also add another DNS server using `nmcli con mod` command as shown here:

  ```
  $ nmcli con mod "static" +ipv4.dns "8.8.8.8"
  ```

- We can change the static IP address and gateway for a connection profile as shown here:

  ```
  $ nmcli con mod  "static"  ipv4.address  "50.50.50.50/24"
  ipv4.gateway  "50.50.50.254"
  ```

- We can assign a secondary IP address to the same interface without a gateway in an existing profile as shown here:

  ```
  $ nmcli con mod "static" +ipv4.addresses "70.70.70.100/16"
  ```

- To activate the changes, the connection profile needs to be activated using up with `nmcli con` command as shown here:

  ```
  $ nmcli con up "static"
  ```

- Delete a connection profile using `nmcli del` command as shown here:

  ```
  $ nmcli del "static"
  ```

- Disable all managed interfaces using `nmcli` command as shown here:

  ```
  $ nmcli net off
  ```

- Bring down an interface by temporarily disconnecting the device as shown here:

  ```
  $ nmcli dev dis enp0s8
  ```

- Bring up an interface by connecting the device as shown here:

  ```
  $ nmcli dev con enp0s8
  ```

Editing network configuration files

In the previous section, we looked at how `nmcli` is used to configure static and dynamic IP addressing. Apart from the NetworkManager command-line interface and GUI interface, we can configure networking manually using network interface configuration files. At any one time, we can either configure networking using network interface files manually or using NetworkManager, but not both simultaneously. The location of the network interface files (scripts) varies from one Linux distribution to another. In the case of CentOS 7, the network interface configuration files are stored in the `/etc/sysconfig/network-scripts/` folder and their naming conventions begin with `ifcfg-<device_name>`.

Configuring networking options in static and dynamic modes

We can configure networking manually in static IP addressing or DHCP IP addressing modes by modifying network interface config files.

Following are the examples to illustrate how networking is configured manually in CentOS 7:

- Dynamic (dhcp) configuration of the ifcfg file is shown here:

- Static configuration of the ifcfg file is explained as follows:

    If more than one value of an IP address, prefix, or gateway is to be assigned in static configuration, then it is suffixed with a number at the end. If multiple DNS server are to be assigned, then they are numbered in their order of lookup, as shown here:

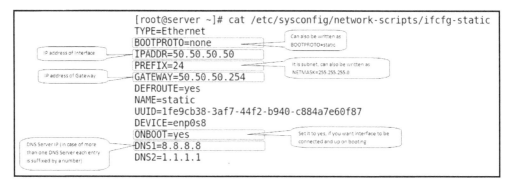

After making the desired changes to the configuration files, the networking service is to be restarted, or you can run the nmcli con reload command. This will make NetworkManager re-read the configuration files and apply changes. When reloading the nmcli configuration, the interface needs to be brought up and down once, for changes to come into effect as shown here:

```
$ nmcli con reload
$ nmcli con down "static"
$ nmcli con up "static"
```

Configuring hostnames and name resolutions

Hostname and DNS servers play an important role in networking as a machine is reachable in a network either by the IP address or hostname. The DNS server is responsible for the IP address to domain name and domain name to IP address conversion. This process of conversion is also known as **name resolution** or **DNS resolution**.

Since CentOS 7, the static host name has been stored in a new file, `/etc/hostname`. In earlier versions, it was stored in the `/etc/sysconfig/network` file. Now, a new command has been introduced with the name `hostnamectl`, to view and modify the hostname of machine.

Displaying and modifying the hostname

The `hostname` command is used to view the hostname or to temporarily modify the hostname at runtime. And the `hostnamectl` command is used to permanently modify the hostname from command line.

Following are the examples to illustrate the usage of hostname command:

- View the fully qualified host name of CentOS 7 using the `hostname` command as shown here:

```
[root@server ~]# hostname
server.example.com
```

- Modify the fully qualified hostname temporarily at runtime, using the `hostname` command as shown here:

```
[root@server ~]# hostname abc.example.com
[root@server ~]# hostname
abc.example.com
```

Following are the examples to illustrate the usage of hostnamectl command:

- View the hostname changes made using the `hostnamectl` command as shown in the following screenshot:

```
[root@server ~]# hostnamectl status                    ─── Using hostnamectl command to view hostname
        Static hostname: server.example.com ─────── Permanent hostname as set in /etc/hostname file
    Transient hostname: abc.example.com ───
              Icon name: computer-vm                   ─── Temporary hostname set using hostname command
                Chassis: vm
             Machine ID: 99e36987a88341d2af68ee2124f9ba6c
                Boot ID: d12f6b5abb8142de8a5083fbc96c2d24
         Virtualization: kvm
       Operating System: CentOS Linux 7 (Core)
            CPE OS Name: cpe:/o:centos:centos:7
                 Kernel: Linux 3.10.0-862.9.1.el7.x86_64
           Architecture: x86-64
```

- Use the `hostnamectl` command to make permanent changes to the hostname as shown in following screenshot:

```
[root@server ~]# hostnamectl set-hostname desktop.example.com
[root@server ~]# hostnamectl status
        Static hostname: desktop.example.com         ─── Setting new hostname using hostnamectl command
              Icon name: computer-vm
                Chassis: vm
             Machine ID: 99e36987a88341d2af68ee2124f9ba6c
                Boot ID: d12f6b5abb8142de8a5083fbc96c2d24
         Virtualization: kvm
       Operating System: CentOS Linux 7 (Core)
            CPE OS Name: cpe:/o:centos:centos:7
                 Kernel: Linux 3.10.0-862.9.1.el7.x86_64
           Architecture: x86-64
[root@server ~]# cat /etc/hostname ─── Display new hostname set in /etc/hostname file
desktop.example.com
[root@server ~]# hostname ─── Display new hostname set using hostname command
desktop.example.com
```

Modifying nameservers (DNS sever)

The order of IP address to domain name and vice-versa lookup is already discussed earlier in this chapter. The information for the DNS server (nameserver) is stored in the `/etc/resolv.conf` file. The nameserver directive is followed by the IP address of a nameserver to query the IP lookup. A maximum of three nameserver directives can be specified in this file to provide backup if one is down.

DNS server entries in `/etc/resolv.conf` are managed by NetworkManager. We should add or modify the DNS server using `nmcli` or GUI NetworkManager if NetworkManager is running.

Following examples are used to explain, how we can view or modify the nameserver of a system:

- Display the nameserver details as shown here:

```
[root@desktop ~]# cat /etc/resolv.conf
# Generated by NetworkManager
search example.com          search → This directive is followed by the list of
nameserver 10.0.3.3         domain name to try with a short host name query

                   nameserver → This directive is followed by the IP
                   address of DNS Server to be queried
```

- We can modify the nameserver entry by adding the DNS server for a specific connection profile using `nmcli` as shown here:

```
$ nmcli con mod <connection_profile> ipv4.dn <ip_of_dns_server>
$ nmcli con mod  "static"  ipv4.dns "8.8.8.8"
```

If NetworkManager is running, then manual modifications made in the `/etc/resolv.conf` file are overwritten by NetworkManager. Hence, for manually modifying and preserving the entries of `/etc/resolv.conf` file, we should first turn off NetworkManager and then modify them as shown here:

```
$ vi /etc/resolv.coonf
search mydomain.com
nameserver 8.8.8.8
nameserver 1.1.1.1
```

Accessing remote logins with SSH

SSH is an OpenSSH client program used for securely logging in to a remote machine for remote administration. It provides an authenticated encrypted communication channel between two hosts over an untrusted network.

Understanding OpenSSH

The SSH component can be categorized into two parts. The first is OpenSSH server (sshd service) which is installed and run on a remote server to accept connections from OpenSSH Client. By default, it runs on port 22 using TCP protocol, which should be allowed by firewalls to accept OpenSSH client connections.

The second component is SSH Client, which should be installed on any client system (Linux, Windows, or macOS) from which you want to connect to the system running OpenSSH server for remote administration.

Thus, the SSH protocol facilitates secure communications between two systems using client-server architecture. SSH encrypts the user login session completely and thereby makes it difficult for intruders to sniff any unencrypted password and eliminates **man-in-the-middle-attack** (**MITM**) probability over the network. SSH authenticates using the private-public key scheme, which further eliminates the impersonation attack on the network.

Executing commands over SSH remotely

Following are the examples to illustrate the basic usage of `ssh` command:

- The `ssh` command can be used to log in to a remote system using the current logged-in username of client requesting connection to ssh sever, as shown in command line and next screenshot:

  ```
  $ ssh <hostname_or_ip_address>
  ```

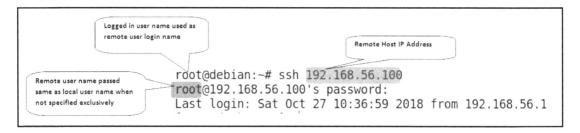

- The `ssh` command can be executed as another user by specifying the username and hostname/IP address as shown here:

  ```
  $ ssh <username>@<hostname_or_ip_address>
  or
  $ ssh -l <username> <hostname>
  ```

An example of execution of ssh command as different user is shown in the following screenshot:

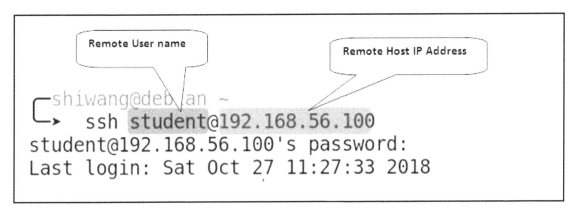

- You can execute a command on the remote system via s s h as shown here:

```
$ ssh <username>@<hostname_or_ip_address> <command_name>
```

An example of executing a command on remote system via s s h is shown in the following screenshot:

```
                                   Command to be run on Remote Host
┌shiwang@debian ~
└> ssh student@192.168.56.100 "/sbin/ip addr show"
student@192.168.56.100's password:
1: lo: <LOOPBACK,UP,LOWER UP> mtu 65536 qdisc noqueue state UNKNOWN group default qlen 1000
    link/loopback 00:00:00:00:00:00 brd 00:00:00:00:00:00
    inet 127.0.0.1/8 scope host lo
       valid lft forever preferred lft forever
    inet6 ::1/128 scope host
       valid lft forever preferred lft forever
2: enp0s3: <BROADCAST,MULTICAST,UP,LOWER UP> mtu 1500 qdisc pfifo_fast state UP group default qlen 1000
    link/ether 08:00:27:48:25:f5 brd ff:ff:ff:ff:ff:ff
    inet 192.168.56.100/24 brd 192.168.56.255 scope global noprefixroute dynamic enp0s3
       valid lft 754sec preferred lft 754sec
    inet6 fe80::ff14:181f:3b44:e69a/64 scope link noprefixroute
       valid lft forever preferred lft forever
3: enp0s8: <BROADCAST,MULTICAST,UP,LOWER UP> mtu 1500 qdisc pfifo_fast state UP group default qlen 1000
    link/ether 08:00:27:68:84:6a brd ff:ff:ff:ff:ff:ff
    inet 10.0.3.15/24 brd 10.0.3.255 scope global noprefixroute dynamic enp0s8
```

Key-based SSH authentication

SSH communication is secured using public key cryptography. When a user connects to the SSH-server using SSH-client for the first time, the SSH program stores the SSH-server public key in the user's home directory inside a file, `known_hosts`, in a hidden folder named `~/.ssh/`, as shown in the following screenshot:

```
[root@desktop ~]# ssh root@192.168.56.102
The authenticity of host '192.168.56.102 (192.168.56.102)' can't be established.
ECDSA key fingerprint is SHA256:9m+GSWBiya9nz6/2x3Xtbupy9q6XMIjE5XGwF9ylvMc.
ECDSA key fingerprint is MD5:55:19:b4:6d:3c:b1:6c:c1:46:8c:08:21:01:ec:de:8f.
Are you sure you want to continue connecting (yes/no)? yes
Warning: Permanently added '192.168.56.102' (ECDSA) to the list of known hosts.
root@192.168.56.102's password:
Last login: Sat Sep 15 06:22:46 2018
```

ECDSA public key fingerprint of ssh-server is stored in ~/.ssh/known_hosts file of client connecting for first time

The following screenshot shows an example of a public key fingerprint of the remote host being stored in the client's known host file:

```
[root@desktop ~]# cat .ssh/known_hosts
192.168.56.102 ecdsa-sha2-nistp256 AAAAE2VjZHNhLXNoYTItbmlzdHAyNTYAAAAIbmlzdHAy
NTYAAABBBM/tS2x+/YKz/TEgo/yhij7yMqVD4YtpN/PvGtBkZ6BvpVB+2Zg6c2brLRgeM8w7BCsRoCv
/A38PXKwuV1CbsAE=
```

Fingerprint of ssh-server in client file

Now, subsequently whenever ssh-client connects to the server, it compares the public key sent by the server to the public key of the server stored in the `~/.ssh/known_hosts` file. If the public key does not match, the client assumes that the network traffic is being hijacked or the server to which the connection is being made is not the same, and hence SSH-client breaks the connection, as shown here:

```
[root@desktop ~]# ssh root@192.168.56.102
@@@@@@@@@@@@@@@@@@@@@@@@@@@@@@@@@@@@@@@@@@@@@@@@@@@@@@@@@@@@@@@@
@    WARNING: REMOTE HOST IDENTIFICATION HAS CHANGED!     @
@@@@@@@@@@@@@@@@@@@@@@@@@@@@@@@@@@@@@@@@@@@@@@@@@@@@@@@@@@@@@@@@
IT IS POSSIBLE THAT SOMEONE IS DOING SOMETHING NASTY!
Someone could be eavesdropping on you right now (man-in-the-middle attack)!
It is also possible that a host key has just been changed.
The fingerprint for the ECDSA key sent by the remote host is
SHA256:4vSDsavF7Q9GbELaOIiCCSOp6aXeyMbm/ESlW5HsbmY.
Please contact your system administrator.
Add correct host key in /root/.ssh/known_hosts to get rid of this message.
Offending ECDSA key in /root/.ssh/known_hosts:1
ECDSA host key for 192.168.56.102 has changed and you have requested strict checking.
Host key verification failed.
```

Fingerprint of ssh-server in client file is not matching with the fingerprint sent by remote host on connection request

It is also a possibility that the server was reformatted or the server key replaced for any legitimate reason. In such circumstances, the user needs to update their `~/.ssh/known_hosts` files by deleting the old keys to enable logging in to the server.

Configuring ssh-keygen for password-less authentication

SSH server has multiple ways of authenticating a client connecting to it. The most popular method is password-based authentication as it is the easiest one, however it is not so secure. Passwords are exchanged with secure mechanisms, however, due to ease of use they are generally not complex or long. This enable the attacker to break the password using brute-force or dictionary attacks. In such scenarios, the SSH keys can provide a secure and reliable means of authentication for clients.

SSH server uses a public key cryptography scheme to authenticate users. In this scheme, a pair of keys are generated, a public key and private key, for authentication. As the name suggests, a private key is kept secret by the client as its compromise can lead to someone logging in to the server without any additional authentication.

The corresponding public key for the secret private key of the client is not kept as secret and is copied to systems the user logs in to. The private key is used to decrypt the message encrypted using the associated public key of the client. Using the key pair, we can also enable the password-less authentication.

The trusted public key of the client is stored in a special file named `authorized_keys` in the `home` directory of user account, used to log in as shown in the following diagram:

Public Key of client, stored in remote host "authorized_keys" files

```
root@Ubuntu-1804:~# cat .ssh/authorized_keys
ssh-rsa AAAAB3NzaC1yc2EAAAADAQABAAABAQCz2CqzCgZvElM2uKmMO/lS+w/PX3QQTeMh/5A1w2IS
zGuPCLoEcSwtNfuu2AURs7BdFQPKi1SDwQf0vI4oRSUbCIC41tuBueAeZmpYSqVVKuke0W7GvRLVvOyB
47RIqs277+PVF8nk0+Z0YQD6naYLNgxRAGcGQF/ik1s+MB6GjlfrnW2QHVE+hVeE1VTi42/47g2xancC
hqwUSul+oHFXUbbXxE4AHhL1tOV7qu0+Qq6fGd+2uGdcyKAhapV9mBDjkJ37UMpA7KZHv2WgoFoHZ6AF
nVe5myJwoQ65BR3jtjasArS1ntO3pMW9/BBJrszwglUx5RZ3C7EuOY0U+eDx root@desktop.exampl
e.com
```

When a client attempts to authenticate the SSH server using keys, a challenge is issued using the public key of the client stored in the server. On successfully decrypting the challenge using the client's private key, the user gets access to the shell of the server.

In addition to password-based and key-based authentication, SSH also supports Kerberos and gssapi and so on for authentication.

Creating a SSH key pair

In this step, the client uses a special utility, `ssh-keygen`, to generate an SSH key pair for authentication with the server. This utility is bundled with OpenSSH and by default it creates a 2048-bit RSA key pair. It supports RSA and DSA, both with different lengths of keys. A key length of 4096 bits is recommended for establishing a secure connection between two machines. The following diagram shows how to create a RSA key pair of 2048-bit:

```
[root@desktop ~]# ssh-keygen -t rsa                    Enter passphrase
Generating public/private rsa key pair.                here, if required
Enter file in which to save the key (/root/.ssh/     rsa):
Enter passphrase (empty for no passphrase):
Enter same passphrase again:                                 Location of Public Key
Your identification has been saved in /root/.ssh/id_rsa.
Your public key has been saved in /root/.ssh/id_rsa.pub.
The key fingerprint is:
SHA256:vvDbwVF2YHAoSCxnjhNojc4oEenLJCYgGcsGNyI2Gyw  root@desktop.example.com
The key's randomart image is:
+---[RSA 2048]----+
|BOo+ o..  .o+    |                                  Location of Private Key
|E=B.+ = . .o .   |
|*X  B  . o .     |
|*+o o .    o .   |
|B .  . S .       |
| o      . . .    |
|       . . o     |
|        o o .    |
|        +..      |
+----[SHA256]-----+
```

It will prompt you to select a location for the keys that will be generated. By default, the keys are stored in the user's home directory, the `~/.ssh` directory, with the private key named as `id_rsa` and the public key as `id_rsa.pub`. The permission on the private key is 600 and it is 644 on public key.

Then, it prompts you to enter an optional passphrase for the key, which is used to decrypt the key on the local machine (client side). Hence, brute-force or dictionary attacks are not possible for this passphrase. The passphrase also provides additional security in case of the system being compromised. For example, it can prevent the attacker from logging in to other servers when SSH keys have already been exchanged in the compromised system. Following image shows the RSA key pair public key used for authentication:

```
|
                                        Public Key of client to be copied at
[root@desktop ~]# ls .ssh/              server for key based authentication
id_rsa  id_rsa.pub  known_hosts
[root@desktop ~]# cat .ssh/id_rsa.pub
ssh-rsa AAAAB3NzaC1yc2EAAAADAQABAAABAQCzzcqzCgZvElM2uKmMO/lS+w/PX3QQTeMh/5A1w2IS
zGuPCLoEcSwtNfuu2AURs7BdFQPKi1SDwQf0vI4oRSUbCIC41tuBueAeZmpYSqVVKuke0W7GvRLVvOyB
47RIqs277+PVF8nk0+Z0YQD6naYLNgxRAGcGQF/ik1s+MB6Gjlfrnw2QHVE+hVeE1VTi42/47g2xancC
hqwUSul+oHFXUbbXxE4AHhL1t0V7qu0+Qq6fGd+2uGdcyKAhapV9mBDjkJ37UMpA7KZHv2WgoFoHZ6AF
nVe5myJwoQ65BR3jtjasArS1nt03pMW9/BBJrszwglUx5RZ3C7Eu0Y0U+eDx root@desktop.exampl
e.com
```

Now, to enable key-based authentication, the public key of client is to be copied to the destination system running SSH server.

Following example illustrate the copying of public key to remote machine using ssh-copy-id command:

- There is one utility, `ssh-copy-id`, which is also bundled with OpenSSH and can be used to copy the key to the remote system. It automatically copies the `~/.ssh/id_rsa.pub` file by default into the remote system as shown here:

```
                                    ⎧ Remote Host IP to copy      ⎫
                                    ⎩ the Public of SSH Client     ⎭

[root@desktop ~]# ssh-copy-id root@192.168.56.101
/usr/bin/ssh-copy-id: INFO: Source of key(s) to be installed: "/root/.ssh/id_rsa
.pub"
/usr/bin/ssh-copy-id: INFO: attempting to log in with the new key(s), to filter
out any that are already installed
/usr/bin/ssh-copy-id: INFO: 1 key(s) remain to be installed -- if you are prompt
ed now it is to install the new keys
root@192.168.56.101's password:

Number of key(s) added: 1

Now try logging into the machine, with:   "ssh 'root@192.168.56.101'"
and check to make sure that only the key(s) you wanted were added.
```

The general syntax of `ssh-copy-id` command is as follows:

`$ ssh-copy-id      username@remotehost`

- The following diagram shows how to do ssh on remote host without giving password:

```
[root@desktop ~]# ssh root@192.168.56.101
Welcome to Ubuntu 18.04 LTS (GNU/Linux 4.15.0-...generic x86_64)

 * Documentation:  https://help.ubuntu.com          ⎧ Logging into Remote Host  ⎫
 * Management:     https://landscape.canonical.com  ⎩ without giving password    ⎭
 * Support:        https://ubuntu.com/advantage


 * Canonical Livepatch is available for installation.
   - Reduce system reboots and improve kernel security. Activate at:
     https://ubuntu.com/livepatch

295 packages can be updated.
25 updates are security updates.

Last login: Wed Oct 31 06:20:17 2018 from 192.168.56.100
```

- Another method of copying the public key into the remote host's `authorized_keys` files using `ssh` command is shown here:

```
$ cat ~/.ssh/id_rsa.pub | ssh student@192.168.56.100 "cat >>
~/.ssh/authorized_keys"
```

Now SSH into the remote host by entering the passphrase when prompted (required only if you give the passphrase while creating the keys).

Configuring and securing SSH logins

Additional security measures can be enabled by modifying the OpenSSH server configuration file `/etc/ssh/sshd_config`, on the remote host. Following are the some steps that can be taken to secure the SSH logins:

1. Now, since we have configured the SSH key-based authentication in the previous section, we can disable the password authentication to secure SSH logins in the SSH server configuration file. Edit the SSH daemon config file on the remote host running the SSH server and set the `PasswordAuthentication` directive value to `no` as shown here:

```
$ vi /etc/ssh/sshd_config
PasswordAuthentication no
```

2. Prohibit direct login as the root user through SSH, as the root user has unrestricted privileges and exists by default on every Linux system. To secure the root user account through SSH, we can do following changes in configuration file:

   - Comment the line with the directive `PermitRootLogin` as shown here:

     ```
     #PermitRootLogin yes
     ```

   - Set the directive `PermitRootLogin` value as `no` as shown here:

     ```
     PermitRootLogin no
     ```

   - Allow only key-based ssh login in the root account by setting the directive `PermitRootLogin` value as `without-password` as shown here:

     ```
     PermitRootLogin without-password
     ```

3. After making changes in the SSH server configuration file
   `/etc/ssh/sshd_config`, restart the `sshd` service to bring the applied changes
   into effect, as shown here:

   ```
   $ systemctl restart sshd
   ```

Transferring files in Linux

We have seen how to secure our communication between the client and remote host server
using SSH. In this section, we will securely transfer files between two connected machines.
CentOS 7 has two popular utilities, `scp` and `rsync`, to secure data transfer between
connected machines.

Secure file transfer using SCP

The `scp` command is used to securely transfer files from a local system to a remote host or
from a remote host to a local system. It uses SSH server for secure (encrypted) data transfer
and for authentication.

The `ssh`, `scp`, and `sftp` are bundled into `ssh` package and gets installed automatically on
installation of `ssh`.

Local to remote filesystem file transfer

The syntax of transferring a file from local system to remote filesystem is as follows:

```
$ scp    <local_filenames>    <username>@<host>:<remote_host_directory>
```

On execution of the preceding command, you will be prompted for the remote user
password. After entering the correct password, file transfer will begin as shown in the
following diagram:

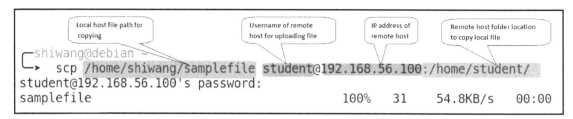

Remote to local filesystem file transfer

The syntax of transferring a file from remote system to local filesystem transfer is as follows:

```
$ scp    <username>@<host>:<remote_host_file>    <local_path>
```

On execution of preceding command you will be prompted for remote user password. After entering the correct password, file transfer will begin as shown here:

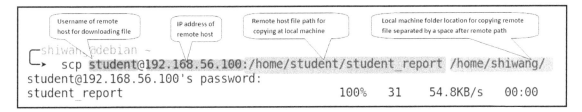

Synchronizing files using rsync

Rsync is another utility that is used to copy files securely and quickly from one system to another. It uses an SSH connection for transfer of data and differs from SCP as it copies only the differences in existing files. Rsync is faster than SCP as it copies only differences when copying files from one directory on a local system to a directory on a remote system, whereas SCP would copy everything.

The following table lists the important options along with their description, that are used with `rsync` command for synchronizing files and folders:

Option	Description
-a	Archive mode (it includes recursion, synchronizing symlinks, preserving permissions, preserving group ownership, times stamps, ownership of files, and synchronizing of device files). It is equivalent of the following options: -rlptgoD
-v	It adds verbosity in the output when synchronization takes place.
-r	Synchronize whole directory tree recursively.
-n	Perform dry-run without making changes.
--remove-source-files	Synchronized files are removed from the sender system.
-z	Compress file data during transmission from source to destination.
-X	Synchronize SELinux contexts from source to destination.
-A	Synchronize ACLs on file.

Synchronizing data locally from one folder to another for backup

The syntax for local synchronization for backup from one folder to another is as follows:

```
$ rsync    -<options>    <source_directory>    <destination_directory>
```

An example of `rsync` command usage to synchronize local files is shown here:

```
[root@desktop ~]# rsync -av /var/log/ /tmp/backup
sending incremental file list
created directory /tmp/backup
./
Xorg.0.log
Xorg.0.log.old
Xorg.1.log
Xorg.9.log
boot.log
boot.log-20181002
```

Synchronizing data from a local to remote host filesystem

The syntax for local to remote host filesystem synchronization is as follows:

```
$ rsync    -<options>    <source_directory>
<username>@<host>:<remote_host_directory>
```

On execution of the preceding command, you will be prompted for a remote user password. After entering the correct password, file synchronization will begin as shown here:

```
root@debian:~# rsync -av /var/log/ student@192.168.56.100:/home/student/backup
student@192.168.56.100's password:
sending incremental file list
created directory /home/student/backup
./
alternatives.log
alternatives.log.1
alternatives.log.10.gz
alternatives.log.2.gz
alternatives.log.3.gz
alternatives.log.4.gz
alternatives.log.5.gz
```

(Local Source Directory) — /var/log/

(Remote Destination Directory) — student@192.168.56.100:/home/student/backup

Synchronizing data from remote host to local filesystem

The syntax for remote host to local filesystem synchronization is as follows:

```
$ rsync      -<options>      <username>@<host>:<remote_host_directory>
<local_directory>
```

On execution of preceding command you will be prompted for remote user password. After entering the correct password, file synchronization will begin as shown here:

```
shiwang@debian ~
└➤  rsync -av root@192.168.56.100:/var/log/  /tmp/backup/
root@192.168.56.100's password:
receiving incremental file list
created directory /tmp/backup
./
Xorg.0.log
Xorg.0.log.old
Xorg.1.log
Xorg.9.log
boot.log
```

(Remote Source Directory) — /var/log/

(Local Destination Directory) — /tmp/backup/

Summary

In this chapter, we began with learning basic networking concepts such as IP address, DNS, gateway, and so on. This was followed by essential networking commands used in CentOS 7. Then we looked at the management of network interfaces using nmcli (NetworkManager command-line interface), the editing of network configuration files for manual configuration, and modifying hostname, DNS server parameters, and so on. Thereafter, we learnt how to securely connect to remote hosts using the SSH Client and password as well as with public keys for authentication. Finally, we looked up how to securely transfer and synchronize files for backup from one host to another using the command line.

In the next chapter, we will learn about how to keep CentOS 7 and its installed applications up to date. We will also learn how to install or remove undesired applications using the command line.

8
Software Package Management

To keep your system up to date and install or remove applications as you choose, Linux supports multiple methods. One method is to use the source code of the application for compilation and installation on your machine. Another one is using pre-built programs or groups of programs known as **packages**, which are ready for installation on a particular distribution.

In this chapter, you will learn how to manage these pre-built software packages using RPM and the YUM utility. You will also learn how to add or remove official and third-party repositories in CentOS 7.

In this chapter, we will cover the following topics:

- Managing applications using RPM
- Managing applications using YUM
- Managing official and third-party repositories
- Creating custom repositories

Managing applications using RPM

RPM (short for **Red Hat Package Manager**) is an open source package management utility developed by Red Hat for RPM-based systems such as RHEL, CentOS, and Fedora. Using the RPM utility, the user can install, remove, update, query, and verify application packages built in the `.rpm` format. You can download `.rpm` packages from repositories containing application packages in `.rpm` format.

An RPM package may or may not require any resource prerequisites. If a rpm package requires any resource, such as a shared library or another package to be available on system before proceeding ahead with that rpm package installation, then those resources are known as dependencies of that package. A package management utility such as YUM automatically resolves the dependencies when a package is installed, while the RPM utility lacks this feature. Using the RPM utility, you can find out a package dependency, but RPM cannot automatically install them. The RPM utility is also known as a low-level package management tool.

Anatomy of a RPM

The naming of each RPM package file follows a standard, as given here:

```
name-version-release.architecture.rpm
```

The naming convention used for RPM packages is shown in the following diagram:

The following table describes the breakdown of various fields used in the naming of RPM packages, and their descriptions:

Field	Description
Name	It consists of a string describing the contents of the application.
Version	It is the version number of the application.
Release	It is the release number of the package set by the packager.
Arch	It describes the architecture of the package. It says for what architecture the package was built: 32-bit, 64-bit, or both: • i386: 32-bit • x86_64: 64-bit • noarch: Not specific to any architecture, can be used on both 32-bit and 64-bit

Using RPM packages for installing an application has the added advantage of manageability (tracking package files, updating the package, removing the package). Almost all software provided by CentOS is in the form of RPM packages.

 An RPM package primarily consists of three components: metadata, files, and scripts. Metadata consists of package name, version, release, builder, date, dependencies, and so on. Files consist of archives of files contained in the package to be installed. The scripts file inside an RPM package is executed when the package is installed, removed, or updated.

What happens when you update an application

When an application is updated, typically, the older version of the package is removed from the system. The existing configuration files are generally retained, but retaining, overwriting, or writing a new configuration file with a different name is decided while creating the package.

In a typical scenario, only one version of an application is installed at a time. However, in certain cases, multiple versions of the same application exist, such as in kernel packages or in a multi-architecture environment where the same package is installed for different architectures (32-bit and 64-bit). A kernel package is designed so that multiple versions can be kept in the system. If a new installation of the kernel fails, the older kernel is always available as a standby. Always remember that the kernel package is never updated using the update option of the RPM utility. It is always installed and not updated.

Using RPM to query options with RPM packages

There are several options that are used in combination with query options. Some popular ones are as follows:

- List all the packages installed in the system:

  ```
  $ rpm -qa
  ```

- Find a specific package installed in the system by piping the output of the previous command to the `grep` command, as shown here:

```
[root@desktop ~]# rpm -qa | grep kernel
kernel-3.10.0-862.9.1.el7.x86_64
kernel-tools-libs-3.10.0-862.9.1.el7.x86_64
kernel-devel-3.10.0-862.el7.x86_64
kernel-3.10.0-862.el7.x86_64
abrt-addon-kerneloops-2.1.11-50.el7.centos.x86_64
kernel-tools-3.10.0-862.9.1.el7.x86_64
kernel-devel-3.10.0-862.9.1.el7.x86_64
kernel-headers-3.10.0-862.9.1.el7.x86_64
```

- Identify the package that installed a file on the system, as shown here:

```
[root@desktop ~]# rpm -qf /etc/httpd/conf/httpd.conf
httpd-2.4.6-80.el7.centos.1.x86_64
```

- Display the list of files installed by an RPM package, as shown here:

```
[root@desktop ~]# rpm -ql httpd
/etc/httpd
/etc/httpd/conf
/etc/httpd/conf.d
/etc/httpd/conf.d/README
/etc/httpd/conf.d/autoindex.conf
/etc/httpd/conf.d/userdir.conf
```

- Display the recently installed RPM package, as shown here:

```
[root@desktop ~]# rpm -qa --last
vsftpd-3.0.2-22.el7.x86_64                 Thu 08 Nov 2018 04:43:19 PM IST
nux-dextop-release-0-5.el7.nux.noarch      Sun 04 Nov 2018 08:47:40 AM IST
epel-release-7-11.noarch                   Sun 04 Nov 2018 08:47:14 AM IST
```

- Display information on the installed package, as shown here:

```
[root@desktop ~]# rpm -qi vsftpd
Name        : vsftpd
Version     : 3.0.2
Release     : 22.el7
Architecture: x86_64
Install Date: Thu 08 Nov 2018 04:43:19 PM IST
Group       : System Environment/Daemons
Size        : 356236
License     : GPLv2 with exceptions
Signature   : RSA/SHA256, Fri 11 Aug 2017 01:47:26 AM IST, Key ID 24c6a8a7f4a80eb5
Source RPM  : vsftpd-3.0.2-22.el7.src.rpm
Build Date  : Thu 03 Aug 2017 11:40:20 AM IST
Build Host  : c1bm.rdu2.centos.org
Relocations : (not relocatable)
Packager    : CentOS BuildSystem <http://bugs.centos.org>
Vendor      : CentOS
URL         : https://security.appspot.com/vsftpd.html
Summary     : Very Secure Ftp Daemon
Description :
vsftpd is a Very Secure FTP daemon. It was written completely from
scratch.
```

- Display the documentation of the file installed by a package, as shown here:

```
[root@desktop ~]# rpm -qdf /usr/bin/wget
/usr/share/doc/wget-1.14/AUTHORS
/usr/share/doc/wget-1.14/COPYING
/usr/share/doc/wget-1.14/MAILING-LIST
/usr/share/doc/wget-1.14/NEWS
/usr/share/doc/wget-1.14/README
/usr/share/doc/wget-1.14/sample.wgetrc
/usr/share/info/wget.info.gz
/usr/share/man/man1/wget.1.gz
```

- Display the documentation installed by package, name as shown here:

```
[root@desktop ~]# rpm -qd yum
/usr/share/doc/yum-3.4.3/AUTHORS
/usr/share/doc/yum-3.4.3/COPYING
/usr/share/doc/yum-3.4.3/ChangeLog
/usr/share/doc/yum-3.4.3/INSTALL
/usr/share/doc/yum-3.4.3/PLUGINS
/usr/share/doc/yum-3.4.3/README
/usr/share/doc/yum-3.4.3/TODO
/usr/share/doc/yum-3.4.3/comps.rng
/usr/share/man/man5/yum.conf.5
/usr/share/man/man8/yum-shell.8
/usr/share/man/man8/yum.8
```

- Display the configuration file installed by the package, as shown here:

```
[root@desktop ~]# rpm -qc vsftpd
/etc/logrotate.d/vsftpd
/etc/pam.d/vsftpd
/etc/vsftpd/ftpusers
/etc/vsftpd/user_list
/etc/vsftpd/vsftpd.conf
```

- Display the list of change information of a specific package, as shown here:

```
[root@desktop ~]# rpm -q --changelog httpd
* Tue Jun 26 2018 CentOS Sources <bugs@centos.org> - 2.4.6-80.el7.centos.1
- Remove index.html, add centos-noindex.tar.gz
- change vstring
- change symlink for poweredby.png
- update welcome.conf with proper aliases

* Mon May 28 2018 Luboš Uhliarik <luhliari@redhat.com> - 2.4.6-80.1
- Resolves: #1560609 - httpd: active connections being terminated when httpd
  gets gracefully stopped/restarted, GracefulShutdownTimeout is not being
  honored

* Mon Jan 08 2018 Luboš Uhliarik <luhliari@redhat.com> - 2.4.6-80
- Related: #1288395 - httpd segfault when logrotate invoked

* Wed Nov 01 2017 Luboš Uhliarik <luhliari@redhat.com> - 2.4.6-79
- Resolves: #1274890 - mod_ssl config: tighten defaults
```

Verifying RPM package signatures

The RPM packages are generally signed by the organization, community, or individual that packages them using the GPG private key. Before installing a package on our system, we should always verify the signature of the package with its public GPG key to ascertain its integrity. The following command is used to check the signature of RPM packages:

```
$ rpm --checksig <packagename.rpm>
```

Using RPM to install packages

To install a package, the -i option is used. It is generally clubbed with the -v and -h options for verbosity and to display the progress of the installation using hash symbols, as shown in the following screenshot:

```
[root@desktop Packages]# rpm -ivh lynx-2.8.8-0.3.dev15.el7.x86_64.rpm
Preparing...
############################### [100%]
Updating / installing...
   1:lynx-2.8.8-0.3.dev15.el7
############################### [100%]
```

The disadvantage of using this method is that RPM is unable to resolve the dependency automatically, and hence it will exit installation in-between if it encounters any unmet dependencies while installing the package.

We can use RPM to install a package forcefully as well, by disabling the dependency check during the installation process using the --nodeps option. This method is not recommended as a program may fail to work after, that is, if it is installed without resolving its dependencies.

An example of forceful installation of a package using the RPM utility is shown in the following screenshot:

```
[root@desktop Packages]# rpm -ivh samba-4.7.1-6.el7.x86_64.rpm
error: Failed dependencies:
        libxattr-tdb-samba4.so()(64bit) is needed by samba-0:4.7.1-6.el7.x86_64
        libxattr-tdb-samba4.so(SAMBA_4.7.1)(64bit) is needed by samba-0:4.7.1-6.el7.x86_64
        samba-common-tools = 4.7.1-6.el7 is needed by samba-0:4.7.1-6.el7.x86_64
        samba-libs = 4.7.1-6.el7 is needed by samba-0:4.7.1-6.el7.x86_64
[root@desktop Packages]# rpm -ivh samba-4.7.1-6.el7.x86_64.rpm  --nodeps
Preparing...                          ################################### [100%]
Updating / installing...
   1:samba-0:4.7.1-6.el7             ################################### [100%]
```

Nodeps option forcefully installs the package without fulfilling the dependencies

Using rpm to remove packages

We can remove a package by specifying the package name with the −e option, as shown here:

```
[root@desktop Packages]# rpm  -ev samba
Preparing packages...
samba-0:4.7.1-6.el7.x86_64
```

We can also remove a package without doing the dependency check. It will forcefully remove the package from the system and any application, depending on that particular package may fail to run. The following diagram shows how to remove a package without checking its dependencies:

```
[root@desktop Packages]# rpm -ev openssl
error: Failed dependencies:
        openssl is needed by (installed) python2-cryptography-1.7.2-2.el7.x86_64
        openssl >= 0.9.8g-12 is needed by (installed) unbound-libs-1.6.6-1.el7.x86_64
        /usr/bin/openssl is needed by (installed) authconfig-6.2.8-30.el7.x86_64
[root@desktop Packages]# rpm -ev openssl --nodeps
Preparing packages...
openssl-1:1.0.2k-12.el7.x86_64
```

Nodeps option to forcefully remove the package without checking the dependencies

Using RPM to upgrade packages

Most of the time, installed packages are automatically upgraded using a high-level package manager such as YUM. However, if a package is not available for upgrade through the central repository, it can be downloaded from the internet and upgraded manually, as shown here:

```
$ rpm -U <file.rpm>
```

We can use either the preceding command or the following command to upgrade a package manually:

```
$ rpm -Uvh <file.rpm>
```

An example of the rpm command to upgrade a package is shown here:

```
[root@desktop Packages]# rpm -Uvh vsftpd-3.0.2-22.el7.x86_64.rpm
Preparing...
############################### [100%]
Updating / installing...
   1:vsftpd-3.0.2-22.el7
############################### [100%]
```

Using RPM to verify packages

Verify the installed files of the package against the files available in the RPM file, as shown here:

```
[root@desktop Packages]# rpm -Vp httpd-2.4.6-80.el7.centos.x86_64.rpm
Unsatisfied dependencies for httpd-2.4.6-80.el7.centos.x86_64:
        httpd-tools = 2.4.6-80.el7.centos is needed by httpd-2.4.6-80.el7.centos.x86_64
missing     /etc/httpd
missing     /etc/httpd/conf
missing     /etc/httpd/conf.d
missing     /etc/httpd/conf.d/README
missing   c /etc/httpd/conf.d/autoindex.conf
```

Importing a RPM GPG key

To verify package integrity before installation, the repository or package author's public GPG key must be imported into our system. The following screenshot shows the command that's used to import the CentOS 7 GPG key:

```
[root@desktop mnt]# rpm --import RPM-GPG-KEY-CentOS-7
[root@desktop mnt]# rpm --import RPM-GPG-KEY-CentOS-Testing-7
```

Display all the imported RPM repositories' GPG keys on the system, as shown in the following screenshot:

```
[root@desktop mnt]# rpm -qa gpg-pubkey*
gpg-pubkey-f4a80eb5-53a7ff4b
gpg-pubkey-baadae52-49beffa4
gpg-pubkey-8fae34bd-538f1e51
```

Managing applications using YUM

YUM (short for **Yellowdog Updater Modified**) is an open source tool that was developed by Red Hat Inc for RPM-based systems. It is a high-level package management tool that's used for easily installing, removing, updating, or searching software packages on systems or in network repositories. It allows us to use a CentOS base and third-party repositories that are created on remote or local servers to install individual packages or groups of packages automatically, after resolving their dependencies.

> In upcoming versions, YUM is being replaced by DNF (which is compatible in its command set). YUM has already been replaced with DNF (Dandified YUM) as the main package manager in Fedora.

Understanding the YUM package manager

The main configuration file of YUM is /etc/yum.conf, and the main directory, which stores the repository configuration file, is /etc/yum.repos.d/. The repository configuration file has got a specific syntax, and it should end with a .repo extension in the /etc/yum.repos.d/ directory.

The repository configuration file contains the URL of the repository, the `repo id`, `repo name`, instructions to use GPG for checking package signatures, and an option to enable or disable the repository.

Using the YUM command line

In this section, we will learn about package management by using YUM on the Linux command line.

Finding an application using yum

We can search for a package name using YUM in multiple ways. The search option with a keyword (package name) lists the package in which the specified keyword is present in the package name itself and in the summary field of packages also. The following example are used to illustrate the working `yum search` command:

- Search for a package by name only using `yum search` command, as shown here:

  ```
  $ yum search <package_name>
  ```

  An example of yum search command to find the package named `whois` is shown here:

  ```
  [root@desktop yum.repos.d]# yum search whois
  Loaded plugins: fastestmirror, langpacks
  Loading mirror speeds from cached hostfile
   * base: mirrors.fibergrid.in
   * extras: mirrors.fibergrid.in
   * updates: mirrors.fibergrid.in
  ========================= N/S matched: whois =========================
  whois.x86_64 : Improved WHOIS client

    Name and summary matches only, use "search all" for everything.
  ```

- Find the package if the search string is available in name, summary, and description fields, as shown here:

```
[root@desktop yum.repos.d]# yum search all "whois"
Loaded plugins: fastestmirror, langpacks
Loading mirror speeds from cached hostfile
 * base: mirrors.fibergrid.in
 * extras: mirrors.fibergrid.in
 * updates: mirrors.fibergrid.in
=========================== Matched: whois ===========================
whois.x86_64 : Improved WHOIS client
apache-commons-net.noarch : Internet protocol suite Java library
```

- Search for a package by package description using the `yum whatprovides` command, as shown here:

```
$ yum whatprovides "*/package_name"
```

An example of the `yum whatprovides` command to find the package name `lynx` is shown here:

```
[root@desktop yum.repos.d]# yum whatprovides "*/lynx"
Loaded plugins: fastestmirror, langpacks
Loading mirror speeds from cached hostfile
 * base: mirrors.fibergrid.in
 * extras: mirrors.fibergrid.in
 * updates: mirrors.fibergrid.in
lynx-2.8.8-0.3.dev15.el7.x86_64 : A text-based Web browser
Repo        : base
Matched from:
Filename    : /usr/bin/lynx
```

- Identify the package that installed a file (absolute path name) on the system using the `yum provides` command, as shown here:

```
[root@desktop yum.repos.d]# yum provides /etc/ntp.conf
Loaded plugins: fastestmirror, langpacks
Loading mirror speeds from cached hostfile
 * base: mirrors.fibergrid.in
 * extras: mirrors.fibergrid.in
 * updates: mirrors.fibergrid.in
ntp-4.2.6p5-28.el7.centos.x86_64 : The NTP daemon and utilities
Repo        : base
Matched from:
Filename    : /etc/ntp.conf
```

Installing applications using YUM

We can install a new package using the YUM utility. The YUM utility will resolve all the dependencies of the package and prompt for confirmation before installation.

The following are examples to illustrate the usage of the yum command for package installation:

- Use the following command to install an application using YUM:

    ```
    $ yum install firefox
    ```

- Install an application without prompting for confirmation by using the $-y$ option:

    ```
    $ yum -y install firefox
    ```

- Install a package without verifying its signature:

    ```
    $ yum install firefox --nogpgcheck
    ```

- Install a downloaded RPM file from a local directory. It automatically downloads the dependencies of the package from the configured repositories:

    ```
    $ yum localinstall <path_to_rpm_file>
    ```

An example of the yum localinstall command is shown here:

```
[root@desktop ~]# yum localinstall /mnt/Packages/bind-utils-9.9.4-61.el7.x86_64.rpm
Loaded plugins: fastestmirror, langpacks
Examining /mnt/Packages/bind-utils-9.9.4-61.el7.x86_64.rpm: 32:bind-utils-9.9.4-61.el7.x86_64
Marking /mnt/Packages/bind-utils-9.9.4-61.el7.x86_64.rpm to be installed
Resolving Dependencies
--> Running transaction check
---> Package bind-utils.x86_64 32:9.9.4-61.el7 will be installed
--> Finished Dependency Resolution

Dependencies Resolved

================================================================================
 Package          Arch        Version           Repository                  Size
================================================================================
Installing:
 bind-utils       x86_64      32:9.9.4-61.el7   /bind-utils-9.9.4-61.el7.x86_64   431 k

Transaction Summary
================================================================================
Install  1 Package
```

Displaying packages and their information with YUM

The following are examples of displaying detailed information of a package using the yum command:

- The usage of the yum info command is shown here:

```
[root@desktop ~]# yum info httpd
Loaded plugins: fastestmirror, langpacks
Loading mirror speeds from cached hostfile
 * base: mirrors.fibergrid.in
 * extras: mirrors.fibergrid.in
 * updates: mirrors.fibergrid.in
Available Packages
Name        : httpd
Arch        : x86_64
Version     : 2.4.6
Release     : 80.el7.centos.1
Size        : 2.7 M
Repo        : updates/7/x86_64
Summary     : Apache HTTP Server
URL         : http://httpd.apache.org/
License     : ASL 2.0
Description : The Apache HTTP Server is a powerful, efficient, and extensible
            : web server.
```

- The usage of the yum list command to display the installed packages list is shown in the command line here:

```
$ yum list installed
```

- The usage of the yum list command to display the installed and available package information using its name is shown in the following screenshot:

```
[root@desktop ~]# yum list vsftpd
Loaded plugins: fastestmirror, langpacks
Loading mirror speeds from cached hostfile
 * base: mirrors.fibergrid.in
 * extras: mirrors.fibergrid.in
 * updates: mirrors.fibergrid.in
Installed Packages
vsftpd.x86_64                        3.0.2-22.el7                    installed
[root@desktop ~]# yum list samba
Loaded plugins: fastestmirror, langpacks
Loading mirror speeds from cached hostfile
 * base: mirrors.fibergrid.in
 * extras: mirrors.fibergrid.in
 * updates: mirrors.fibergrid.in
Available Packages
samba.x86_64                         4.7.1-9.el7_5                   updates
```

- The `yum list` command can also be used to display all available packages in repositories from the YUM database, as shown in command line here:

```
$ yum list
```

Removing applications using yum

The following are examples to illustrate the usage of the `yum command` for removing an application package:

- The `yum` command can be used to remove a package with all its dependencies, as shown in the command line here:

```
$ yum remove firefox
```

- The `yum` command can also be used with the -y option to remove an application without prompting for confirmation, as shown in the command line here:

```
$ yum -y remove firefox
```

Updating applications and the system using yum

We can see whether there are any updates available for the packages installed on our system by executing the command line, as shown here:

```
$ yum check-update
```

We can also update an installed application and its dependencies to the latest stable version using the `yum` command. In this process, YUM preserves the existing configuration files, except in cases where it is mandatory to update the configuration file for working on an updated version of the application, as shown in command line here:

```
$ yum update httpd
```

We can update our system and installed application together in a single command by not specifying any application name to the `yum update` command, as shown in command line here:

```
$ yum update
```

While updating the system or application, all applications except the kernel are updated immediately at runtime. The latest kernel version comes into effect only after rebooting the system. We can use the `uname -r` command to view the running kernel version.

Managing groups of applications using YUM

In CentOS 7, related packages that serve a common purpose are grouped under one category. We can also install a particular group containing related packages, in place of installing them one by one, as shown in the following examples:

1. Display all the package groups by using the `yum grouplist` command, as shown here:

   ```
   $ yum grouplist
   ```

2. Install a specific package group of related packages by using the `yum groupinstall` command, as shown here:

   ```
   $ yum groupinstall "Development Tools"
   ```

3. Update packages in an existing installed package group by using the `yum groupupdate` command, as shown here:

   ```
   $ yum groupupdate "Administration Tools"
   ```

4. We can also remove an installed group of packages from the system by using the `yum groupremove` command, as shown here:

   ```
   $ yum groupremove "Development Tools"
   ```

We can display information about mandatory, default, and optional packages that are installed or not installed with the group in the system by using the `yum groupinfo` command. The output of this command displays the list of packages in that group, with each package name displayed with a symbol in front of them. The following table lists the symbol and its corresponding meaning, as follows:

Symbol	Meaning
=	Package was installed as part of the group and is presently installed on the system.
+	Package is not installed on the system. It will get installed if the group is installed or updated.
_	Package is not installed on the system and it will not get installed if the group is installed or updated.
No symbol	Package is installed on the system, but it was not installed through the group.

An example of the `yum groupinfo` command to find the information of packages installed with a group is shown in the command line here:

```
$ yum groupinfo "System Administration Tools"
```

Using YUM history

YUM keeps a record of all the past install and remove transactions in a log file that is, `/var/log/yum.log`. An example to display the record of yum transactions kept in a log file is shown in the following screenshot:

```
[root@desktop ~]# tail /var/log/yum.log
Nov 04 06:44:42 Installed: epel-release-7-11.noarch
Nov 04 08:46:06 Erased: epel-release-7-11.noarch
Nov 04 08:47:14 Installed: epel-release-7-11.noarch
Nov 08 16:51:42 Erased: ipa-client-4.5.4-10.el7.centos.3.x86_64
Nov 08 16:51:45 Erased: sssd-1.16.0-19.el7_5.5.x86_64
Nov 08 16:51:46 Erased: sssd-ad-1.16.0-19.el7_5.5.x86_64
Nov 08 16:51:48 Erased: sssd-ipa-1.16.0-19.el7_5.5.x86_64
Nov 08 16:51:50 Erased: 32:bind-utils-9.9.4-61.el7.x86_64
Nov 08 19:45:25 Installed: 32:bind-utils-9.9.4-61.el7.x86_64
Nov 08 19:46:16 Installed: 32:bind-utils-9.9.4-61.el7.x86_64
```

We can display the history of installed and removed packages with the `yum` command, as shown here:

```
[root@desktop ~]# yum history
Loaded plugins: fastestmirror, langpacks
ID     | Login user           | Date and time     | Action(s)    | Altered
-------------------------------------------------------------------------------
    10 | root <root>          | 2018-11-08 19:46  | Install      |     1 <
     9 | root <root>          | 2018-11-08 19:45  | Install      |     1 ><
     8 | root <root>          | 2018-11-08 16:51  | Erase        |     5 ><
     7 | root <root>          | 2018-11-04 08:47  | Install      |     1 >
     6 | root <root>          | 2018-11-04 08:46  | Erase        |     1 <
     5 | root <root>          | 2018-11-04 06:44  | Install      |     1 >
     4 | root <root>          | 2018-10-05 00:38  | Install      |     3
     3 | student <student>    | 2018-08-13 23:06  | I, U         |   179 EE
     2 | student <student>    | 2018-08-13 22:46  | Install      |     1
     1 | System <unset>       | 2018-07-13 19:30  | Install      |  1474
history list
```

We can undo a previous transaction using the `yum history undo` command, as shown here:

```
[root@desktop ~]# yum history undo 9
Loaded plugins: fastestmirror, langpacks
Undoing transaction 9, from Thu Nov  8 19:45:23 2018
    Install bind-utils-32:9.9.4-61.el7.x86_64 @/bind-utils-9.9.4-61.el7.x86_64
Resolving Dependencies
--> Running transaction check
---> Package bind-utils.x86_64 32:9.9.4-61.el7 will be erased
--> Finished Dependency Resolution

Dependencies Resolved

================================================================================
 Package          Arch          Version              Repository          Size
================================================================================
Removing:
 bind-utils       x86_64        32:9.9.4-61.el7      installed           431 k

Transaction Summary
================================================================================
Remove  1 Package
```

Managing application repositories using YUM

To manage application repositories using YUM, do the following:

- Display only all enabled repositories in the system using the `yum repolist` command, as shown here:

  ```
  $ yum repolist
  ```

- Display all available (enabled or disabled) repositories in the system using the `yum repolist all` command, as shown here:

  ```
  $ yum repolist all
  ```

- We can install a package from a specific repository by enabling it for runtime only. It is used to install a package from a specific repository when it exists in more than one repository, as shown in command line here:

  ```
  $ yum --enablerepo=epel install httpd
  ```

- We can permanently enable or disable a repository by using the `yum-config-manager` utility. It makes necessary changes in the file stored in the `/etc/yum.repos.d/` directory, as shown in command line here:

  ```
  $ yum-config-manager  --enable <repo id>
  ```

> The `yum-config-manager` utility can also be used to create a client repo configuration file inside `/etc/yum.repos.d`, as shown in the following command line:
> ```
> $ yum-config-manager        \
>            --addrepo=http://repo.example.com/7/x86_64/
> ```

Handling other miscellaneous options of yum

The YUM utility also provides an interactive shell using the `yum shell` command for performing multiple tasks in one go. To exit from the YUM shell, type `exit` or `quit`, or press *Ctrl + D*. The example in the following screenshot illustrates the usage of the `yum shell` command:

```
[root@desktop yum.repos.d]# yum shell
Loaded plugins: fastestmirror, langpacks
> install lynx
Loading mirror speeds from cached hostfile
 * base: mirrors.fibergrid.in
 * elrepo: mirror-hk.koddos.net
 * epel: mirror.vinahost.vn
 * extras: mirrors.fibergrid.in
 * nux-dextop: mirror.li.nux.ro
 * updates: mirrors.fibergrid.in
> run
--> Running transaction check
---> Package lynx.x86_64 0:2.8.8-0.3.dev15.el7 will be installed
--> Finished Dependency Resolution
```

YUM keeps all the enabled repositories' cached packages and other data in the `/var/cache/yum` directory. Here, YUM creates a subdirectory for each repository. We can clean or empty the cached directory to save space at any time by executing the following command:

```
$ yum clean all
```

We can display the usage information of YUM by using the following command:

```
$ yum help
```

Managing official and third-party repositories

Sometimes, the desired software is not available in the base (official) repositories of CentOS 7. In such scenarios, CentOS 7 and other Linux communities have contributed to several third-party repositories that can be used to install a variety of applications that are not available in official repositories. This section discusses various popular third-party repositories that are available for CentOS 7.

Official repositories of CentOS 7

By default, CentOS 7 provides the base repository, the updates repository, and the extras repository. These repositories are managed by the CentOS community and are sufficient for completing most of the daily operations requirements.

Third-party repositories

These are the repositories that are not managed by the official CentOS community. Sometimes, we need to add them to our YUM database of repositories to download and install certain software, which is not available in CentOS official repositories. However, if these are added, they should be managed separately to prevent any unintended or conflicting updates from them.

The following is a list of certain repositories that have certain additional CentOS packages that are not available in the CentOS base or updates repository:

- **Extra Packages for the Enterprise Linux (EPEL) repository**: This repository is maintained by the Fedora community and is one of the most trusted third-party repositories that can be added in your system. We can add this repository to our system with the following command:

  ```
  $ yum install epel-release -y
  ```

- **Community Enterprise Linux Repository (ELRepo)**: This is an Enterprise Linux repository that provides hardware-related RPM packages. It includes filesystem drivers, graphics, sound, webcam, video, and network drivers, and the latest kernel packages. We can add this repository to our system with the following command:

```
[root@desktop ~]# rpm --import https://www.elrepo.org/RPM-GPG-KEY-elrepo.org
[root@desktop ~]# rpm -Uvh https://www.elrepo.org/elrepo-release-7.0-3.el7.elrepo.noarch.rpm
Retrieving https://www.elrepo.org/elrepo-release-7.0-3.el7.elrepo.noarch.rpm
Preparing...                        ############################### [100%]
Updating / installing...
   1:elrepo-release-7.0-3.el7.elrepo  ############################### [100%]
```

- **Nux-desktop repository**: This repository provides desktop and multimedia-related packages for Enterprise Linux. Some popular multimedia software such as VLC media player, mplayer, and so on are available through this repository. Some of the packages in this repository have some dependencies that are resolved with the EPEL repository. At the same time, it is strongly recommended not to use this repository with RPMForge or the ATRPMS repository as it may lead to conflict between packages and dependencies. Also, RPMForge is a dead project and is not being maintained. We can add the Nux-desktop repository to our system with the following command:

  ```
  $ yum install epel-release
  $ rpm -Uvh \
  http://li.nux.ro/download/nux/dextop/el7/x86_64/nux-dextop-release-
  0-5.el7.nux.noarch.rpm
  ```

- **Remi repository**: This is a third-party repository, mainly famous for providing the latest versions of the PHP stack, MySQL, and related software used in Enterprise Linux. It also requires the EPEL repository to be installed on CentOS before installing it. We can push the remi repository to our system with the following commands:

  ```
  $ yum install epel-release
  $ rpm -Uvh https://rpms.remirepo.net/enterprise/remi-release-7.rpm
  ```

 The remi repository is not enabled by default on installation. To install packages using this repository, we need to first enable it.

- **RPM fusion repository**: This third-party repository offers some free and non-free add-on packages that the Fedora project or Red Hat do not want to share with Enterprise Linux. We can add this repository to our system with the following command:

  ```
  $ rpm -Uvh
  https://download1.rpmfusion.org/free/el/rpmfusion-free-release-7.no
  arch.rpm
  ```

There are many third-party repositories available; some of them are not maintained, whereas some of them have conflicting packages. For more information about repositories, such as which repositories should be avoided and which are recommended, you can go to the following wiki page of CentOS:
https://wiki.centos.org/AdditionalResources/Repositories.

Creating custom repositories

Creating a YUM repository is one of the easiest and best ways to install software or security updates on multiple systems over LAN. We can download all the packages from the internet repository or from the DVD and host them on the local server, which will be known as the YUM server. Other Linux machines on the LAN can be configured to download the required packages from the local YUM server and they will be known as the YUM clients. This saves internet bandwidth, provides offline installation of packages to clients, and speeds up the update process.

In this section, we will create a custom repository of the packages shipped in the CentOS 7 DVD and share this repository to clients using an FTP server, as follows:

1. Mount the media containing the packages. In our case, it will be the CentOS 7 DVD, as shown here:

```
[root@desktop ~]# mount -o loop /dev/sr0 /mnt/
```

2. Install the FTP server package, vsftpd, from the mounted DVD, as shown here:

```
[root@desktop ~]# cd /mnt/Packages/
[root@desktop Packages]# rpm -ivh vsftpd-3.0.2-22.el7.x86_64.rpm
Preparing...
############################### [100%]
Updating / installing...
   1:vsftpd-3.0.2-22.el7
############################### [100%]
```

3. Now, enable the service to start `vsftpd` on boot automatically and start the service, as shown here:

```
[root@desktop Packages]# systemctl enable vsftpd
Created symlink from /etc/systemd/system/multi-user.target.wants/vsftpd
.service to /usr/lib/systemd/system/vsftpd.service.
[root@desktop Packages]# systemctl start vsftpd
```

4. Install the `createrepo` package to create a local repository database. If the internet is connected to our system, we can use YUM to install the `createrepo` package, as shown in command line here:

$ yum install createrepo -y

If you don't have an internet connection, then install the package using the RPM package manager, as shown here:

```
[root@server Packages]# rpm -ivh createrepo-0.9.9-28.el7.noarch.rpm
error: Failed dependencies:
        deltarpm is needed by createrepo-0.9.9-28.el7.noarch
        libxml2-python is needed by createrepo-0.9.9-28.el7.noarch
        python-deltarpm is needed by createrepo-0.9.9-28.el7.noarch
```

We got the preceding error because in our system the `createrepo` package dependencies were not installed. So, we met the dependencies of `createrepo` package. First, install the following packages in the same order that's shown here:

```
[root@server Packages]# rpm -ivh libxml2-python-2.9.1-6.el7_2.3.x86_64.rpm
Preparing...                          ############################### [100%]
Updating / installing...
   1:libxml2-python-2.9.1-6.el7_2.3   ############################### [100%]
[root@server Packages]# rpm -ivh deltarpm-3.6-3.el7.x86_64.rpm
Preparing...                          ############################### [100%]
Updating / installing...
   1:deltarpm-3.6-3.el7               ############################### [100%]
[root@server Packages]# rpm -ivh python-deltarpm-3.6-3.el7.x86_64.rpm
Preparing...                          ############################### [100%]
Updating / installing...
   1:python-deltarpm-3.6-3.el7        ############################### [100%]
[root@server Packages]# rpm -ivh createrepo-0.9.9-28.el7.noarch.rpm
Preparing...                          ############################### [100%]
Updating / installing...
   1:createrepo-0.9.9-28.el7          ############################### [100%]
```

5. Store the packages in the `ftp` folder to build the local repository, as shown here:

```
[root@server Packages]# mkdir /var/ftp/pub/myrepo/
[root@server Packages]# cp -ar /mnt/Packages/*.* /var/ftp/pub/myrepo/
[root@server Packages]# createrepo -v /var/ftp/pub/|
```

6. Restore the SELinux tag on packages copied from the DVD, as per the `vsftpd` server files, as shown here:

```
[root@server Packages]# restorecon -Rvv /var/ftp/pub/|
```

7. Create a YUM server configuration file with the `.repo` extension in the `/etc/yum.repos.d/` directory, as shown in command line here:

   $ vim /etc/yum.repos.d/localserver.repo

   The content of the `localserver.repo` file is shown here:

```
[localserver]
name=CentOS 7 Local Server
baseurl=ftp://192.168.56.100/pub/
enabled=1
gpgcheck=0
```

8. Enable the local YUM server repository and clean the yum cache by using the `yum` command, as shown here:

   $ yum clean all

   After cleaning the previous cache of the YUM database, build the YUM database of the repository from scratch with the command that's shown here:

```
[root@server Packages]# yum repolist
Loaded plugins: fastestmirror
Loading mirror speeds from cached hostfile
 * base: mirrors.fibergrid.in
 * epel: mirrors.tuna.tsinghua.edu.cn
 * extras: mirrors.fibergrid.in
 * updates: mirrors.fibergrid.in
repo id            repo name                                      status
base/7/x86_64      CentOS-7 - Base                                 9,911
*epel/x86_64       Extra Packages for Enterprise Linux 7 - x86_64 12,742
extras/7/x86_64    CentOS-7 - Extras                                 432
localserver        CentOS 7 Local Server                           3,971
updates/7/x86_64   CentOS-7 - Updates                              1,614
repolist: 28,670
```

You can use any other application such as a web server or an NFS server for sharing the packages of the YUM server (system serving the packages) to the YUM client (system downloading the packages). We also need to open the corresponding application port in the firewall to allow access for YUM clients for downloading packages from the YUM server.

Summary

In this chapter, we began with learning methods to keep your system and application software up to date. We learned how package management utilities such as RPM and YUM are used to install, remove, or update application packages. We had a look at different third-party repositories for CentOS 7. Finally, we wrapped up this chapter by creating or own custom repository and making it available for clients. Keeping your system and applications updated is vital to make sure they are free from any vulnerabilities. This helps in securing your information and making the system safe from malware and hackers.

In our next chapter, we will learn some of the essential utilities of CentOS 7. We will see how system logging works and how you can manage system services. Then, we will understand the functionality of the firewall and SELinux for hardening system security.

Overview of Essential Advance Utilities

9

In this chapter, we will learn some advanced and essential concepts related to the system, such as logging, controlling system services, firewalls, and **Security Enhanced Linux** (**SELinux**). Logging plays a key role in debugging and troubleshooting system applications. A solid understanding of logging will make your daily operations easier to handle and will also give you a deep insight into the application's functioning.

In this final chapter, we will learn the different logging mechanisms available in CentOS 7, such as journald and rsyslog. By now, you have seen how to install, update, and remove applications. Now, we will see how to control these applications and system services using the systemd and systemctl utilities. Finally, we will understand the basic usage of firewalld and SELinux to secure running services and harden the security of the system.

We will cover the following:

- Understanding system logging
- Working with rsyslogd and journald
- Understanding control of systems and services
- Working with systemd and systemctl
- Understanding SELinux concepts
- Working with SELinux
- Understanding firewall concepts in CentOS 7
- Working with firewalld

Understanding system logging

Most application programs and the kernel write their event information in log files maintained at different locations. It helps in keeping track of activities that are taking place on the system and also forms an essential part of system auditing. Monitoring of log files helps in spotting any unusual activity in the system. Logging also helps in troubleshooting any application problems. By convention, Linux uses the `/var/log/` directory for storing logs in the system.

Starting with CentOS 7, we have two logging services that exist in the system:

- Rsyslog service
- Systemd-journald service

> System time service should be properly configured before configuring log services, as time is an important component of log files.

Working with rsyslog

The rsyslog service centrally collects the log messages from different applications running in the Linux system. It collects the logs based on their type and their priorities, and stores them persistently in the `/var/logfollows:/` directory.

The following table lists some important log files maintained by rsyslog, along with their description:

Log file path	Description
`/var/log/messages`	Most standard log messages are stored here, except authentication logs, email logs, and some application debugging logs.
`/var/log/secure`	Authentication logs containing errors and other messages are stored here.
`/var/log/maillog`	Mail server logs are stored here.
`/var/log/boot.log`	Boot/system startup messages are logged here.
`/var/log/cron`	It stores cron job (scheduler) logs.
`/var/log/wtmp`	Login activity logs are kept here.
`/var/log/dmesg`	Kernel messages are stored here.
`/var/log/cups`	Printing service logs are stored here.

`/var/log/samba`	Samba service logs are kept here, not managed by rsyslog. The Samba service directly writes logs here.
`/var/log/httpd`	This directory contains Apache web server logs, not managed by rsyslog. Apache directly writes logs in these files.
`/var/log/audit/`	Contains the `auditd` service logs and SELinux log files.

 Rsyslogd is an application in Linux systems, based on the syslog project that started in 1980. It uses syslog protocol to log events in the system with certain extended features, such as the RELP protocol and buffered operation support. Sometimes, syslog is also used in the context of rsyslog in Linux.

Configuring rsyslogd sections

The rsyslogd service is used by most of the applications running in Linux for logging events. The rsyslogd service uses three main components for handling the log messages of various applications in the system:

- **Facility**: It represents the type of process
- **Priority or severity**: It represents the severity of the message
- **Destination/location**: It describes the location where the log messages are sent to or logged

The configuration file for the rsyslogd service is stored in two locations:

- In the main configuration file, `/etc/rsyslog.conf`
- In the files stored with `.conf` extensions inside the `/etc/rsyslog.d/` directory

The main configuration file, `/etc/rsyslog.conf`, contains the information on what is to be logged and where it should be stored. It is divided into three different sections displayed in capital letters, as shown:

- `#### MODULES ####`: The modules section is used to configure advanced features of rsyslogd.

- `#### GLOBAL DIRECTIVES ####`: The global directives section is used to specify globally configurable parameters.

- `#### RULES ####`: It is the most important section, and contains the rules to specify what is to be logged and where it is to be logged. We will discuss this more in the *Rsyslogd rules* section of this chapter.

Documentation for rsyslog can be accessed from the `man` command as follows:

```
# man 5 rsyslog.conf
```

Rsyslogd facilities and priorities

Facilities represent the fixed list of internal system processes that produce the log messages.

The following table lists the common facilities keywords that are available in CentOS 7 and their descriptions:

Facility	Description
`auth` or `authpriv`	It represents authentication-related subsystem messages such as login
`cron`	It represents the crond service and any scheduled application messages
`daemon`	Generic name used to represent the various daemon subsystem messages
`kern`	It represents kernel messages
`lpr`	It represents legacy print service messages
`mail`	It represents all mail program messages
`mark`	It is for internal use and not to be used with any application
`news`	It represents the messages generated by NNTP
`security`	Same as `authpriv` and not used anymore
`syslog`	It represents the messages of the syslog daemon
`user`	It represents the messages generated by the user space
`uucp`	It represents the messages generated by the UUCP subsystem
`local0-local7`	It represents the custom unused facilities provided by the system to the user for sending messages generated by user defined services
`*`	It matches all the facilities

Priorities represent the severity or priority of messages that are logged for any service. There are different priority levels that can be used to determine the type of event that can be logged, such as `debug`, `info`, `emerg`, `alert`, and so on, for the specified service.

The following table lists the severity/priority levels with their description and assigned number for priority:

Assigned number	Priority	Severity description
0	emerg	Generates message when system is unusable
1	alert	Action must be taken immediately, available service is about to be discontinued
2	crit	Generates message when critical condition occurs
3	err	Non-critical error condition
4	warning	Warning condition
5	notice	Informational message for event that needs attention to prevent future issues
6	info	Generates informational messages for normal service operation
7	debug	Debugging-level messages for service operation

If the wild card * is specified in the priority field, then it represents all types of severity (messages). If none is written in the severity field, then it means none of the messages of the corresponding facility will be added in the specified log files. The none is used to prevent logging of same message in different log files, as shown in the following diagram:

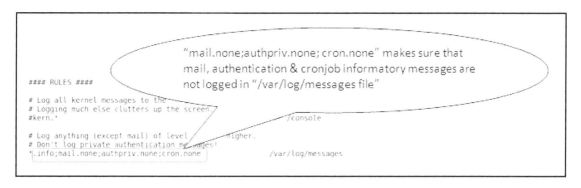

Rsyslogd rules

The ####RULES#### section of /etc/rsyslog.conf contains directives to define the logging of messages. The syntax of the directive used in /etc/rsyslog.conf file is as follows:

`facility.priority`   `destination`

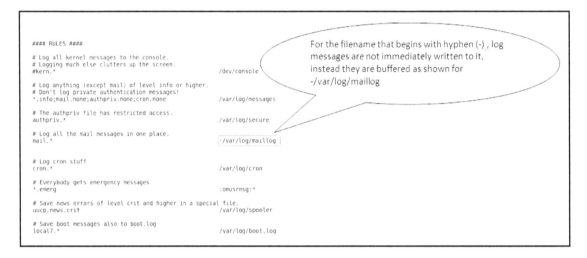

The following are examples that illustrate the usage of directives defined in the /etc/rsyslog.conf file for logging of messages:

- To log all information messages of the kernel, we can specify a different log file as follows:

```
$ vi /etc/rsyslog.conf
kern.info /var/log/kernel
```

- We create a debug.log file in the /var/log/ directory to collect debugging priority messages from all services as shown in the following command line:

```
$ vi /etc/rsyslog.conf
*.debug /var/log/debug.log
```

- After making the required changes in the /etc/rsyslog.conf file, restart the rsyslog service to bring changes into effect as shown in the following command line:

```
$ systemctl restart rsyslog
```

After making the preceding changes, the debugging messages will not appear in the `/var/log/messages` file.

Log file rotation

Log rotation prevents the filling up of the `/var/log` directory. Old log files are renamed with `filename-datestamp` on rotation. The `datestamp` indicates the date on which it was rotated (archived) as shown in the following table:

Existing log	Archived log
`/var/log/messages`	`/var/log/messages-20180530` (rotated on May 30, 2018)

Logrotate is the utility that takes care of rotating the log files periodically. A cron job is run nightly with the script named `/etc/cron.daily/logrotate` for log rotation. The rotation of log files is carried out as per the configuration of log rotation program stored in the following two locations:

- `/etc/logrotate.conf`
- `/etc/logrotate.d/*` (any file inside this directory)

Most log files are rotated weekly; however, the `logrotate` command rotates some logs faster or slower or on certain conditions, such as on reaching a certain size.

After rotation of logs, the log watch program discards the old archive of log files to conserve disk space (typically 4 weeks or after a certain number of rotations). A new log file is created during rotation and the service is notified. On installation of a new application, the application adds its log file to `logrotate` management by dropping its logging configuration file inside the `/etc/logrotate.d/` directory.

An example of creating a custom log file is as follows:

```
# vi / etc/logrotate.d/<application_name>
/var/log/path_to_log_file {
rotate 3
size 2M
monthly
postrotate
/bin/systemctl reload httpd
endscript
}
```

These are the important commands used in the `log rotation` file:

- `rotate 3`: Keeps the last three versions of the file and deletes the oldest
- `size 2M`: Rotates the log file on reaching 2 MB in size
- `monthly`: It is another alternative to size; if size has not reached 2 MB, then rotate the file on a monthly basis

Analyzing syslog entries

The system logs generated by the rsyslogd service are stored in the `/var/log/` directory in various files. The oldest message is kept at the top of the log and new log entries are appended at the bottom of the log file in a standard format, as shown in the following diagram:

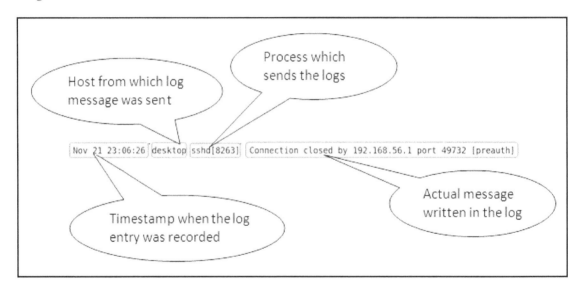

Monitoring live log file traffic using the tail command

While performing troubleshooting, it is required to view the logs being generated by an application when it is being run. Using the `tail` command with the `-f` option does this. In one Terminal, we will execute the application we want to troubleshoot, and in another Terminal, we will execute the `tail` command as shown in the following:

```
# tail -f </path_of_log_file>
```

It displays the 10 lines from the bottom of the filename specified, and keeps the file open to view the new lines that are being written to it. Once we are done viewing logs, we can close the log file by pressing *Ctrl + C*.

For example, to monitor the failed login attempts on the system, on one Terminal, open /var/log/secure, and in another Terminal, execute the ssh command on the same system as shown in the following screenshot:

```
┌─shiwang@debian ~
└→  ssh root@192.168.56.100                                                                    255 ↵
root@192.168.56.100's password:
Last login: Thu Nov 22 06:21:21 2018 from 192.168.56.1
[root@desktop ~]#

⊞                                        root@desktop:~ 111x15
[root@desktop ~]#
[root@desktop ~]# tail -f /var/log/secure
Nov 22 06:19:29 desktop sshd[5076]: Disconnected from 192.168.56.1 port 48066
Nov 22 06:19:29 desktop sshd[5076]: pam_unix(sshd:session): session closed for user root
Nov 22 06:20:13 desktop sshd[14057]: Accepted password for root from 192.168.56.1 port 59266 ssh2
Nov 22 06:20:14 desktop sshd[14057]: pam_unix(sshd:session): session opened for user root by (uid=0)
Nov 22 06:21:21 desktop sshd[14141]: Accepted password for root from 192.168.56.1 port 59268 ssh2
Nov 22 06:21:21 desktop sshd[14141]: pam_unix(sshd:session): session opened for user root by (uid=0)
Nov 22 06:23:21 desktop sshd[14208]: Connection closed by 192.168.56.100 port 40318 [preauth]
Nov 22 06:23:34 desktop sshd[14057]: Received disconnect from 192.168.56.1 port 59266:11: disconnected by user
Nov 22 06:23:34 desktop sshd[14057]: Disconnected from 192.168.56.1 port 59266
Nov 22 06:23:34 desktop sshd[14057]: pam_unix(sshd:session): session closed for user root
Nov 22 06:24:10 desktop sshd[14224]: Accepted password for root from 192.168.56.1 port 59274 ssh2
Nov 22 06:24:10 desktop sshd[14224]: pam_unix(sshd:session): session opened for user root by (uid=0)
```

Using the logger command

Although most applications are configured to write logs in the log file automatically, we can use the logger command to write messages to rsyslogd also. The logger command writes the log messages in the log file as per the facility and priority specified with the logger command. By default, it sends the logs to the facility named as user with priority named as notice (user.notice). The logger command can be used inside a shell script to create logs, as shown in the following examples:

- If we send a log message of information priority to the rsyslog program, then it will get stored in the /var/log/boot.log file as shown in the following command line:

    # **logger -p local7.info "Sample log entry using logger command"**

- We can send any log message to the default log file, /var/log/messages, by using logger command as shown in the following command line:

    # **logger "Log file entry using logger"**

For more information on logging, refer to the man pages of the `logger`, `tail`, `rsyslog.conf`, and `logrotate` commands.

Working with systemd-journald

This daemon provides a non-persistent method of advanced log management for collecting and displaying messages from the kernel, boot programs, and other services running in CentOS 7. The journald stores these messages in a journal maintained in binary format, which can be accessed using the `journalctl` command. The default behavior of the journal is non-persistent across reboot. It forwards the messages to rsyslogd for permanent central storage and processing.

Finding events with the journalctl command

In CentOS 7, the `systemd-journal` is stored in the `/run/log/journal/` directory, as shown in the following screenshot:

```
[root@desktop ~]# ls /run/log/journal/   -l
total 0
drwxr-s---+ 2 root systemd-journal 60 Nov 21 15:58 99e36987a88341d2af68ee2124f9ba6c
```

When we execute the `journalctl` command as root without any options, then it shows the full system journal, from the oldest log entry to the latest as shown in the following command line:

```
# journalctl
```

The `journalctl` command uses color coding to highlight the severity of messages, as shown in the following table:

Priority	Description of text highlighting used in logs
`Error`, `crit`, `alert` or `emerg`	Text is red
`Notice` or `warning`	Text is bold
`Info` or `debug`	Regular text

Different options are used with the `journalctl` command to limit the searches of the journal to the desired output:

- `Journalctl -n`: By default, using the `-n` option with `journalctl` will display the last 10 log entries. We can also specify the number of log entries to be displayed in the output as shown in the following screenshot:

```
[root@desktop ~]# logger -p user.crit "Testing log"
[root@desktop ~]# journalctl -n 5
-- Logs begin at Wed 2018-11-21 15:58:52 IST, end at Thu 2018-11-22 06:52:57 IST. --
Nov 22 06:47:31 desktop.example.com nm-dispatcher[14604]: req:1 'dhcp4-change' [enp0s3]: start running ordered
Nov 22 06:50:01 desktop.example.com systemd[1]: Started Session 112 of user root.
Nov 22 06:50:01 desktop.example.com systemd[1]: Starting Session 112 of user root.
Nov 22 06:50:01 desktop.example.com CROND[14654]: (root) CMD (/usr/lib64/sa/sa1 1 1)
Nov 22 06:52:57 desktop.example.com root[14680]: Testing log
lines 1-6/6 (END)
```

- `Journalctl -p`: We can filter the output of the journal by specifying the priority of the log entries using the `-p` option. We can specify either name or number of the priority level to display the log entries of the specified or higher-level priority, as shown in the following screenshot:

```
[root@desktop ~]# journalctl -p err
-- Logs begin at Wed 2018-11-21 15:58:52 IST, end at Thu 2018-11-22 06:58:39 IST. --
Nov 21 15:59:49 desktop.example.com spice-vdagent[1540]: Cannot access vdagent virtio channel /dev/virtio-ports
Nov 22 06:41:32 desktop.example.com root[14547]: Testing log
Nov 22 06:52:57 desktop.example.com root[14680]: Testing log
Nov 22 06:58:39 desktop.example.com root[14758]: Alert type of testing log made using logger
lines 1-5/5 (END)
```

- `Journalctl -f`: The `-f` option is similar to the `-f` option used with the `tail` command; it displays the last 10 lines of the journal and keeps it open to display the new entries as they are written in the journal, until you press *Ctrl + C* as shown in the following screenshot:

```
[root@desktop ~]# journalctl -f
-- Logs begin at Wed 2018-11-21 15:58:52 IST. --
Nov 22 06:57:29 desktop.example.com nm-dispatcher[14728]: req:1 'dhcp4-change' [enp0s3]: start running ordered
scripts...
Nov 22 06:58:39 desktop.example.com root[14758]: Alert type of testing log made using logger
Nov 22 07:00:01 desktop.example.com systemd[1]: Started Session 113 of user root.
Nov 22 07:00:01 desktop.example.com systemd[1]: Starting Session 113 of user root.
Nov 22 07:00:01 desktop.example.com CROND[14782]: (root) CMD (/usr/lib64/sa/sa1 1 1)
Nov 22 07:01:01 desktop.example.com systemd[1]: Started Session 114 of user root.
Nov 22 07:01:01 desktop.example.com systemd[1]: Starting Session 114 of user root.
Nov 22 07:01:01 desktop.example.com CROND[14809]: (root) CMD (run-parts /etc/cron.hourly)
Nov 22 07:01:01 desktop.example.com run-parts(/etc/cron.hourly)[14813]: starting 0anacron
Nov 22 07:01:01 desktop.example.com run-parts(/etc/cron.hourly)[14820]: finished 0anacron
```

Limiting journalctl output to a specific time: The `journalctl` command can be used to with two more options, `--since` and `--untill`, to specify a time range and display the log messages of that duration. The following `journalctl` query shows all logs recorded between `18:05:00` and `18:10:00`:

```
# journalctl --since 18:05:00 --until 18:10:00
```

We can use the `journalctl` command to display today's journal entries only as shown in the following command line:

```
# journalctl --since today
```

We can also use the `journalctl` command to display extra fields attached to the log entries by enabling the verbose output on the journal as shown in the following command line:

```
# journalctl -o verbose
```

The following table lists some of the important fields of the `journalctl` command that are used to filter the query:

Field name	Description
_COMM	It filters the journal based on the name of the command
_EXE	It is used to filter the query based on the path of the executable for the process
_PID	It filters the journal based on the PID of the process
_UID	It filters the journal based on the UID of the user running the process
_SYSTEMD_UNIT	It filters the journal based on the systemd unit that started the process

For example, for listing the journal messages that originated from a systemd process with PID 1 can be filtered using the following command:

```
# journalctl _PID=1
```

The `journalctl` command can also be used to list all the journal messages send by the `sshd` service, as shown in the following command line:

```
# journalctl _SYSTEMD_UNIT=sshd.service
```

The `journalctl` command can also be used to view the journal log messages since last boot as shown in the following command line:

```
# journalctl -b
```

Configuring systemd-journald to store logs persistently

systemd-journal is stored in the /run/log/journal directory, which is cleared on system reboot. Its configuration file is /etc/systemd/journald.conf, which can be used to fine-tune journal parameters such as the amount of filesystem to be used for storing the journal (default value is 10%).

systemd-journal is configured in such a way that if the /var/log/journal/ directory exists in the system, then it logs journal entries in that directory instead of /run/log/journal/. The same concept is used to made systemd-journal storage persistent across reboot. The following steps are to be taken to make systemd-journal persistent:

1. Create the /var/log/journal/ directory as root user as shown in the following command line:

   ```
   # mkdir /var/log/journal
   ```

2. Make the owner of the directory created as root and group as systemd-journal with permissions 2755 as shown in the following command line:

   ```
   # chown root:systemd-journal /var/log/journal
   # chmod 2755 /var/log/journal
   ```

3. Reboot your system or send the USR1 signal to systemd-journald as shown in the following command line:

   ```
   # killall -USR1 systemd-journald
   ```

4. Make sure systemd-journal is persistent after reboot by listing a new directory containing journal log files inside the /var/log/journal directory as shown in following command line:

   ```
   # ls /var/log/journal
   ```

Understanding how to control the system and services

From a user or system administrator point of view, it is essential to understand how to manage various services installed on your system. A user should be able to enable a service at boot time and start or stop it when required.

Earlier, the Linux system and services were managed by SysV init or BSD init. Later on, their management was further improvised by adding utilities such as service and chkconfig, in addition to shell scripts. More recently, starting with CentOS 7, system and service management is now done with systemd. Systemd has replaced initd as the first process of CentOS 7.

In the next section, you will learn how to manage services running on your system. You will learn how to use systemd and its components, responsible for switching the system from the kernel space to the user space and managing system processes thereafter.

Defining essential terms

This section we will define the essential terms related to system and services management.

What is a daemon?

A daemon is a process that waits or runs in the background, executing several tasks. It listens for connections using a network socket.

What is a socket?

When a client connection is established, a socket is created and passed by systemd to a daemon or it creates a daemon for itself. In Linux, sockets are used mainly to establish client communication with the daemon.

What is systemd?

From CentOS 7 onward, systemd has replaced the init process as the first process (PID=1) that is started by the kernel when Linux boots up. It manages the system and services in the system for the Linux kernel by providing an interface between applications and the kernel. After starting systemd, it starts logging activities, mounting the filesystem and devices, starts other services, and finally provides the user with a login shell. These tasks are carried out by systemd with the help of different libraries and utilities such as `systemctl`, `journalctl`, `hostenamectl`, `localectl`, `timedatectl`, `systemd-cgls`, and so on, which it installs with itself. It manages the various system resources through objects known as units.

What are units?

In systemd, units are objects that systemd knows how to manage and operate. They represent different system resources and they are defined using configuration files called unit files. These unit files are are kept in the `/usr/lib/systemd/system/` directory by default. Only those units whose unit files are stored in the `/lib/systemd/system` directory can be started or stopped during a session. These files are installed in the system by the application's RPM files. Units are the replacement of old init scripts that were used before CentOS 7.

What is systemctl?

It is a replacement for the service and `chkconfig` command in CentOS 7. The `systemctl` command is used to manage the different types of systemd objects (units). Systemd has 12 unit types, which can be listed with the command shown in the following screenshot:

```
[root@desktop ~]# systemctl -t help
Available unit types:
service
socket
busname
target
snapshot
device
mount
automount
swap
timer
path
slice
scope
```

The following table lists some popular units and their descriptions:

Unit types	Description
Service	These types of units have a `.service` extension and represent the system services. This unit is used to start daemons such as the web server. If no unit name is specified with `systemctl`, then the service is assumed as the default unit.
Socket	These types of units have a `.socket` extension and represent **inter-process communication (IPC)** sockets.
Path	These type of units have a `.path` extension and are used to delay the activation of a service until a specific filesystem change occurs.

Target	These types of units have a `.target` extension and represent a group of units.
Slice	These types of units have a `.slice` extension and they represent a management unit of processes.

Working with systemd and systemctl

This section describes how systemd and systemctl are organized and how important objects (units) are managed using systemd.

Viewing states of service with systemctl

The service unit is one of the most important units of `systemd`, which is managed using `systemctl`. If no unit type is specified, `systemctl` shows the status of the service unit, if it exists. The following is the syntax to view any unit:

```
# systemctl     status     name.type
```

Here, name is the service name and type is the unit type, such as service, socket, path, and so on. The example in the following screenshot illustrates the usage of the `systemctl` command for viewing the status of a service:

```
[root@desktop ~]# systemctl status sshd.service
  sshd.service - OpenSSH server daemon
   Loaded: loaded (/usr/lib/systemd/system/sshd.service; enabled; vendor preset: enabled)
   Active: active (running) since Wed 2018-11-21 15:59:25 IST; 1 day 13h ago
     Docs: man:sshd(8)
           man:sshd_config(5)
 Main PID: 962 (sshd)
    Tasks: 1
   CGroup: /system.slice/sshd.service
           └─962 /usr/sbin/sshd -D
```

Keyword to describing the state of service. It can be loaded, active, inactive, enabled, disabled or static

```
Nov 21 23:06:20 desktop.example.com sshd[8263]: pam_succeed_if(sshd:...
Nov 21 23:06:22 desktop.example.com sshd[8263]: Failed password for ...
Nov 21 23:06:25 desktop.example.com sshd[8263]: pam_succeed_if(sshd:...
Nov 21 23:06:26 desktop.example.com sshd[8263]: Failed password for ...
Nov 21 23:06:26 desktop.example.com sshd[8263]: Connection closed by...
Nov 21 23:06:26 desktop.example.com sshd[8263]: PAM 2 more authentic...
Nov 22 06:20:13 desktop.example.com sshd[14057]: Accepted password f...
Nov 22 06:21:21 desktop.example.com sshd[14141]: Accepted password f...
Nov 22 06:24:10 desktop.example.com sshd[14224]: Accepted password f...
Nov 23 02:43:21 desktop.example.com sshd[30483]: Accepted password f...
Hint: Some lines were ellipsized, use -l to show in full.
```

The following table lists the various statuses of services, along with their descriptions:

Status	Description
Loaded	Unit configuration file is processed successfully
Active (running)	Running with one or more active processes
Active (exited)	Successfully completed a one-time configuration
Active (waiting)	Running and waiting for an event to take place
Inactive	Not running currently
Enabled	Will get started at boot time
Disabled	Will not get started at boot time
Static	Cannot be enabled directly, but may be started by another enabled unit automatically

Viewing unit files with systemctl

As a system administrator or user, sometimes it is necessary to find out the current status of systemd unit files. This helps in fine-tuning of system. We can configure services to be in active and loaded state or in an inactive state after booting of system, using the systemctl command.

The following table lists the commands used to view the unit files and their descriptions:

Command	Description
# systemctl	Displays the state of all the different units that are active and loaded on startup
# systemctl --type=service or # systemctl list-units --type=service	Displays the state of only service units that are active
# systemctl --type=service –all or # systemctl list-units --type=service --all	Displays the state of all service units loaded, whether active or inactive
# systemctl --failed --type=service	Displays all services that failed
# systemctl is-active sshd	Displays whether the particular service is currently active or not
# systemctl is-enabled sshd	Displays whether the particular service in enabled to start at boot time or not
# systemctl list-unit-files --type=service	Displays the enabled, disabled, or static settings of all units of the specified type
# systemctl status sshd.servisystemctlce -l	Displays detailed status information about the specified service

Unit dependencies and unit file structure

Services are started as standalone, or sometimes as dependencies of other services. For example, let's assume a socket unit is enabled, but the service unit with the same socket name is not, then the service will automatically get started when a request is made on the network socket. Similarly, the service can also be triggered by the path unit when a filesystem path condition is met. The following command is used to list the dependency tree of the specified unit:

```
# systemctl list-dependencies sshd
```

Starting with CentOS 7, `systemd` provides a uniform interface to start unit files from their storage loaction. The locations of the unit file stored in the system are as follows:

- `/usr/lib/systemd/system/`: It contains system default unit files
- `/etc/systemd/system`: It contains system-specific parameters to modify the default behavior of systemd
- `/run/systemd/system/`: It contains the runtime configuration of unit files

The structure of a unit file is shown in the following screenshot:

```
[root@desktop ~]# cat /usr/lib/systemd/system/vsftpd.service
[Unit]
Description=Vsftpd ftp daemon
After=network.target

[Service]
Type=forking
ExecStart=/usr/sbin/vsftpd /etc/vsftpd/vsftpd.conf

[Install]
WantedBy=multi-user.target
```

The preceding unit file can be broken down into following three sections:

- **Unit**: This section describe the unit type and its dependencies, if any. It also contains the `After` statement and the `Before` statement. These statements define the dependencies of the unit. The `Before` statement says that this unit should be started before the specified unit. The `After` statement says that this unit should be started after starting the specified units.
- **Service**: This section contains a description of how to start and stop the service. The line beginning with the `ExecStart` parameter describes how to start the unit and the line beginning with the `ExecStop` parameter describes how to stop the unit.

- **Install**: This section contains a line beginning with the `WantedBy` parameter, which states the target of this application. Target units are the equivalent of runlevels, which we had in CentOS 6 and earlier versions.

Managing daemons using systemctl

Services can be started at boot time by creating a link to the unit files in the systemd configuration directory using the `systemctl` command. Earlier enabling of a service to start it automatically at boot time was managed using `chkconfig`. An example to illustrate the usage of `systemctl` command to disable or enable a unit file is shown in the following diagram:

```
[root@desktop ~]# systemctl disable sshd
Removed symlink /etc/systemd/system/multi-user.target.wants/sshd.service.
[root@desktop ~]# systemctl enable sshd
Created symlink from /etc/systemd/system/multi-user.target.wants/sshd.service to /usr/lib/systemd/system/sshd.service.
[root@desktop ~]# systemctl is-enabled sshd
enabled
```

Masking services

To prevent conflict between similar types of services that perform a certain function, masking is used. For example, for a firewall, CentOS 7 has both `iptables` and `firewalld` services; however, it is recommended to use only one at a time. Hence, one of the two firewall services is masked to prevent conflict between the two services. Masks prevent the accidental startup of a service by creating a `symlink` of the service file to `/dev/null` as shown in the following screenshot:

```
[root@desktop ~]# systemctl mask chronyd
Created symlink from /etc/systemd/system/chronyd.service to /dev/null.
[root@desktop ~]# systemctl unmask chronyd
Removed symlink /etc/systemd/system/chronyd.service.
```

If a service is disabled, it will not get started automatically at boot even by other unit files; however, a user can still start that service manually. A mask service has the advantage here, as it cannot be started manually or automatically.

The following table lists the different `systemctl` commands used to manage a service:

Command	Description
`# systemctl status <unit>`	Displays detailed information of unit state
`# systemctl stop <unit>`	Stops the running service
`# systemctl start <unit>`	Starts the stopped service
`# systemctl restart <unit>`	Restarts (stop and then start) a service
`# systemctl reload <unit>`	Reloads configuration of a running service by rereading its config file
`# systemctl mask <unit>`	Completely disables a service from starting at boot time automatically, or manually any time
`# systemctl unmask <unit>`	Unmasks a masked service, making it available for the user to enable it or start manually
`# systemctl enable <unit>`	Sets the service to start automatically at boot time
`# systemctl disable <unit>`	Disables a service from starting automatically at boot time
`# systemctl poweroff`	Shuts down the system
`# systemctl reboot`	Restarts the system

Controlling the boot process using systemd

During the boot process, when the kernel image and initramfs image get loaded, initramfs starts the first process on the system, which is systemd with the process ID 1. This systemd process further takes over control in the final stages of system booting and performs the following operations:

- Reads the configuration files from the `/etc/systemd/` directory
- Reads the files linked by `/etc/systemd/system/default.target`
- Executes the `/etc/rc.local file`

Systemd target units are responsible for determining and starting the services automatically on the system after booting up. In this section, we will learn how to control the execution of a set of services on startup. These services will collectively define the state of our system such as it is in single user mode or multi-user mode with networking enabled, and so on.

What are systemd targets?

Target units are used for grouping and ordering other units. `systemd` manages starting several related process at the same time with the help of target units. Some targets, such as `multi-user.target`, define a specific state of the system and can be considered as more robust and flexible equivalents of SysV runlevels. At the same time, other targets do not offer any additional functionality except grouping units to manage dependencies effectively. The target unit configuration files are stored in the `/usr/lib/systemd/system` directory.

The following table lists important targets, along with their equivalent runlevels and their descriptions:

Equivalent runlevel	Target unit	Description
0	`poweroff.target`	Shuts down and powers off the system
1	`rescue.target`	Sulogin prompt with basic system initialization
2, 3, 4	`multi-user.target`	Non-graphical multi-user text-based login only
5	`Graphical.target`	Graphical multi-user and text-based login
6	`Reboot.target`	Shuts down and reboots system

Some targets are part of another target: `graphical.target` includes `multi-user.target`, which in its turn depends on `basic.target` and others. We can view these dependencies from the command line by executing the command line shown in the following screenshot:

```
[root@desktop ~]# systemctl list-dependencies graphical.target   | grep target
graphical.target
● └─multi-user.target
●   ├─basic.target
●   │ ├─selinux-policy-migrate-local-changes@targeted.service
●   │ ├─paths.target
●   │ ├─slices.target
●   │ ├─sockets.target
●   │ ├─sysinit.target
●   │ │ ├─cryptsetup.target
●   │ │ ├─local-fs.target
●   │ │ └─swap.target
●   │ └─timers.target
●   ├─getty.target
●   ├─nfs-client.target
●   │ └─remote-fs-pre.target
●   └─remote-fs.target
●     └─nfs-client.target
●       └─remote-fs-pre.target
```

We can view the available targets that are currently loaded on the running system by using the following command line:

```
# systemctl list-units --type=target --all
```

We can view all the targets that are installed on the system by using the following command line:

```
# systemctl list-unit-files --type=target --all
```

Switching your targets at runtime

In CentOS 7, an administrator can switch to different target (runlevel) at runtime by using the `systemctl isolate` command, which was done using the `telinit` command in CentOS 6. We can only isolate to those targets that have `AllowIsolate=yes` set in their unit files. For example, we can switch to `multi-user.target` from `graphical.target` with the following command:

```
# systemctl isolate multi-user.target
```

The preceding command will bring the user to runlevel 3. To switch back to runlevel 5, execute the following command:

```
# systemctl isolate graphical.target
```

Changing the default target of the system

During the booting up of the system, systemd activates `default.target`, which is generally a symbolic link in the `/etc/systemd/system/` directory to either `graphical.target` or `multi-user.target`. It is equivalent to the default runlevel, which the system administrator used to set in the `/etc/inittab` file.

The following table lists the `systemctl` commands that are used to manage default targets along with their description:

Command	Description
`# systemctl get-default`	Views the existing default target
`# systemctl set-default graphical.target`	Sets the default target to `graphical.target` (graphical shell)
`# systemctl set-default multi-user.target`	Sets the default target to `multi-user.target` (text-based shell)

An example to change the default target by using the `systemctl` command is shown in the following screenshot:

```
[root@desktop ~]# systemctl get-default
graphical.target
[root@desktop ~]# systemctl set-default multi-user.target
Removed symlink /etc/systemd/system/default.target.
Created symlink from /etc/systemd/system/default.target to /usr/lib/systemd/system/multi-user.target.
```

Understanding SELinux concepts

SELinux is an additional layer of security to protect the system. The permission set by users manually is a kind of security control that works at the user's discretion, while SELinux is a mandatory access control for securing the system. Its main role is to protect data when a system service is compromised. SELinux consists of a set of security rules that determine which process can access which files, directories, or ports.

SELinux contexts

When SELinux is enforced in the system, it check for rules on which process can access which files, directories, and ports. Every file, process, directory, and port has a special security label known as an SELinux context, which is a name used to determine whether a process can access a file, directory, or port. By default, the policy does not allow any interaction unless an explicit rule grants access.

SELinux labels have different contexts: user, role, type, and sensitivity. The targeted policy is the default policy enabled in CentOS 7, which defines its rules based on the third context, which is the type context. Type context names generally end with _t.

Viewing SELinux context

Most of the Linux commands have the -z option to display SELinux contexts. For example, `ps`, `ls`, `cp`, and `mkdir` all use the -z option to display or set SELinux contexts of a file, directory, process, or port.

The following are examples that illustrate the usage of -Z option with several commands for displaying the SELinux context:

- The `ps` command can be used to view processes along with their SELinux contexts:

    # **ps axZ**

- The `ps` command can also be used with option `-ZC`, to view the SELinux context of a process specified as an argument as shown in the following example:

    # **ps -ZC sleep**

- The `ls` command can be used with `-Z` option to view the SELinux context of files in a directory as shown in the following command line:

    # **ls -Z /home**
    # **ls -Z /var/www**

- The `cp` command can be used with the `-A` option to preserve the SELinux context of a file or directory while performing the copy operation as shown in the following command line:

    # **cp -A /tmp/demo /var/www/html/**

Generally, the context of the parent directory is assigned to the child, when we create a new file with the `vim`, `cp`, or `touch` command.

To get a clearer and deeper insight into SELinux concepts, let's consider the workings of an Apache web server in the absence and presence of SELinux controls:

- **In the absence of SELinux**: In this case, the web server is running on port 80, which is opened in the firewall to allow access for service web pages. Let's assume the attacker has compromised the Apache service due to a vulnerability in it. After compromising it, the attacker will gain access to the document root with the permissions of the Apache user and Apache group. Hence, an attacker can create and write files in the /var/www/html/, /tmp, and /var/tmp directories.

- **In the presence of SELinux enforcing mode**: In this case, SELinux checks for the rules given in the targeted policy, which are based on type context. The SELinux context type for Apache web server process is httpd_t and SELinux context type of files and directories in /var/www/html is httpd_sys_content_t. The SELinux context type of files and directories in /tmp and /var/tmp is tmp_t in enforcing mode.

The targeted policy rule permits the process running as `httpd_t` to access files and directories with the context `httpd_sys_content_t`, so access to files or directories in `/tmp/` and `/var/tmp/` is not permitted. Thus, even if a malicious user compromises the web server, they cannot create or write a file in the `/tmp/` or `/var/tmp` directories. The damage caused by the user will remain restricted to the `/var/www/html` folder as shown in the following diagram:

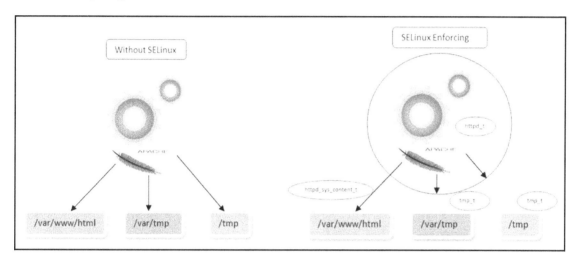

Working with SELinux

This section deals with various commands used to manage the SELinux context and enforced policies applied on files, directories, processes, and ports.

Changing SELinux modes

SELinux has three modes of operation, mentioned in the following table:

SELinux mode	Description
Enforcing	In this mode, rules are available and applied. SELinux logs the activities and protects the system.
Permissive	In this mode, rules are available but not applied. This mode is mainly used for troubleshooting. This mode is used to temporarily allow access to content that SELinux was restricting in enforcing mode. In this mode, SELinux logs the denied actions. System reboot is not required to switch from enforcing to permissive mode and vice versa.

Disabled	In this mode, rules are not available. It completely disables SELinux. A system reboot is required to disable or switch from enforcing or permissive mode to disabled mode, as it completely relabels the files.

Using setenforce for runtime changes

We can change the SELinux modes from enforcing to permissive and vice versa during runtime by using the `setenforce` command. Before and after changing the SELinux mode, we must ensure the current mode by using the `getenforce` command.

The following are examples that illustrate the usage of the setenforce and getenforce commands:

- To display the current SELinux mode, use the following command:

    ```
    # getenforce
    ```

- To change the current SELinux mode from enforcing to permissive, use either of the following commands:

    ```
    # setenforce 0
    or
    # setenforce Permissive
    ```

- To change the current SELinux mode from permissive to enforcing, use either of the following commands:

    ```
    # setenforce 1
    or
    # setenforce Enforcing
    ```

- To view detailed SELinux information, use the following command:

    ```
    # sestatus
    ```

Another way to temporarily change the SELinux mode is by passing a parameter to the kernel at boot time. Passing a kernel argument of `enforcing=0` will boot the system in permissive mode for that instance and `selinux=1` will boot the system in enforcing mode.

Setting default modes of SELinux

The configuration file of SELinux is `/etc/selinux/config`. It determines the mode and policy of SELinux at boot time. We can modify the `/etc/selinux/config` file and set the `SELINUX=permissive` parameter to change the default mode of SELinux, as shown in the following diagram:

```
[root@desktop ~]#  cat /etc/selinux/config

# This file controls the state of SELinux on the system.
# SELINUX= can take one of these three values:
#     enforcing - SELinux security policy is enforced.
#     permissive - SELinux prints warnings instead of enforcing.
#     disabled - No SELinux policy is loaded.
SELINUX=enforcing                                    Default SELinux Mode
# SELINUXTYPE= can take one of three two values:
#     targeted - Targeted processes are protected,
#     minimum - Modification of targeted policy. Only selected processes are protected.
#     mls - Multi Level Security protection.
SELINUXTYPE=targeted
                                                     Default SELinux Policy
```

 In previous releases of CentOS, the SELinux configuration file was stored at `/etc/sysconfig/selinux`. Now, in CentOS 7, this file is a `symlink` of `/etc/selinux/confg`.

If any kernel argument of `enforcing=0` for permissive mode or `selinux=0` for disabling SELinux is passed at boot, then it will override the current configuration set in `/etc/selinux/config`.

Modifying file context

As mentioned earlier, generally, the parent directory SELinux context is assigned to the newly created file, if it is created using the `vim`, `cp`, or `touch` command.

If a file is moved using the `mv` command, or copied using the `cp -a` command, the original SELinux context will remain unchanged.

Often, we need to modify the file context as per the destination directory, so that a process can access the file object when required. In the following sections, we discuss the different utilities that can be used to achieve this.

Using restorecon for restoring the default context

Using the restorecon command is the most popular and preferred way of modifying the SELinux context of a file or directory. As is visible from the name of the restorecon command, it is used to restore the default context of a file or directory by reading the default rules set in the SELinux policy. If the wrong context is applied, restorecon automatically corrects it from the policy of the filesystem.

In the following example, we simulate a problem scenario, in which a file has incorrect syntax and we correct it using the restorecon command:

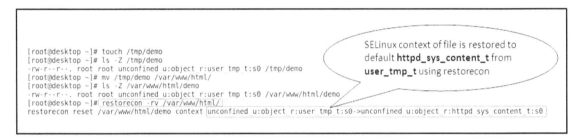

The restorecon command is a part of the policycoreutil package, so in order to use this command, this package should be installed on the system.

Using chon for context management

The chcon command can also be used with the _t option to change the context of the file. This method of modifying the context of the file is not recommended, as errors can happen while using it. The chcon command, when used, writes the new context to the filesystem, but the policy remains unchanged. Hence, changes made using this command get overwritten on relabeling the SELinux context on the filesystem.

An example of `chcon` command usage is shown in the following diagram:

```
                                    ┌─────────────────────────────────────┐
                                    │  SELinux context of file is modified │
                                    │  to httpd_sys_content_t from         │
                                    │  user_tmp_t using chcon              │
                                    └─────────────────────────────────────┘
[root@desktop ~]# ll -Z /var/www/html/
-rw-r--r--. root root unconfined_u:object_r:user_tmp_t:s0 abc
[root@desktop ~]# chcon -t httpd_sys_content_t /var/www/html/abc
[root@desktop ~]# ll -Z /var/www/html/
-rw-r--r--. root root unconfined_u:object_r:httpd_sys_content_t:s0 abc
```

Using semanage for context management

The `semanage` command writes the new context to the SELinux policy, which is used to apply the file context at the relabeling of the file labels or while setting the default file context using `restorecon`. It uses an extended regular expression to specify the path and filenames for applying those rules (new file context). The most commonly used extended regular expression with `semanage fcontext` is `(/.*)?`. This expression matches the directory listed before the expression and everything in that directory recursively.

An example of `semanage` command usage is shown in the following diagram:

```
                                    ┌─────────────────────────────────────┐
                                    │  Semanage command to add the        │
                                    │  rules of SELinux for default context│
                                    │  on directory                       │
                                    └─────────────────────────────────────┘
[root@desktop ~]# mkdir /demo
[root@desktop ~]# touch /demo/sample
[root@desktop ~]# ls -Z /demo/
[root@desktop ~]# semanage fcontext -a -t httpd_sys_content_t "/demo(/.*)?"
[root@desktop ~]# restorecon -Rvv /demo/
restorecon reset /demo context unconfined_u:object_r:default_t:s0->unconfined_u:object_r:httpd_sys_content_t:s0
restorecon reset /demo/sample context unconfined_u:object_r:default_t:s0->unconfined_u:object_r:httpd_sys_content_t:s0
[root@desktop ~]# ls -Z /demo/
-rw-r--r--. root root unconfined_u:object_r:httpd_sys_content_t:s0 sample
```

The `semange` command is a part of the `policycoreutil-python` package. In order to use the `semanage` command, make sure this package is installed in the system.

Modifying port context

SELinux does much more than just restricting the access of processes to files based on SELinux labels. It can also control the network traffic by restricting access to unauthorized ports for a service. By default, the SELinux policy allows the `ssh` service to access port, 22/TCP . In the following example, we allow `ssh` to run on another port 2525/TCP, in addition to its default port, as shown in the following steps:

1. The `semanage` command can be used with the `port` sub-command to list the current port assigned to a service as shown in the following screenshot:

```
[root@desktop ~]# semanage port -l | grep ssh
ssh_port_t                      tcp      22
```

- We can also use the `semanage` command for granting access to any custom port for a particular service. In the following screenshot, the `semanage` command is used to add the selected port to the access list of a particular service:

```
[root@desktop ~]# semanage port -l | grep ssh
ssh_port_t                    tcp      22
[root@desktop ~]# semanage port -a -t ssh_port_t -p tcp 2525
[root@desktop ~]# semanage port -l | grep ssh
ssh_port_t                    tcp      2525, 22
```

- The `semanage` command can also be used to remove an association of a port to a particular service as shown in the following screenshot:

```
[root@desktop ~]# semanage port -l | grep ssh
ssh_port_t                    tcp      2525, 22
[root@desktop ~]# semanage port -d -t ssh_port_t -p tcp 2525
[root@desktop ~]# semanage port -l | grep ssh
ssh_port_t                    tcp      22
```

Managing SELinux Booleans

SELinux Booleans are switches that contains a set of rules to make a selective adjustment in behavior to an SELinux policy. SELinux Booleans provide an easy interface to change the behavior of an SELinux policy rule.

The following are examples that illustrate the usage of the getsebool and setsebool commands for managing SELinux Booleans:

- The `getsebool` command can be used with the `-a` option to display the list of all SELinux Booleans and their current values as shown in the following command line. The output of this command is passed to a grep filter to narrow down the results:

  ```
  # getsebool -a
  ```

- The output of the `getsebool -a` command can be filtered down using `grep` as shown in the following command line:

  ```
  # getsebool -a | grep ftp
  ```

- The `setsebool` command can be used to modify (switch on or off) the value of a SELinux Boolean at runtime as shown in following command line:

  ```
  # setsebool ftp_home_dir on
  ```

- Modify runtime value as well as the default values of the SELinux Boolean simultaneously by using the `setsebool` command with the `-P` option as shown in the following command line:

  ```
  # setsebool -P ftp_home_dir on
  ```

Managing SELinux troubleshooting

SELinux provides an essential layer of security beyond the discretionary access control set by the user. It prevents any unauthorized attempt to access a resource such as a file by a running process. Here, the process that attempt to access a resource could be a genuine process or it could be a compromised process. Disabling SELinux is not considered good practice. Sometimes, when a binary or application is installed from a third party, it does not contain any appropriate SELinux context, which may lead to restrictions in running that service properly. In those circumstances, SELinux is run in permissive mode and new rules are created based on the denial of service messages captured in log files. In most cases of SELinux troubleshooting, it has been observed that access control restrictions are applied by SELinux due to incorrect type context on a file. This issue can be easily resolved using the `restorecon` command, which sets the default context on files from SELinux rules given in a policy. Using this method, we can keep our SELinux in enforcing mode and the security of our systems intact.

Modifying the mode of SELinux Booleans by turning their values on and off is also used sometimes to relax or harden the SELinux controls for running a service. For making an appropriate change in SELinux rules or policies, the primary requirement is to understand the problem correctly. In this, the monitoring of SELinux violations by going through logs plays an important role. For logging SELinux messages to /var/log/messages and /var/log/audit/audit.log in an easily understandable format, the setroubleshoot-server package should be installed on the system with the following command:

```
# yum install setroubleshoot-server -y
```

Using sealert for troubleshooting

Each SELinux violation is assigned a **unique identifier** (**UUID**). This UUID is used with the sealert command to produce a summary of a report for a specific incident.

For example, let's create a file in root's home directory and move this file into /var/www/html/. Now, try to access that file through the web browser or from the command line using curl as shown in the following diagram:

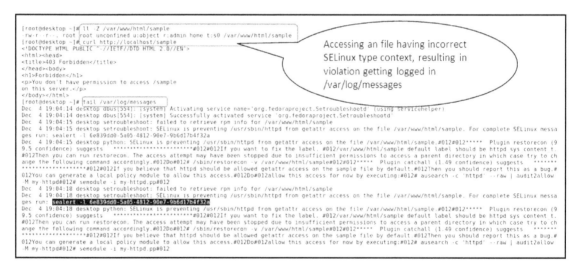

The error report of the SELinux violation can be viewed now, using the UUID and sealert command, as shown in the following screenshot:

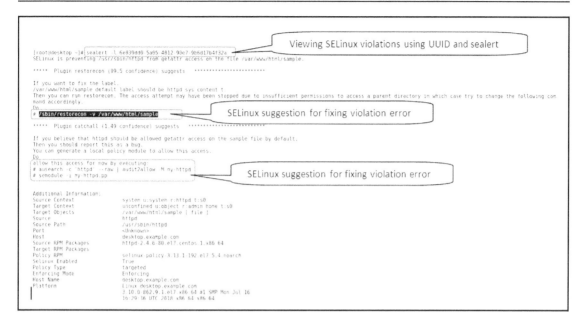

On applying the suggestions of the SELinux violation given in the `sealert` report, it will remove the error and allow access to the file using the `curl` command as shown in the following screenshot:

```
[root@desktop ~]# /sbin/restorecon -v /var/www/html/sample     ──── Applying SELinux suggestion received in sealert
/sbin/restorecon reset /var/www/html/sample context unconfined_u:object_r:admin_home_t:s0->unconfined_u:object_r:httpd_sys_content_t:s0
[root@desktop ~]# curl http://localhost/sample
SELinux logging test file
```

Understanding firewall concepts in CentOS 7

Operating system security generally follows a defense in depth model, where security is implemented at different layers in the system. Starting from policies and procedure, physical controls, network perimeter security, host security, application security, and so on, several elements are secured to harden the security of a system. In this, a firewall helps in securing the system, as well as applications, by limiting access to the system. Firewall rules filter packets based on specific criteria, such as IP addresses, port and protocol, and so on.

In Linux, firewall rules are managed by the network filtering subsystem available in the kernel and known as **netfilter.** The netfilter framework enables the system to inspect, modify, drop, or reject any incoming, outgoing, or forwarded network packet programmatically.

The `iptables` command is the most popular tool used to interact with netfilter and manage the firewall. The `iptables` command only manages the IPv4 rules in the firewall. For management of IPv6 rules, the `ip6tables` command is used, and for software bridges, the `ebtables` utility is used. However, managing the firewall using the `iptables` utility is not user friendly and requires a good understanding of both the firewall and `iptables` command. Thus, to overcome the complexity of `iptables` and incorporate some advanced features, a new utility, `firewalld`, was designed.

Firewalld concepts

In CentOS 7, a new utility called **firewalld** has been introduced to interact with netfilter. It can be used to configure and monitor the firewall rules for IPv4, IPv6, and for software bridges. Furthermore, applications can interact with `firewalld` to add or change firewall rules, such as a requesting for a port opening with the help of the D-bus messaging system. firewalld supports both runtime configuration and persistence configuration. It is installed by default in the CentOS Base installation, but if it is not available, then user can install it is using the following command lines:

```
# yum install firewalld -y
# systemctl start firewalld
# systemctl enable firewalld
```

firewalld is not compatible with the `iptables` service, so it is strongly recommended to not use them simultaneously on the same system. Either use `firewalld` and disable `iptables` (`iptables`, `ip6tables`, and `ebtables`), or use `iptables` and disable `firewalld`.

Firewalld zones

The firewalld segregates incoming traffic into zones. Each zone is a collection of rules. To select which zone is to be used for an incoming connection, firewalld uses the following three rules to match in the given order:

- **The source address** on the incoming packet is matched with the source address rule configured for the zone. If the source address matches, the packet is routed through that zone.

- If the source address does not match, then the **incoming interface** for a packet is matched with the interface set up for the zone and that zone is used.
- If neither the incoming interface of the packet nor the source address of a packet matches, then the rules given in the **default zone** are applied on that packet. The default zone is one of the other zones defined by the system or user. By default, the public zone is set as the default zone. The example of `firewall-cmd` to list the available zones and default zone is shown in the following screenshot:

```
[root@desktop ~]# firewall-cmd --get-zones
block dmz drop external home internal public trusted work
[root@desktop ~]# firewall-cmd --get-default-zone
public
```

The following table lists the predefined zones available in `firewalld` and their descriptions:

Zone	Description
trusted	Allows all incoming traffic.
home	This zone is used for home networks. In this zone, incoming traffic is rejected unless it is related to outgoing traffic or it matches the predefined services of zone, such as `ssh`, `mdns`, `ipp-client`, `samba-client`, or `dhcpv6-client`.
internal	This zone has the same rules as defined in the home zone. It is generally used for internal networks.
work	In this zone, all incoming traffic is rejected, unless it is related to outgoing traffic or it matches some predefined services of the zone, such as, `ssh`, `mdns`, `ipp-client`, or `dhcpv6-client`:
public	In this zone, all incoming traffic is rejected, unless it is related to outgoing traffic or it matches some predefined services of the zone, such as `ssh` or `dhcpv6-client`.
external	In this zone, all incoming traffic is rejected, unless it is related to outgoing traffic or it matches some predefined services of zone, such as `ssh`. Outgoing IPv4 traffic forwarded from this zone is masqueraded (NAT) to make it originate from the outgoing network interface.
dmz	`dmz` is the demilitarized zone. Only selected incoming connections with limited access to the internal network are allowed. All other traffic is rejected.
block	Reject all incoming traffic with an `icmp-host-prohibited` message. Only incoming traffic related to connections originating from the outgoing traffic of the system is allowed.

`drop`	In this zone, all incoming traffic is dropped (without any ICMP errors) unless it is related to outgoing traffic.

Firewalld services

The other main component of firewalld is services. There are certain default services that are used to allow or deny access to traffic on specific ports, for a particular network service in the firewall. Each service has got a configuration file that describes its requirements, such as what TCP or UDP ports are required for service operation. Users can list all the available services in firewalld with the command shown in the following screenshot:

```
[root@desktop ~]# firewall-cmd --get-services
RH-Satellite-6 amanda-client amanda-k5-client bacula bacula-client bitcoin bitcoin-rpc bitcoin
-testnet bitcoin-testnet-rpc ceph ceph-mon cfengine condor-collector ctdb dhcp dhcpv6 dhcpv6-c
lient dns docker-registry dropbox-lansync elasticsearch freeipa-ldap freeipa-ldaps freeipa-rep
lication freeipa-trust ftp ganglia-client ganglia-master high-availability http https imap ima
ps ipp ipp-client ipsec iscsi-target kadmin kerberos kibana klogin kpasswd kshell ldap ldaps l
ibvirt libvirt-tls managesieve mdns mosh mountd ms-wbt mssql mysql nfs nfs3 nrpe ntp openvpn o
virt-imageio ovirt-storageconsole ovirt-vmconsole pmcd pmproxy pmwebapi pmwebapis pop3 pop3s p
ostgresql privoxy proxy-dhcp ptp pulseaudio puppetmaster quassel radius rpc-bind rsh rsyncd sa
mba samba-client sane sip sips smtp smtp-submission smtps snmp snmptrap spideroak-lansync squi
d ssh synergy syslog syslog-tls telnet tftp tftp-client tinc tor-socks transmission-client vds
m vnc-server wbem-https xmpp-bosh xmpp-client xmpp-local xmpp-server
```

For the secure configuration of firewalld, each service should be allowed access in the correct zone.

The services configuration file is stored in the following two directories:

- `/usr/lib/firewalld/services`
- `/etc/firewalld/services`

These services files are configured in XML format. An example of the `ftp.xml` file is shown in the following screenshot:

```
[root@desktop ~]# cat /usr/lib/firewalld/services/ssh.xml
<?xml version="1.0" encoding="utf-8"?>
<service>
  <short>SSH</short>
  <description>Secure Shell (SSH) is a protocol for logging into and executing commands on rem
ote machines. It provides secure encrypted communications. If you plan on accessing your machi
ne remotely via SSH over a firewalled interface, enable this option. You need the openssh-serv
er package installed for this option to be useful.</description>
  <port protocol="tcp" port="22"/>
</service>
```

Managing firewalld

Firewalld can be managed in the following two ways.

Using the firewalld-cmd command-line tool

This is the most common method of managing firewalld configurations (both running as well as permanent). In this section, we have described the management of firewalld with this tool. It can perform all the jobs that are performed using the firewalld-config GUI tool. This tool is a part of the `firewalld` package.

Using the firewalld-config graphical tool

Firewall-config is a graphical tool that is used to modify and view the running (in-memory) configuration of firewalld, as well as permanent (on hard disk) configuration. This tool is a part of the firewall-config package. It is invoked from the command line by typing `firewall-config`.

The configuration files of firewalld are stored inside the `/etc/firewalld/` directory. Firewalld supports two types of configurations:

- **Runtime or in-memory configurations**: The in-memory configurations of firewalld are lost on reloading firewalld or after rebooting of system.
- **Permanent or on-disk configurations**: This configuration remains after reboot and is applied on reloading firewalld.

Working with firewalld

Before starting firewalld, we need to ensure that `iptables`, `ip6tables`, and `ebtables` are not running, as they conflict with firewalld.

The following are examples that illustrate the usage of firewalld-cmd command:

1. Stop the conflicting service of `iptables`, `ip6tables`, and `ebtables` using the following command:

```
# systemctl stop iptables
# systemctl mask iptbales
# systemctl stop ip6tables
# systemctl mask ip6tables
# systemctl stop ebtables
# systemctl mask ebtables
```

2. The following command is used to `start` and enable `firewalld` in CentOS 7:

```
# systemctl start firewalld
# systemctl enable firewalld
# systemctl status firewalld
```

3. Now, the first step in configuring `firewalld` should be to check the existing zones and services that are configured by default and the zones and services that the user has not configured:

- List all the zones in `firewalld` by using the following command line:

```
# firewall-cmd --get-zones
```

- List only active zones of `firewalld` by using the following command line:

```
# firewall-cmd --get-active-zones
```

- List the current default zone by using the following command line:

```
# firewall-cmd --get-default-zone
```

- List the services available for configuration with `firewalld` by using the following command line:

```
# firewall-cmd --get-services
```

4. After making any changes in the `firewalld` configuration, it is mandatory to reload it to bring the applied changes into effect. By default, all changes made are runtime changes only. We can make them permanent by using the `--permanent` option. It will preserve the configuration changes across reboot. Now, let's change the default zone using the `firewalld-cmd` command as follows:

```
# firewall-cmd --set-default-zone=internal
```

After updating the default zone, we should confirm the setting of the current default zone by using the following command line:

```
# firewall-cmd --get-default-zone
```

5. Now, let's add a port to the public zone using `firewall-cmd` permanently by using the following command line:

```
# firewall-cmd --permanent --zone=internal --add-port=80/tcp --
permanent
```

In the preceding command, if we don't add the `--permanent` option, then changes will get lost after reloading the `firewalld` configuration. We can reload the `firewalld` configuration by using the following command line:

```
# firewall-cmd --reload
```

Now, see the status of recently added TCP port 80 in `firewalld`:

```
# firewall-cmd --zone=internal --list-ports
```

We can also use the `firewall-cmd` command to view the complete configuration for a zone. In the following example, we list the complete configuration of the internal zone:

```
# firewall-cmd --zone=internal --list-all
```

6. In the following example, we use the `firewall-cmd` command to remove TCP port 80 from the internal zone as shown in the following command line:

```
# firewall-cmd --zone=internal --remove-port=80/tcp
```

7. Add a service to a zone in `firewalld`. The following example shows how to add an `ftp` service in the `firewalld` internal zone:

```
# firewall-cmd --zone=internal --add-service=ftp
```

8. List the services in a zone by using the following command line:

```
# firewall-cmd --list-services --zone=internal
```

9. Remove a service from a zone in `firewalld` by using the following command line:

```
# firewall-cmd --zone=internal --remove-service=ftp
```

10. The user can drop all incoming and outgoing packets of an active connection when there is a breach in the network by using the panic options of `firewall-cmd` as shown in the following command line:

```
# firewall-cmd --panic-on
```

On execution of the preceding command, any ping, `ssh`, or web-related activity on the system will be blocked. To turn off this feature, execute the following command:

```
# firewall --panic-off
```

 Besides the `firewall-cmd` configuration rules that we have discussed in this section, firewalld has two more options for adding firewall rules, direct rules and rich rules.

Summary

In this chapter, we began by learning what the different types of logging in the Linux system are, and how to use them effectively for debugging and troubleshooting Linux systems. Then, we learned about managing system services to optimize system performance. This was followed by understanding SELinux concepts to harden the security of applications and the system. Finally, we looked at how to filter the incoming and outgoing packets in the system using the firewalld framework.

Linux is all about learning by doing. If you have practiced the commands given in each chapter, together with the theoretical part, you will feel more comfortable while working on Linux. This book is written for novice Linux users, yet a seasoned Linux user will also have something to take away from each chapter. With this, our fascinating journey of kick-starting Linux with the CentOS 7 operating system comes to an end. If you have any queries, I would like to hear it from you. You can reach me at shiwangkalkhanda@outlook.com.

Other Books You May Enjoy

If you enjoyed this book, you may be interested in these other books by Packt:

Mastering Ubuntu Server - Second Edition
Jay LaCroix, Recommended for You

ISBN: 9781788997560

- Manage users, groups, and permissions
- Encrypt and decrypt disks with Linux Unified Key Setup (LUKS)
- Set up SSH for remote access, and connect it to other nodes
- Add, remove, and search for packages
- Use NFS and Samba to share directories with other users
- Get to know techniques for managing Apache and MariaDB
- Explore best practices and troubleshooting techniques
- Get familiar with scripting
- Automate server deployments with Ansible

CompTIA Linux+ Certification Guide
Philip Inshanally

ISBN: 9781789344493

- Understand the Linux system architecture
- Install, upgrade, and manage Linux system packages
- Configure devices and maintain the Linux filesystem
- Manage the Shell environment, write scripts, and manage data
- Set user interfaces and desktops in the Linux operating system
- Automate system admin tasks and manage essential system services
- Manage SQL server on Linux and log locally and remotely with rsyslogd
- Administer network and local security

Leave a review - let other readers know what you think

Please share your thoughts on this book with others by leaving a review on the site that you bought it from. If you purchased the book from Amazon, please leave us an honest review on this book's Amazon page. This is vital so that other potential readers can see and use your unbiased opinion to make purchasing decisions, we can understand what our customers think about our products, and our authors can see your feedback on the title that they have worked with Packt to create. It will only take a few minutes of your time, but is valuable to other potential customers, our authors, and Packt. Thank you!

Index

www.ingramcontent.com/pod-product-compliance
Lightning Source LLC
Chambersburg PA
CBHW080624060326
40690CB00021B/4811